RENEWING
THE AMERICAN
DREAM

A Citizen's Guide for Restoring Our Competitive Advantage

Frank Islam • George Muñoz • Ed Crego

Published in the United States by IMC Publishing

Book cover design by Kevin Baier

Table of Contents

SECTION III: Working on the Dream   151

A Citizen's Call to Arms

Dear Fellow Citizen:

2009 was the worst of times for the United States. We were involved in two wars of necessity. One war had been proclaimed. It was—and is—a war that is being fought for us by a small group of brave troops in a valley nation far away.

The other war had not been declared, even though it is the one that will determine our destiny as a nation. This war must be fought by all of us in the homeland. This second war is one to renew America and the American Dream. This war can only be won by creating a sustainable competitive advantage that restores the economic and social fabric of the United States.

Winning this war is not the job of government or business. It is ours. As citizens, we need to arm ourselves and join forces to win it. This is not simply about casting a vote or toeing the party line. It is about education and engagement. It is about doing what is necessary to renew America and the American Dream.

We have written this book because we believe that many Americans do not recognize the gravity of America's current situation. They think that these tough times will inevitably pass and America will recover to where it was before. In this book, we make the case that America's decline is real and could be permanent. The purpose of this book is to enlist your participation in reversing that decline. We provide it as a guide to help facilitate that participation.

We are not politicians or economists—nor are we representatives of big business or academics. Rather, we are three Americans who have lived the American Dream and who want to contribute to sustaining and growing it.

On December 23, 1776, during the darkest days of the Revolutionary War, Thomas Paine wrote, "These are the times that try men's souls. The summer soldier and the sunshine patriot will, in this crisis, shrink from their service; but he that stands by it now, deserves the love and thanks of man and woman."

We face a different but equally formidable crisis today. We ask you to join arms with us as fellow citizens in the twenty-first-century brigade to address that crisis. We are confident that united, we will be victorious in winning this war to renew America and the American Dream.

Preface: The Dream at Risk

"We are all in the same boat in a stormy sea, and we owe each other a terrible loyalty."

G. K. Chesterton

IF 2009 WAS THE WORST OF YEARS, 2000–2009 WAS THE WORST OF decades. It was *the decade of decline*.

It was a lost decade for American workers. The average citizen took it on the chin. There was zero net job creation. The median income and the net worth of American households declined for the first time since these figures have been tracked. Income inequality was at the highest level since the Great Depression.

In spite of this, few have come to the recognition that the United States is at war on the home front. America and the American Dream are threatened—not by terrorists but by the enemy within.

The enemy within is our inability to grasp the severity of the country's current situation and to work together to resolve it. We need to come to a fundamental understanding that America's position as the world's economic and social leader is at serious risk. We are at a critical crossroads.

2010–2019 will be **the decisive decade**. The decisions we make and the actions we take in this decade will determine the future of America and the American Dream for all of us.

Some might think that our condition is a result of the economic collapse of 2008. Nothing could be further from the truth. The meltdown made things worse. It, however, was simply the manifestation of a 3-D effect that has been pushing us toward crisis for some time.

Over the past quarter of a century, the United States has become a:

- **Deficit Nation**—We are all familiar with the country's fiscal deficit and trade deficit. There is another deficit, however, that is of equal importance in terms of the future of the country and the American Dream—a civic deficit. We have become a nation of cynics and skeptics, while at the same time, we are less informed and involved in the political and social process.

- **Debtor Nation**—In the past decade, many of us went credit crazy. As a result, both businesses and consumers became substantially overleveraged. With the economic meltdown of 2008, things completely destabilized. The economy is deleveraging and moving toward a new "normal." No one can project that normal exactly. But as George Muñoz can attest to what he saw in most other countries when he was the head of the Overseas Private Investment Corporation (OPIC), "normal" for them was having a small economic elite class, a few in the middle class, and most in the lower ranks.

- **Divided Nation**—America's political system is becoming increasingly bipolar and dysfunctional. Extreme conservatives to the right; extreme liberals to the left. In between, there is little reasoned discussion or debate. This divide is being deepened and widened to almost seismic proportions by certain elected officials, talk-show hosts, media pundits, and radical ideologues who promote divisiveness and rabble rousing.

The consequence of this condition is doubt about the future—considerable doubt. Doubt about what lies ahead for us, for our children, and for our grandchildren. Doubt is neither good nor bad. How we respond to doubt matters. Who responds to doubt matters even more.

Unfortunately, as we watched the responses to the economic crisis throughout 2009, what we saw was "government as usual" and "business as usual" thinking and action. This increased, rather than reduced, America's doubt and anxiety.

In the public sector, strategic thinking and reasoning were not central to most of the debates in Washington, D.C. Too much of the focus was on promoting partisan positions. Too frequently, getting legislation passed or blocked was seen as an end and not a means. Problems and issues were looked at in bits and pieces and in isolation. The dots were not connected. There was an obsession with process and not performance.

In the private sector, most banks were hesitant to make loans—overcompensating for the excesses of the 2006–2008 time frame. All of the major financial institutions were repaying their bailout loans so that they could pay their executives substantial bonuses. Wall Street firms continued to engage in the same type of practices that put the economy at risk in the first place. The majority of businesses hunkered down, shed more jobs, and attempted to cut their way to profitability.

ENTERPRISE USA: A NEW PARADIGM

Based upon this behavior and the mediocre economic results of 2009, we came to the conclusion that what was needed was an alternative approach—a new problem-solving paradigm. We present such a paradigm in this book.

It entails looking at the United States as an enterprise. Call it Enterprise USA—a shared venture with business, government, community-based, and nonprofit organizations working together in order to revitalize all aspects of America and the American Dream. At the heart of that venture is you—the twenty-first-century citizen.

Renewing the American Dream requires a multifaceted approach including:

- Defining a twenty-first-century competitive advantage for the nation
- Redirecting government
- Redirecting business
- Renewing leaders, organizations, and individuals
- Implementing an integrated renewal process

- Implementing policies and programs that: create jobs, rejuvenate the middle class, reignite the manufacturing sector, unleash the potential of small businesses and entrepreneurs, ensure a vital news media, and advance America's role in the world.

We devote a chapter to each of these areas and make recommendations for how to accomplish those goals in this book. We also introduce a three-part Renewal Framework that we have developed for thinking about and acting upon the American Dream:

- **The American Dream Construct**—comprised of eight forms of capital
- **The American Dream Platform**—comprised of enduring promises, rules and regulations, and programs and initiatives
- **The American Dream Process**—comprised of leadership, organizational and individual renewal combined with proper preparation, involvement, and execution.

The Renewal Framework provides the organizational structure for the book and is the foundation for Enterprise USA.

The framework presents our perspective as businesspeople. It is based on our belief in facts, evidence-based analysis, and rational decision making. It is based on the understanding that the response to our nation's current situation cannot be about grand ideas, ideologies, or governmental polices or programs alone. Nor can, or should, it be the exclusive province of politicians, lobbyists, and special interests.

Our analysis and recommendations are grounded in recognition that the American Dream is a continuous journey. That journey began, and is sustained, by the contributions of individual citizens. As Adlai Stevenson once put it, "As citizens of this democracy, you are the rulers and the ruled, the law-givers and the law-abiding, the beginning and the end."

We believe this fervently. That is why we have written this book as a resource and reference guide for what we term twenty-first-century citizens—those citizens who are: interested, issue-oriented, informed, independent, and involved.

Twenty-first-century citizens are willing to stand up and speak out—not as advocates for entrenched positions or as members of political parties. They are prepared to confront doubt directly and engage in nonpartisan problem solving. As committed and collaborative individuals, they recognize that they are:

- Entitled to think
- Required to reason
- Empowered to act

The American Dream and that "shining city upon a hill" have begun to slip into the shadows. As twenty-first-century citizens, we have the capacity and the capability to revive the dream. We can not do it alone, but we can as part of a shared venture—an enterprise devoted to bringing us closer together, instead of moving us further apart.

WHY US? WHY NOW?

When the three of us first got together to talk about writing this book, we thought we were an unusual trio to be considering the task. We're not politicians, economists, lobbyists, academics, talking heads, journalists, actors, or athletes.

The more we thought about it, we concluded that this point of differentiation was one of the very things that qualified us to talk about the American Dream and its current status. We are businesspeople and citizens who are seriously concerned about the future of America and the American Dream.

We have had the good fortune to lead and work in private- and public-sector organizations. We represent some of the diversity that is America: George Muñoz—a Hispanic American. Frank Islam—a Muslim Indian American. Ed Crego—of European American heritage.

Each of us has lived the American Dream. The great thing about the United States of America is that while our stories which follow are personal, they are not unusual. They are representative of what can be accomplished in the United States of America.

- George Muñoz comes from a large family. He has 11 siblings and grew up in South Texas. He is from the boomer generation, which means that, despite his family's modest surroundings, he believed everything was possible. There is no one who believes in the American Dream more than George. He got his B.A. in accounting from the University of Texas and his law degree from Harvard Law School and a master's in public policy from the Kennedy School of Government at Harvard. After starting his legal career at Mayer Brown in Chicago, George continued his education and got his fourth college degree—a master's in taxation from DePaul University. He is such a believer in the importance of education that he served as the president of the Chicago Board of Education during its difficult years in the 1980s and pushed through "school reform" aimed at reducing the dropout rate. In 1993, he was appointed by President Clinton and confirmed by the U.S. Senate to serve as an assistant secretary and the chief financial officer of the United States Treasury Department. During Clinton's second term, George served as the president of OPIC. George has become an internationally known business attorney, CPA, and investment banker. He also serves on a number of corporate boards, including Marriott International, Altria Group, and the National Geographic Society.

- Frank Islam grew up in a middle-class family of four siblings in India. Frank left India at the age of 15 to pursue the American Dream and to become an entrepreneur. He got his B.S. and M.S. in computer sciences from the University of Colorado at Boulder. He worked at two major information technology firms in Washington, D.C., before purchasing the QSS Group, Inc., in 1994 for $45K. Within 13 years, he took that firm from one employee to a workforce of more than 2,000 and revenues of approximately $300M. For those accomplishments, Frank's firm was consistently near the top of the Inc. 500, and Frank was recognized by Ernst and Young as Maryland Entrepreneur of the Year in 1999 and by the Small Business Administration (SBA) as Small Business Person of the Year in 2001. Frank sold the QSS Group to Perot Systems in 2007 and currently heads his own investment group and a private foundation that supports educational, cultural, and artistic causes worldwide. He also serves on the advisory council to the Export-Import Bank of the United States.

- Ed Crego grew up in a blue-collar family of five boys in Streator, Illinois. Ed was the first in his family to go to college. He got his B.A. and M.A. in political science from the University of Illinois at Chicago. Ed is a serial entrepreneur. He started his first management consulting firm in 1974 and has founded or been a partner in four others. Ed's areas of specialization included strategic planning, customer loyalty, and change management. His clients run the gamut from closely held and entrepreneurial businesses to large public and private sector entities. He has written or been a contributing author of six books and has also been a featured speaker for organizations such as the American Management Association, the Conference Board, and the American Marketing Association. Ed currently heads his own consulting firm, which concentrates on helping organizations manage transitions, turnarounds, and transformations.

Our natural tendency as entrepreneurs and citizens who have lived the dream was to not want to believe that America was on a downward trend. Based upon our analysis of all of the available evidence, however, we concluded that the United States was in a crisis. What are the dimensions of that crisis?

We talked about the *decade of decline* at the beginning of this preface. Here is what we looked like as a nation at the end of 2009 as a result of that decline:

- The annual budget deficit was above $1.4 trillion and rising
- 1 out of 5 Americans was un- or underemployed
- 1 out of 8 mortgages was in default or foreclosure
- 1 out of 8 Americans was on food stamps
- 1 out of 9 families couldn't make minimum payments on credit cards

In turbulent times such as these, we would have expected our political and business leaders to come together much as they did after

9/11. Instead, what we saw was ritualistic Kabuki theatre within the Washington Beltway and inertia outside of it. We witnessed a congressional system that was highly dysfunctional and virtually incapable of doing problem solving.

We were disappointed and dismayed. We learned that we were not alone. As we talked with others, we realized that many of you shared our perceptions and concerns about America's fragile condition and the lack of shared leadership to confront it. From the UPS driver to the waitress in the coffee shop, nearly everyone we spoke with was disgruntled and disillusioned. They were all trying to make sense of the current situation, searching for answers, and looking for ways to make a difference.

This convinced us of the necessity for this book. It persuaded us that we are all in this together and that as citizens, we have the right and responsibility to speak out and to make our voices heard. We present our analyses and recommendations here. Use them as a starting point. Accept what makes sense. Reject what does not. Add your ideas and stir the pot. The important thing is that you participate.

We do not profess to have all the answers or even to know all the right questions. We do believe that it is imperative, however, for citizens to take a more proactive and prominent role in the quest for America's future. That is why we have written this book.

Although we deal with the current state of things, we don't see our work as a current affairs book. We see it, instead, as a future affairs book. It takes a hard look at where we are right now virtually in real time and sets out a course of action which we, as citizens, can embrace to participate more fully in creating the country's future in this *decisive decade*.

Our hope is that the book will advance the cause of Enterprise USA and help bring the citizen's voice to the forefront in the national debate and dialogue on the future of America. If that occurs, the American Dream will not be at risk. It will be in good hands—the hands of the American people. We are confident, beyond the shadow of a doubt, that in those hands the American Dream will prevail.

1 | Competitive Advantage for the Twenty-First Century

"What's good for General Motors is good for the country, and vice versa."

Charlie Wilson, GM Chairman, 1952

THE UNITED STATES HAS STOOD ALONE ATOP THE WORLD STAGE FOR nearly a quarter of a century. It has enjoyed a competitive advantage on almost all fronts. Now as we stare into the second decade of the twenty-first century, America's primacy is challenged. Whether on the playing fields or battlefields, in the boardrooms or in the anterooms, nothing seems for certain anymore.

The United States has been, and still is, a champion. To stay a champion and to renew the American Dream, however, we need to win the race for competitive advantage. The race will not go to the swiftest, but to the one who understands the critical requirements for success going forward, prepares properly, and perseveres.

THE FINAL FOUR: THE INTERNATIONAL PLAYING FIELD

Every year in the third month on the calendar, a euphoric condition called "March Madness" consumes the American sports-loving public. That's the time when the NCAA selects 65 teams to compete for the national collegiate basketball title. The condition continues unabated while the competing teams are reduced to 32, 16, 8, and then, the Final Four. The condition intensifies as the field is reduced to 2, and finally ends when a winner emerges.

The lesson here is not about winning or losing but about what is required to get to the Final Four: a good coach, talented players, interdependence, discipline, a sound game plan, the ability to adjust and change the plan, and to win the game despite a change in circumstances. It struck us that the Final Four is a useful metaphor for thinking about global competitiveness, economic success, and leadership in the twenty-first century.

There are more than 190 countries in the world. About half of them are major economic players. The G-8 contains most of the top-seeded contenders except China and India. However, the real test of success is getting to be one of the Final Four. To get there, you have to prepare, plan well, play as a team, and execute to perfection.

Until about the middle of 2008, it appeared that a new Final Four was emerging for the next quarter century. America still looked like a presumptive member—although not a shoo-in. China and India had become much stronger and were looking like definite contenders. The European Union appeared to be gaining ground. Russia, with its oil and natural resources, was staging a reemergence and looked like it was becoming competitive again. Brazil was emerging as a potential challenger. In addition, smaller countries like Iceland and Ireland had vibrant economies and were shaping up as players to be reckoned with, even if they weren't big enough to make it all the way to the Final Four.

Then, the global marketplace had a meltdown and everything went up for grabs. The bad news for the United States was that we suffered greatly. The good news was that we were not alone. The meltdown was truly international—in great part because many of the international banks and economic powers were interconnected to the unregulated and improperly supervised financial practices that imploded. The sudden interruption in consumption also hurt those countries that depended on exports to America.

The better news for us is that we may be relatively more able to recover than other nations because of the maturity and diversity of the

American economy. The sad news is that countries like Iceland and Ireland may be permanently damaged. In 2009, Iceland declared bankruptcy and Ireland predicted a decline of more than 10 percent from the high point in its Gross Domestic Product (GDP).

HANDICAPPING THE FIELD

The key questions that need to be answered are: "Who will make it to the Final Four?" and "What do we need to do to ensure the United States' continued presence and potential leadership in this elite group?" We share thoughts on this later in this chapter. We should, however, also say that it's anybody's guess, and it all depends . . . In basketball parlance, it's a jump ball.

The two tables that follow present performance data and projections on some of the leading candidates for the Final Four. These data were drawn from information gathered and reported by the International Monetary Fund.[1]

Table 1.1: GDP Performance in 2008 and 2007			
Country	2008 GDP (Rank) [Billions USD]	2007 GDP (Rank) [Billions USD]	% Increase 2007–2008
United States	14,264,600 (1)	13,807,550	3.31%
Japan	4,923,761 (2)	4,384,380	12.30%
China	4,401,614 (3)	3,382,445	30.13%
Germany	3,667,513 (4)	3,320,913	10.44%
United Kingdom	2,674,085 (6)	2,803,404	−4.61%
Russia	1,676,586	1,294,383	29.53%
India	1,209,686	1,102,351	9.74%

The primary conclusions we draw from this data are:

- In 2008, the GDP of the U.S. was nearly three times as much as that of its nearest competitor Japan
- 2008 was a good year for both Russia and China
- 2008 was a terrible year for the United Kingdom
- 2008 was a "so-so" year for the United States

The United States still held a relatively enviable position entering 2009. As the following table shows, though, things are projected to change dramatically over the next 5 years.

Table 1.2: GDP Estimates 2009–2014			
Country	**2009 GDP Estimate [PPP*]**	**2014 GDP Estimate [PPP*]**	**% Increase 2009–2014**
United States	14,002,739	16,927,843	20.89%
China	8,511,092	14,437,715	69.63%
India	3,469,059	5,236,705	50.95%
Japan	4,122,547	4,906,560	19.02%
Germany	2,772,927	3,149,214	13.57%
Russia	2,145,764	2,732,434	27.34%
United Kingdom	2,159,320	2,545,696	17.89%

* PPP = Purchasing power parity calculations derived from calculations of the International Monetary Fund compiled in April 2009.

If these estimates are realized, the reality becomes the following:

- China and India will have incredible growth in GDP over this 5-year period and leapfrog to numbers two and three in terms of GDP
- Although still lagging the U.S., China will be much closer to it in GDP, and together, the two will clearly be the dominant economic forces in the world
- Russia will climb ahead of the United Kingdom
- Germany will experience very slow growth

PERFORMANCE ON THE FIELD IN 2009

That's how things stood at the end of 2008. Let's examine how things shaped up in 2009 for the potential Big Three of the foreseeable future—China, India, and the United States.

The World Bank projected a 2009 GDP for China of 6.5 percent. China's GDP grew 6.1 percent in the first quarter and 7.9 percent in the second quarter of 2009. Based upon this, as of September 2009, the Asian Bank was forecasting 8.2 percent GDP growth for China for the year.

Much of China's strong performance was attributed to a massive government stimulus package and "a surge in bank lending and vigorous fixed assets investments." As China's exports declined, it concentrated on driving growth internally. However, China still managed to topple Germany as the biggest exporter of manufactured goods. What was most astounding about China's performance in 2009 is that more cars were manufactured and sold there than in the United States. Just a few years ago, China was not projected to pass the U.S. in this area until 2025. Can this be a harbinger of things to come in other economic areas?

The World Bank's 2009 GDP projection for India was 5.1 percent. In November, India reported that GDP grew 7.9 percent for the quarter ending in September as opposed to 6.1 percent in the first quarter, resulting in the government raising its 2009/2010 GDP growth projections from 6.5 percent to 7 percent. As with China, much of this performance was attributed to government stimulus spending.

In contrast to India and China, the United States' performance in the first three quarters of 2009 was anemic. GDP in the U.S. declined 5.5 percent and 0.7 percent, respectively, in quarters one and two, and grew 2.8 percent in quarter three. As those statistics show, things were especially bleak for the U.S. at the beginning of the year.

In the period from the beginning of October 2008 through the end of March 2009, the U.S. economy went through its worst two quarters in more than 60 years. In the first quarter of 2009, business investment declined at a record pace. Domestic demand fell at the fastest rate in almost 3 decades. Exports fell at the highest rate in 4 decades while imports fell at the fastest rate in more than 6 decades. By midyear, however, things started to stabilize and an extremely fragile recovery was underway at the end of the third quarter of 2009. The American economy had an unexpected growth spurt in the fourth quarter but most of that was driven by companies replenishing their inventories. Exports strengthened somewhat but consumer spending weakened and unemployment remained high.

GOVERNMENT POLICIES AND COMPETITIVE ADVANTAGE

Given this comparative performance during 2009 and future World Bank projections, it should be obvious that the United States' position as the world economic leader is at risk. Congress, in general, does not appear to have grasped this. They seem oblivious to the fact that there is an intricate linkage between enacted government policies and the nation's competitive advantage. They are caught up in partisan debates, blame placing, and scapegoating.

The debates that are held in the halls of Congress should not be about liberal or conservative alternatives. They should be about whether the choices that are made create a sustainable competitive advantage for the United States in an increasingly competitive world marketplace. This is what will matter to us and future generations more than anything else.

To focus only on budget deficits or global alliances that can never be realized is the "silly season." The silly season aligns both parties against the nation's and the citizens' cause, which is known as common sense.

Republicans and Democrats need to find a common enemy or foe. We're not talking about Afghanistan, Pakistan, Iraq, or Iran. We're talking about economies that eventually could surpass us and reduce the United States' economic status.

Just as the nation needs a strong defense, it needs a strong offense. It can create that offense by looking at all policies in terms of whether they enable the country to maintain economic momentum in the short term and provide the basis for substantial and sustainable growth in the long term.

THE NEED TO MAKE THE BUSINESS CASE

This is the strategic approach and thinking process that the Obama administration could have taken coming into office in presenting its four major policy priorities of healthcare, education, energy, and the environment. A strong business case could have been made for the critical economic importance of each of these areas and the contribution that they would make to ensuring that the nation maintains or restores its competitive advantage.

Instead, the administration initially chose to cast those priorities more in moral and humanitarian terms, rather than applying business logic and building a broad base of "customer support" for its agenda. Let's take healthcare as an example.

The primary customers that were contacted to initiate the healthcare reform process were the insurance companies, pharmaceutical companies, durable medical equipment providers, hospitals, and doctors. The primary focus for healthcare reform was to try to get as close to universal coverage as possible. The primary designers for all of the various versions of the healthcare bills were members of the House and the Senate.

How could this have been handled differently? First, the primary customers could have been small business owners and individuals (9.1 percent of the insured population) who provide their own coverage. Both of these groups pay significantly higher premiums for comparable insurance than large organizations and those with group coverage. (For example, a small business pays 18 percent more for coverage of its employees than a large business.) These groups could have been assured that reform would cut their costs and bring them to parity. Their buy-in could have created an interested and motivated constituency to support health insurance reform.

Second, the primary focus could have been placed squarely on improving quality while decreasing cost. It is estimated that between 100,000 to 200,000 Americans die every year because of preventable medical errors in hospitals. Taxpayers pay $50 billion per year to cover Medicare recipients in the last 2 months of their lives. The World Health Organization ranks the United States as thirty-seventh in terms of the quality of healthcare provided as a country. In 1970, we spent $75 billion on healthcare. By 2008, that had mushroomed to $2.2 trillion. The United States spends twice as much per capita ($7,129) on healthcare as any other country.[2]

Third, the White House could have taken the lead in proposing its strategic plan and solution for the healthcare cost problem. It could then have made the business case for it to both the members of Congress and the American public.

Unfortunately, that's not what happened. No comprehensive and convincing plan or marketing and sales message was created or communicated to persuade the average citizen of the facts and to connect emotionally with them in a way that would rally their support. In the absence of that, discussions on death panels and pulling the plug on granny dominated in the media. No one understood the public option, and it became a synonym for socialized medicine.

As a result, the healthcare bill debate dragged on endlessly with virtually the same points being debated over and over again. It reminded us of the movie *Groundhog Day*.

The House passed its version of the healthcare bill in November 2009. The Senate finally got a bill out on Christmas Eve of the same year. In January 2010, Democrats were shuttling back and forth from Capitol Hill to the White House, working at a feverish pitch to bring a healthcare bill forward for passage. Senator Harry Reid opined that a bill was imminent. Then, on January 19, an election was held in Massachusetts to replace Ted Kennedy as the senator from that state. Scott Brown (R) beat Martha Coakley (D) for Kennedy's seat. All bets were off and healthcare went up for grabs.

In response, the president focused on healthcare in his State of the Union address. He convened a summit to discuss it. The White House drafted its own version of a healthcare bill for consideration. The president lobbied the Hill to persuade moderate Democrats to vote for the bill and took to the road to build public support for it. The bill gained some momentum because of Anthem Blue Cross of California's request for a 39 percent increase in premiums for 2010 and the huge 2009 profits announced by Anthem and several other insurance companies.[3]

The result was that in the week of March 22, 2010, the healthcare reform legislation was passed along party lines. One part of the journey was completed. The more important one was about to begin. Republicans in Congress immediately proclaimed that they would campaign to repeal the bill and attorney generals (mostly Republican) from more than a dozen states filed suits saying the legislation was unconstitutional.

It seems unlikely to us that the healthcare bill will be repealed or declared unconstitutional. Therefore, the challenge ahead of the nation in healthcare in this decade will be to take that bill as a foundation and directly address the two root causes of our healthcare crisis: out-of-control costs and poor quality.

This bill did not deal with either of these causes adequately. In the week the legislation passed, *The New York Times* ran a lead article in its business section on March 22 titled, "In Health Care Reform, Boon for Hospitals and Drug Makers."[4] And, the April issue of *Harvard Business Review*, which was released in mid-March, contained a section titled "Spotlight on Fixing Health Care."[5] That section included a graph titled "Premium Price, Poor Performance" and highlighted the following statistics:

- 55 percent—the chance of receiving care in the United States that meets generally accepted standards

- 25 percent—the decrease in inpatient mortality from community-acquired pneumonia after the implementation of a standard protocol

- 50 percent—the estimated amount of healthcare spending that goes toward unnecessary bureaucracy, duplicative tests, and other waste

The healthcare bill will expand coverage and may reduce the health insurers' bottom line somewhat but appears designed to do precious little in the areas of cost and quality. So, in our opinion, when it comes to healthcare reform—the song, "We've Only Just Begun" comes to mind. Real reform will come only when we bend the cost curve down and the quality curve up. That's what the business case for the remainder of this decade—now that there is something to build on—must be all about.

We know that one senator gets the need for making the business case for healthcare reform—Mark Warner (D-VA). Shortly after the Senate voted to debate the healthcare bill on the floor of the Senate, he sent out an e-mail to supporters stating, "If we do not work toward real healthcare reform, families will face rising premiums, employers will remain at a competitive disadvantage in the global marketplace, and federal budget deficits will go from bad to worse." Warner promised that along with colleagues, he would introduce amendments "focused on bending the cost curve and delivery system reform." We agree completely with the need for this type of approach, and that is why we advocate so forcefully for it here.

Just as with healthcare, there are comparable analyses that could, and should, be done on education, energy, and the environment. Competitive advantage should be central to all of the future plans that are advanced in these areas.

THE NEED FOR ADDITIONAL PRIORITIES

It's not just about making the case for the policy priorities. It's also making sure that they are the *right* priorities handled in the *right* way and in the *right* order.

In this regard, we feel that the healthcare debate and the stimulus bill caused us to take our eye off the ball on what should have been the top priority from the beginning of 2009—jobs. That may sound like Monday morning quarterbacking, but we are comfortable saying it because that is the recommendation that we were on record providing well before January 2009.

We've shared our perspective on the problems with the approach to healthcare. Let's turn our attention next to The American Recovery and Reinvestment Act of 2009 (ARRA, or the stimulus bill).

Our major criticism of the stimulus bill is that it had everything in it but the kitchen sink. That's because the bill was crafted around existing government departments so it conformed to the structure of government instead of the underlying economic crises or their root causes. As a result, the bill had lots of lightbulbs, but there was no tree.

The bill was not meant to be a strategic solution to the economic crisis or make us more competitive globally. The ARRA was intended to stimulate, and it appears that it did. The conventional wisdom from a wide array of economists as 2009 drew to a close was that the stimulus made things better, rather than worse, and saved jobs.

One calculation of the jobs saved or created by October 30, 2009, as reported by recipients and the Bureau of Labor Statistics (BLS), was 640,000. The Council of Economic Advisors estimated that jobs saved or created by the end of the fourth quarter "raised employment to what it otherwise would have been by 1½ to 2 million."[6] Neutral economists agreed that the bill saved or created jobs—but their estimates were more in the one million to 1½ million range.[7] We should note that "jobs saved" is an interesting metric but not one that's in the standard set employed by the BLS.

The problem is that these economists—as they frequently do—were answering the wrong question. The right question is "What would have happened in the economy if Congress had passed a massive jobs bill at the beginning of the year—say, one devoted to putting 3–4 million citizens to work in 2009—instead of a stimulus bill where jobs and money trickled out?"

We don't have a crystal ball, but we do have business experience and insights to draw upon. Our assessment is that we would have been much better off with a jobs bill, rather than a stimulus bill. That is why we advocate so strongly for such a bill in Chapter 4 of this book. It is also why we devote chapters to five additional short- and long-term priority areas that matter for creating competitive advantage: (1) manufacturing, (2) small business and entrepreneurs, (3) middle income, (4) media, and (5) the world.

We are not saying that education, energy, and the environment do not matter—they do. But they must be addressed as part of an integrated and appropriately prioritized response and as the basis for a competitive advantage, and not as a series of independent policy or legislative initiatives.

THE CRITICAL NEED FOR A DEFICIT AND DEBT REDUCTION PLAN

The U.S. deficit has exploded. The budget deficit for the fiscal year that ended on September 30, 2008 was $459 billion. By the end of the fourth quarter of 2009, the deficit had ballooned to $1.4 trillion. That's over a tripling in 1 year. As a result, at the beginning of 2010, the official debt stood at $12.3 trillion. In addition, there were another $40 to $50 trillion in debt for unfunded off-balance-sheet obligations for programs such as Medicare and Social Security.[8]

Part of the growth of the deficit was attributable to the fact that President Obama put the Iraq and Afghanistan wars on the books—the prior administration had kept them off the balance sheet. The other part was primarily attributable to the money spent on the stimulus bill and the bailouts of all types from Wall Street to Motor City to Main Street.

Needless to say, as businesspeople, we don't consider the deficit a good thing. Unfortunately, given the country's current economic need, it is necessary and unavoidable. Deficit reduction must be an absolute. It, however, must be handled with extreme care and in a planned manner to avoid the unintended consequences of creating larger deficits by taking actions that reduce future revenues by an amount greater than expenses are cut.

The bipartisan Committee for a Responsible Federal Budget (the committee) understands this. It cautions that now is not the time to tighten the deficit reduction knot when it writes, "Under current conditions, however, it makes no sense to withdraw aggregate demand until the economy is stronger. Economic growth and the financial sector are expected to be weak for the next few years as recovery takes hold. As the '1937 lesson' of the Great Depression in the United States illustrates, fiscal and monetary policy can be tightened too soon following a financially crisis-induced downturn."

The committee offers six lessons based upon its examination of deficit reduction strategies that countries worldwide have employed over the past 30 years. They boil down to two key factors:

1. Put a deficit reduction (fiscal consolidation) plan in place as soon as possible

2. Phase that plan in gradually

The committee pointed out that public debt was 55 percent of GDP in September 2009 and that without significant adjustment, would go to 87 percent by 2020 and 181 percent by 2035. It also noted that "The International Monetary Fund recently called the U.S. situation 'unsustainable.'" [9] By early 2010, a variety of approaches were being recommended to deal with the deficit and debt problem, and it seemed that some type of plan would be put into place within the next year or so.

In his FY 2011 budget, the president called for balancing the primary (noninterest) budget by 2015 and stabilizing the debt-to-GDP ratio by the end of the decade. The bipartisan Peterson–Pew Commission on Budget Reform set out a six-step proposed approach that would "require significant policy changes and raising taxes and cutting spending." Its recommended steps would result in stabilizing the debt by 2018.[10]

Conservative Congressman Paul Ryan (R-WI) presented a radical alternative to the Peterson-Pew Commission and the president's approaches in his Roadmap for the American Future. The center lanes for Ryan's "roads" included capping government spending and major changes to Social Security, Medicare, and Medicaid tax policy, including actively promoting the privatization of Social Security for future generations.[11]

Finally, David Walker, former comptroller general of the United States, provided a number of excellent ideas for addressing America's fiscal problems in his book, *Comeback America: Turning the Country Around and Restoring Fiscal Responsibility*. These include saving Social Security through means such as wage indexing and modest reductions to cost-of-living adjustments and collecting revenue more fairly by establishing some type of consumption tax and rationalizing the corporate tax structure. Walker's unique contribution was calling for "work on an agenda of transformational reforms" in three major areas: national defense, government, and fixing our dysfunctional democracy.[12] We agree with Walker's call to action in these areas.

We also agree with the IMF and the committee that the present course is unstable and unsustainable. That is why we propose later in this chapter that a deficit reduction plan be incorporated as a central element in a Twenty-First-Century Competitive Advantage Plan for the United States. That plan must be structured carefully to avoid putting the brakes on too quickly and thrusting the economy into a tailspin, which would destroy any chance of ever reducing the budget deficit or the nation's debt. In our opinion, however, that's only half of the battle.

THE CRITICAL NEED TO REBUILD THE OPPORTUNITY SOCIETY

Addressing the budget deficit and debt is necessary, but it's not sufficient to create the basis for a twenty-first-century competitive advantage. Serious and equivalent consideration must be given to what needs to be done to build a vibrant and growing national economy that enables individuals and entities to generate the level of revenue required to correct this problem.

Our concern is that the deficit and debt reduction issues will be studied in isolation. Aggregate and large-scale assumptions will be made about revenue. A scalpel and micrometer will be employed to make cuts in expenses. Little to no attention will be paid to factors related to the nation's ability to grow and how that growth translates into individual wealth generation or well-being. Making this conversion is what has enabled the United States of America to become the "Opportunity Society," which provided the economic basis for the "American Dream." (For more on the current status of the Opportunity Society, see Chapter 5: The Middle Class Matters in this book.)

GDP is the broad measure that is typically used to look at a country's economic growth. It can be defined simply as the total value of the output of a country's goods and services. Conventional economic theory is that as GDP goes up, unemployment goes down, and the standard of living goes up. As the United States' GDP improved in the last two quarters of 2009, that didn't happen, and it appears it may not happen in 2010 or anytime in the near future.

Economic theory is having a difficult time explaining this. The United States is experiencing a jobless recovery, wage deflation or stagnation, and a situation in which income inequality in the country is at its highest level in recorded history. We believe that these are issues and areas that must be addressed as part and parcel of putting together a Twenty-First-Century Competitive Advantage Plan.

Therefore, at the same time projections are being made about future GDP growth, we need to examine and project the impact of that growth on future Individual Economic Well-being (IEW). This is because while there may be a strong correlation between GDP and the general economic conditions of a country at the macrolevel, there can be very little at the micro- or individual level.

There are a variety of reasons for this, including the facts that GDP was never intended to function as an indicator of well-being, and GDP is insensitive to the distribution of income within a country.[13] As Nobel Prize-winning economist Joseph Stiglitz puts it, "No single measure can capture what is going on in a modern society, but the GDP measure fails in critical ways. We need measures that focus on how the typical individual is doing (measures of median income do a lot better than measures of average income) . . ."[14]

If we want to maintain America and the American Dream, we need to develop economic measures for the twenty-first century that examine these connections and build the crosswalk from a nation's overall productivity and output to the individual economic well-being of its citizens. We are not economists. So, we are not professionally qualified to do this. It does not take an economist, however, to know that it needs to be done.[15]

Economists need to continue to study and help us to make new inferences and develop insights on the interrelationships between growth in GDP and IEW. Economics does not create jobs or improve the human condition directly. However, data from economic studies can be used by government and business decision-makers for that purpose.

Our economy can be restored by these leaders and hardworking Americans if given the chance. That chance derives from building a competitive advantage for the nation and its citizens. That is why we advocate the need for incorporating a sophisticated IEW analysis and projections into the work of the National Global Competitiveness Commission. If this does not occur, the result, as the old joke goes, may be: "The operation was a success, but the patient died."

SWOT OR BE SWATTED

The real question is "Where do we go from here?" No one can predict with any accuracy when and how the economic turmoil will end for the United States or for its primary competitors. What can be predicted is that things will look very different for all economies for a very long time. To stay or break into the Final Four, a nation will have to be able to prepare and respond to those differences.

Part of what businesses are doing to decide how to maneuver through this minefield is conducting strategic assessments employing what is known as a SWOT analysis (Strengths, Weaknesses, Opportunities, Threats). Applying the Strengths and Weaknesses component of that approach to the United States, we can see what strengths we can leverage and what weakness we must eliminate in order to secure competitive advantage.

In April 2009, Harvard Business School Professor Michael Porter identified a number of "core" strengths and weaknesses for the United States, including those listed in the table that follows.

Table 1.3: United States Strengths and Weaknesses Analysis[16]	
Strengths	**Weaknesses**
• Innovation: science, technology, R&D • Entrepreneurship • Free and open competition • Capital markets (uncertain) • Economic decentralization • Dynamism and flexibility	• Human resources challenges: the need to restructure public education, access to higher education • Distortions in the international trading system • Falling U.S. leadership in international economic development • Weak transitional "security blanket" • Retraining system • Pension security • Health insurance access and mobility • Unnecessary costs of doing business • Burdensome regulations • High cost/high complexity tax system • Energy inefficiency • High healthcare costs

The American Competitiveness Council pinpointed four key weakness areas for the United States to address to compete effectively in the future:

1. Talent/Skills—The largest number of job openings over the next 10–15 years will be in middle-skilled jobs.

2. Investment in Research and Technology—Federal investment in scientific research is at its lowest level in 50 years.

3. Infrastructure—$1.6 trillion will be needed to bring infrastructure—roads, bridges, schools, the electric grid, telecommunications—to a good condition.

4. Energy—Today, 80 percent of the world's oil reserves are owned by national oil companies; Americans consume on average almost five times more energy per capita than the worldwide average.[17]

We would add the following additional strengths and weaknesses to this group.

Table 1.4: United States Additional Strengths and Weaknesses	
Strengths	**Weaknesses**
• Small businesses • American democracy • Free news media • Capital markets (uncertain) • Citizen initiatives • World leadership	• Growing undereducated minority underclass • Shrinking middle class with less disposable income • Declining capacity to manufacture cutting edge products • Dysfunctional Congress • Media outlets focused on "reality shows" that are less real and informative than those a civil society requires • Multinational corporations with agendas that conflict with that of the nation

Even with our additions, the list of strengths and weaknesses is not exhaustive. They do, however, provide a starting point for initiating the type of planning that will be required to achieve competitive advantage in the future.

RENEWING AMERICA'S COMPETITIVE ADVANTAGE RECOMMENDATIONS

Historically, the United States has been a planning-averse nation. Through a combination of factors, we have made that aversion work for us through the second half of the twentieth century. Part of the reason for that success was the incredible growth spurt fueled by government programs and policies after World War II. Another part was the collapse of communism in the mid-1980s and a relatively weak field of international competitors for almost a quarter of a century thereafter.

That was then. This is now. Major international competitors have upped the ante and are moving toward parity. We can either ignore this or recognize that what got us *here* will not get us *there*. We prefer the latter alternative and recommend a three-pronged approach for enhancing the nation's capacity for doing strategic and transformational thinking and planning for competitive advantage:

Competitive Advantage Primary Recommendation

1. Establish a national global competitiveness commission to develop a twenty-first-century competitive advantage plan for the United States

Competitive Advantage Subsidiary Recommendations

2. Form regional competitiveness councils to piggyback on the national plan and to develop regional solutions

3. Encourage enhanced local economic development and competitiveness planning

Our primary recommendation follows. The subsidiary recommendations are presented in the Appendix to the book.

1. Establish a national global competitiveness commission to develop a twenty-first-century competitive advantage plan for the United States.

The National Global Competitiveness Commission should be a commission similar to the 9/11 Commission in its bipartisan nature and the unfettered scope of its reach, but different from the commission in its composition. The task force should be nonpartisan, not bipartisan. Its members should be drawn from national leaders with expertise and experience in business, politics, government, civic and community service, and academia. The task force should be led by representatives from the business, civic/community, and governmental sectors. While it should include a few former elected officials, they should be a minority of the membership.

The charge to the task force should be to conduct a thorough and in-depth SWOT analysis and strategic assessment of the United States' current position, and to develop a comprehensive competitive advantage strategic plan for the U.S. At a minimum, that plan should clearly spell out a vision, goals, strategies, strategic action programs, implementation requirements, facilitating factors, potential obstacles or barriers, and critical success factors. The plan should include a budget and cost-benefit analysis for its implementation. It should also include a phased-in approach for reducing the deficit (fiscal consolidation) by a fixed percent per year before the end of this decade. The deficit reduction plan should be developed based upon a review of competing perspectives, such as those provided by the Peterson-Pew Commission on Budget Reform and the Center on Budget and Policy Priorities.[18] Finally, the plan should present GDP and IEW projections, along with the assumptions underlying them.

Sufficient time should be spent to do the planning right, meaning 18–24 months. The commission should present its plan to various stakeholder groups, such as the government, U.S. Chamber of Commerce, the National Association of Manufacturers, small business owners, and labor representatives for review and comments. The final plan should be provided to the president and U.S. Congress for consideration and action.

The commission should be paid for by a mix of public and private funds. It should also solicit volunteer-contributed time to assist in the research and analysis from organizations such as businesses, consulting firms, universities, and civic organizations.

The commission will not have to start from scratch. As we noted earlier in this chapter, the Competitiveness Council has done excellent work and analyses that can be used as a starting point. Other groups of all stripes and persuasions, such as the Heritage Foundation, Cato Institute, the New America Foundation, Center for American Progress, Brookings Institution, the American Enterprise Institute, the United States Business and Industry Council, the Center on Budget and Policy Priorities, and the Economic Policy Institute have also done studies of merit. This full body of work should be reviewed and considered as input by the commission in the analysis phase of its planning.

You might argue that our elected officials already are doing this planning when they write laws or develop policy. Unfortunately, nothing could be further from the truth. A law is not a plan. A policy is not a plan.

Moreover, as we note later in the book, Congress is understaffed and frequently has to depend on lobbyists and think tanks to do its primary and secondary research. Those groups have agendas. They are hired guns for their cause, as they should be. When it comes to an issue as critical as the future of this great nation, we adamantly believe that we need more objective and neutral data. We need real strategic planning and foresight. Professor James Galbraith from the University of Texas makes an excellent case for this:

> ". . . Because markets cannot and do not think ahead, the United States needs a capacity to plan. To build such a capacity, we must, first of all, overcome our taboo against planning. Planning is inherently imperfect, but in the absence of planning, disaster is certain . . . At this juncture in history, the United States needs to come to grips with its position in the global economy and prepare for the day when the unlimited privilege of issuing never-to-be paid chits to the rest of the world may come to an end."[19]

In early 2010, President Obama appointed a National Commission for Fiscal Responsibility and Reform headed by ex-Senator Alan Simpson (R-WY), and Erskine Bowles, former White House chief of staff for Bill Clinton, to take an in-depth look at the country's deficit and debt problem. This was an important and essential action. But, it is an insufficient response to the nation's situation because it deals primarily with the expense side of the equation. We need a holistic plan that positions the United States and its citizens for success going forward. If there is one lesson that we should remember from the Great Depression, it is that premature deficit reduction retards growth and recovery and can lead to a double-dip recession.

While the past decade was one of economic decline for the United States, it was one of significant growth for China, India, and Brazil. The United States can ill afford for this decade to be the same. Given the new world realities and the country's delicate condition, the United States can not depend on the "invisible hand" to solve its problems. It must take things into its own hands.

In his State of the Union address, President Obama acknowledged that he understood this requirement when he stated, "Well, I do not accept second place for the United States of America. As hard as it may be, as uncomfortable and contentious as the debates may be, it's time to get serious about fixing the problems that are hampering our growth."[20] It is time to get serious. It is time for the president to rally and challenge each and every one of us to the common cause of doing our personal and collective best to win this worldwide competition.

Creating and maintaining the United States' competitive advantage for both the short term and long term requires doing the right type of planning and teamwork at all levels. It also depends on the ability to execute and the will to persevere. These are themes that we will repeat again and again throughout this book as we address the essential areas and actions for creating Enterprise USA and renewing the American Dream.

Section I

Assessing the Dream

Many of us have taken the American dream for granted. However, most of us have probably done little thinking about the dream and what will be required to maintain and renew it.

We devote the next two chapters of this book to these considerations:

- Chapter 2: Reflections on the Dream
- Chapter 3: The Renewal Framework

In the chapters, we provide a working definition of the dream, put it into context, and furnish a general framework for analyzing and acting upon it. We can use this shared understanding and perspective to identify common ground and ways in which we can work together as citizens to renew America and the American dream.

2 | Reflections on the Dream

"We need a new spirit of community, a sense that we are all in this together, or the American Dream will continue to wither. Our destiny is bound up with the destiny of every other American."

Bill Clinton

THE UNITED STATES OF AMERICA IS A NATION OF DREAMERS AND doers. Our country was founded on the premise that if you can conceive it and believe it, you can achieve it. Since then, each generation has thought that anything and everything was possible—except for the impossible which takes just a little bit longer.

For more than 200 years, no hope has been too large and no dream has been too far out of reach. We all felt that our children would be better off and accomplish more than we did. Now, for the first time in the short history of this country, those dreams appear to be fading.

THE NATURE OF THE DREAM

Each of us has a personal definition or conceptualization of the American Dream. Based upon our own experiences as American Dreamers and discussions with others, here are some of the ingredients that we believe form the essence of the dream for the majority of us.

The American Dream is the opportunity each and every citizen has to realize one's personal potential and to achieve success, generally measured as economic security. The fundamental elements of the dream are getting educated and working hard in order to have a good job that pays decent wages, provides adequate benefits, puts food on the table, a roof over one's head, and allows for retirement with dignity.

A core precept of the dream is that doing this will ensure that America continues to grow and prosper and that each generation will have a better life than the previous one. Two other essential aspects of the dream are: a concern for the common good; and, pride in our nation and its standing in the world.

EVERY PICTURE TELLS A STORY

What is the status of the American Dream today? The real story is told in human terms, not statistics. We're sure you have your own stories of Americans who are under- or unemployed, whose homes have been foreclosed on, and who are going without healthcare insurance because they can't afford it. Maybe you've experienced this yourself. We'd like to share some of the stories with which we are familiar:

- There is a nice home on the corner of Presidents Boulevard and Washington Drive in Sarasota, Florida, that is currently up for a short sale. It was owned by two young brothers who ran a residential construction company in Illinois. When the construction boom times were going well, they bought the home as a vacation getaway—part of their American Dream. When residential real estate development collapsed, their business went with it. They continued to make the payments on the home for as long as they could. But eventually, they could not afford to do so. They gave the property back to the bank and became the victims of a double whammy—forced out of business in Illinois and foreclosed on in Florida.

- John used to be an executive with Blue Cross and Blue Shield. He had been underemployed for almost 5 years and is now unemployed. He no longer carries health insurance because he can't afford it. John will turn 65 in 2 years and become eligible for Medicare. He's taking the gamble that he'll beat the odds till then.

- Al has a law degree and an M.B.A. He's in his 50s and has had an excellent career as a management consultant. He spent the bulk of his career with larger firms and had some good independent project work until approximately 2 years ago. Al has been actively searching for a job since then. He's willing to relocate or to go back out on the road. He hasn't had a single job offer.

- A family-owned business manufactured Mexican food products for 45 years and employed over 100 people. The company never had a product quality problem or a customer problem. Nevertheless, because of the economic downturn, its bank stopped lending and called in the loan and the business collapsed. The demand for the product is still there, but the bank found it more profitable to invest in things other than small businesses.

We're sure you can add a dozen stories to this list. In fact, given the unemployment rate and underemployment rate, the impact is ever present. You just have to stop and look around to see it.

You may be the husband who is staying home to take care of the kids while your wife is working. You may be the ex-middle manager who is working as a greeter at Wal-Mart. You may be the baby boomer who gave up your job to be a caregiver for your parents and now you're concerned about who will care for you when you need it. You may be the recent recipient of a B.A., M.B.A., or Ph.D. working as a waitress or volunteering because the position that you thought would be there when you graduated doesn't exist.

THE DREAM DISTORTED

Whatever the case and wherever we look, the signs abound that the American Dream is diminishing and becoming more and more unachievable. While it may seem that this is the direct result of the economic and market collapse of 2008, it is not.

We Americans have had concerns regarding the potential of achieving the American Dream for some time. As David Kamp noted in his excellent *Vanity Fair* article of April 2009, "Rethinking the American Dream":

"A CNN poll taken in 2006 found that more than half of those surveyed, 54 percent, considered the American Dream unachievable—and CNN

noted that the numbers were nearly the same in a 2003 poll it had conducted. Before that, in 1995, a Business Week/Harris Poll found that two-thirds of those surveyed believed the American Dream had become harder to achieve in the past 10 years, and three-fourths believed that achieving the dream would be harder still in the upcoming 10."[1]

So, the American Dream was not pushed into decline or put into jeopardy by the events of 2008 alone. There's something else going on that is much broader and more cultural, contextual, and longer term in nature.

One of the key factors that we believe has influenced the decline of the American Dream is what we refer to as "the Expectations Escalator." Since the late 1960s, the mantra for many Americans has been more, more, and more—and more is never enough.

Consistent with this interpretation, the construction of what constitutes the American Dream has been expanded and expectations have increased exponentially. As a result, the gap between an idealized "dream state" and an individual's personal reality becomes unachievable. It's not that many of us didn't acquire possessions beyond our wildest dreams or needs. For example, consider:

- **The McMansion**—a massive home built on the entire lot in a suburb where a modest bungalow or ranch-style home once stood. The footprint of the previous residence on this site would fit into the master bath of the mansion.

- **The Hummer**—a tanklike vehicle (fortunately, soon to go the way of the dinosaur) that could not perform well either on- or off-road, but did prove that people will pay almost any amount for an adult toy.

- **Cartier bags, Air Jordan tennis shoes, iPods**—pick your favorite extravagance purchased not for functionality or necessity, but because we could.

How many of us can honestly say we did not participate in some way in the unnecessary gluttony and self-indulgence that came to represent the American Dream of the past quarter century?

Over time, how we view the family unit has also changed. In the 1950s, television sitcoms were almost exclusively about the perfectly functional family: *Ozzie and Harriet, Father Knows Best, My Three Sons,* and *Leave It to Beaver.* Every major channel had its version of a frame house and white picket fence. Back then, we wondered why our family couldn't be as perfect as those portrayed on the television screen.

Since the 1970s, TV's version of the family unit has changed. The dominant stereotype has become the dysfunctional family: *All in the Family, Rosie, the Simpsons*; even the Huxtables had their problems, and the list goes on.

Today, every major broadcast and cable channel has its version of bramble bushes and briar patches. Now, when we watch television, we thank our lucky stars that while our family may not be perfect, we're not as screwed up as those folks are.

As a nation, we've become obsessed with so-called reality TV. What's real about the reality TV shows is that they have real people in very unreal situations doing unreal things in an attempt to get rich quick or to achieve instant notoriety. That's because their producers can make very real profits because these shows cost so much less than the made-for-TV sitcoms or docudramas.

The other thing that's real about these shows is that they appeal to a lot of us. Consider the following: *The Apprentice, Flip This House, American Idol, Survivor,* and *The Amazing Race.* Add to the mix, *Jerry Springer, Dr. Phil, Dog the Bounty Hunter.* Leaven it with *Ozzy Osbourne and The Osbournes, Flavor of Love with Flavor Fav, Jon and Kate Plus 8,* and the list goes on.

A BLURRED VISION

Those reality shows remind us a lot of the Roman Empire when the people would flock to the coliseum to give thumbs-up or thumbs-down to contestants in the ring to decide who would live and who would die. The shows today may not be about life and death, but, in our opinion, the behavior of both the participants and the reactions of the viewing public seem no less barbaric.

They speak volumes about how a relatively large segment of our society has come to see and define the American Dream. When we first wrote the preceding line, we thought we might be overstating the case.

Then, we stumbled upon a book by Robert Burgess titled, *America in Focus.*

Burgess is a focus group expert who has been conducting focus groups for 2 decades. In Chapter 1 of his book, Burgess identifies the following three major components of the "The New American Dream" based upon his focus group findings:

1. Americans <u>crave</u> financial success/wealth.
2. In the quest for money and wealth, anything goes. <u>Anything</u>.
3. Americans want to build wealth <u>right now</u>.[2]

We assume that Burgess does not mean to extrapolate from his focus group to the entire American population. We believe that he does capture a real dilemma regarding the dream and what it has become for too many of us.

In our opinion, there are a number of factors that have driven this distortion or blurring of the dream over the past 3 decades. These include:

- **Arrogant Complacency:** Mike Ribaudo coined this term in the early 1980s to refer to the Big Three automobile manufacturers. We apply it here to the perspective or attitude of the nation as a whole that emerged from the mid-1980s until 9/11, and then reemerged again shortly thereafter. Others have referred to this state as "Extreme Exceptionalism": We were bigger than, better than, smarter than anyone else. We were too big to fail. Or so we thought.

- **Conspicuous Consumption:** As a nation, we went debt-drunk and credit-crazy. We went from being the bread basket and manufacturer for the world to becoming its shopping mall.

- **The Desire for Instant Gratification:** Before credit became easy to obtain, we had Christmas clubs, S&H green stamps, and put things on layaway. Once we were able to finance our homes with ARMs and no money down, we used them as ATMs and lost the discipline to save and the need to defer a purchase. We were nudged into purchasing virtually everything and anything that we wanted immediately—because we could and because our neighbors were also doing it.

- **It's All about Me:** As a society, we became far too self-centered for far too long. Now we are suffering the consequences and will be for some time.

- **Irrational Exuberance:** The behavioral economist Robert Shiller wrote a book with this title.[3] In a thumbnail sketch somewhat over-simplified, Shiller said that we are much less rational in our decision making than we think we are. We tend to overestimate the potential of good things happening while underestimating risk. "The market will always go up." "Our home values will always appreciate." "We'll always get that next promotion, job, or raise." As a result, we frequently plunge in where wise men fear to tread.

A PIVOTAL MOMENT

When things look bleak, we believe there is an opportunity—a pivotal moment for each of us and the United States.

This isn't just about national security or somebody else's job. It's about our domestic and economic security and all of our jobs and future opportunities for this and future generations. It's about who we are and who we will be, what we believe in and what we will stand for. It's about a fight for our future that will demand equal measures of aspiration, inspiration, and perspiration.

What is different about this moment in time is that for the first time in a very long time, we as Americans have begun to express doubts about our future as individuals and as a nation. As a result, both personal and societal issues have come to the forefront:

- Loss of self-esteem
- Lack of personal confidence
- Lack of earning power
- Lack of upward mobility
- Lack of opportunity
- Lack of trust in our basic institutions
- Questions about the competitiveness of the United States in a world economy

- Diminished international status of the United States as a moral leader and role model for the world

If we allow these concerns to overwhelm us and lose our collective confidence, they can plunge us into a national abyss. If, on the other hand, we use these concerns and issues to reflect upon who we are individually and as a country, we can begin to move forward and change the trajectory. We can rebuild the American Dream.

As a nation, we need to engage in a national dialogue and joint and cooperative efforts to restore the dream. There are three basic requirements for accomplishing this:

- Reframing the Dream
- Reinforcing Hope
- Rebuilding Confidence

REFRAMING THE DREAM

The restoration process must begin with the American Dream itself. What is the American Dream, anyway? Some people trace the American Dream to the following words from the Declaration of Independence:

> "... hold these truths to be self-evident, that all men are created equal, they are endowed by their Creator with certain inalienable Rights, that among these are Life, Liberty and the pursuit of Happiness."

Indeed, those words may be the origin of the concept. The actual term, however, was first used by James Truslow Adams in his book *The Epic of America*, written in 1931:

> "... a dream of a land in which life should be better and richer and fuller for everyone, with opportunity for each according to ability and achievement. It is a difficult dream for the European upper classes to interpret adequately, and too many of us ourselves have grown weary and mistrustful of it. It is not a dream of motor cars and high wages merely, but a dream of social order in which each man and each woman shall

be able to attain to the fullest stature of which they are innately capable, and be recognized by others for what they are, regardless of the fortuitous circumstances of birth or position."[4]

We weren't promised fame or fortune by the Declaration of Independence or in the dream's original conceptualization by Mr. Adams in 1931. What we were promised were a few simple but meaningful things: equality, life, liberty, and the pursuit of happiness (not a guarantee of happiness, we must note), a land in which life should be richer and fuller for everyone, a social order in which each man and woman should be able to attain the fullest stature of which they are innately capable (opportunity for each according to ability and achievement), and to be recognized by others for what we are and what we accomplish.

This is the American Dream reframed and right-sized. It is not an outrageous dream. It is not a pipe dream. It is a realistic dream—a dream that was founded on a brilliant and unprecedented promise.

REINFORCING HOPE

We are living in trying times—times that foster and promote pessimism, skepticism, and cynicism. We have heard many people say they are working harder and harder to make less and less. We've also had people at all steps on the economic ladder say to us this is "scary, very scary; never seen anything like this in our lifetimes."

As we discussed earlier in this chapter, for a variety of reasons, our faith or belief in the American Dream and our own prospects for success have been strained, if not shattered. How do we deal with this?

We do it by staying focused on the facts, emphasizing the positive and not being paralyzed by the negative. That's not being an optimist. That's not being a pessimist. That's what we call being a "positive realist." Positive realism is what's required to move forward constructively and work through and around obstacles.

While hope is not a strategy, it is a necessary but not sufficient condition for surviving in tough times. As Captain Chesley "Sully" Sullenberger proved when he successfully landed his plane in the Hudson River in January 2009 in what became known as the "Miracle on the Hudson"—hope floats. Of course, it helped significantly that Sully had the skill and experience to pull this off and that there were tugboats at the scene almost immediately to save the passengers before the plane sank. Hope floats—but only for a while.

REBUILDING CONFIDENCE

Hope is the emotional glue that will hold us together, both individually and collectively, during this stressful period. It is the starting point. Hope, however, will not turn things around. It will not rebuild confidence.

Nor can President Barack Obama. On Sunday, April 5, 2009, *The New York Times* ran an article by Peter Baker titled, "Obama and The Confidence Game." A sidebar in that article read, "Americans are feeling a bit bewildered. Can the President give us back our gumption?"

The answer to that question was, and is, an unequivocal "NO!" Confidence is borne of positive progress and end results. The confidence game in a recovery or recession is won on the playing field. Words can inspire hope, but it takes results to give us confidence.

Positive progress and end results in this instance will depend upon:

- Addressing the right issues
- Developing the appropriate policies, plans, and programs
- Managing execution with a laser-beam focus
- Demonstrating an unprecedented level of pragmatism, patience, and perseverance in the face of adversity

All of these elements will be important for rebuilding confidence and restoring the American Dream. The essential requirement for success, however, will be a meaningful partnership among the key stakeholders in society and active citizen participation in initiating and implementing solutions. This will enable us to reestablish the sense of community and shared destiny that made America great. That will enable the United States to continue to be the land for and home of dreamers and doers.

3 | The Renewal Framework

"I do not believe in a fate that will fall on us no matter what we do. I believe in a fate that will fall on us if we do nothing. So, with all the creative energy at our command, let us begin an era of national renewal. Let us renew our determination, our courage, and our strength. And let us renew our faith and our hope."

Ronald Reagan

In 1773, the Boston Tea Party and town hall meetings were important means for developing the American democracy. In stark contrast, the tea parties and town hall meetings held in the late summer and early fall of 2009 became vehicles for potentially derailing it. It's not because of the citizen participation. That was a good thing. It was because of the manner of that participation.

Some of the healthcare town halls were disrupted. Others were shut down by unruly protesters. A few were canceled. These town halls were labeled "town brawls" by the news media. As *The New York Times* described it:

> "The traditional town hall meeting . . . had been hijacked, overrun by sophisticated social networking campaigns—those on the right protesting so loudly as to shut down public discourse and those on the left springing into action to shut down the shut downs."[1]

Some might characterize the explosive town halls as democracy in action. We believe it was more a case of democracy in traction—traction created by a small group of partisan agitators with an agenda and a limited amount of knowledge. They came to the meetings to create chaos and block communication, rather than to exchange information and engage in a civil dialogue.

Unfortunately, these events were not isolated instances. They reflect an evolving trend toward diminished knowledge and insights regarding the operations and underpinnings of our democratic society.[2] Both American democracy and the American Dream depend upon informed citizens. Informed citizenship requires an understanding of:

- The American Dream Construct
- The American Dream Platform
- The American Dream Process

THE AMERICAN DREAM CONSTRUCT

The American Dream and capitalism are frequently thought of synonymously. Capitalism is an essential requirement for the dream, but it is not the dream. The American Dream is the ability to be all that you can be in a nation that allows you that freedom.

American capitalism is what facilitates the accomplishment of the dream. American capitalism is a much broader construct than just economic or financial capital. It is comprised of at least eight forms of capital as depicted in the illustration that follows.

Figure 3.1: The American Dream Construct

Each form of capital has its own unique characteristics:

- **Individual Capital:** the capacity, capabilities, and resources that each of us has that enables us to achieve personal success.
- **Social Capital:** the connections among individuals and social networks and how those connections work to achieve our goals.
- **Economic Capital:** the collective wealth of the nation in terms of its financial and natural resources.
- **Intellectual Capital:** the collective IQ of the nation, including its intelligence and emotional maturity.
- **Organization Capital:** the composite strengths of the nation's business, government, and nonprofit organizations.
- **Community Capital:** the place-based strengths of each community within the nation.
- **Spiritual Capital:** The religious and moral strengths of the citizens of the nation.
- **Institutional Capital:** The aggregate strengths of the country's foundational organizations (public sector, private sector, and social).

Together, these forms of capital define the context within which an individual can realize his or her potential and shape the parameters of "the common good." They are the engine of the American Dream machine.

If the engine is hitting well on all eight cylinders, the dream thrives. If one or more cylinders are sluggish, the dream stalls.

Consider the U.S. today. How well is the engine tuned? Are there cylinders misfiring that need to be adjusted? If so, which ones?

THE AMERICAN DREAM PLATFORM

As noted in Chapter 2, some people trace the American Dream to the phrase in the Declaration of Independence, ". . . all men are created equal, they are endowed by their Creator with certain inalienable Rights, that among those are Life, Liberty and the pursuit of Happiness."

That phrase is part of the foundation for the dream, but only part. As depicted in the following illustration, the platform for the American Dream has three components.

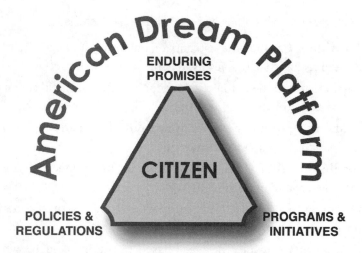

Figure 3.2: The American Dream Platform

Enduring Promises

The Declaration of Independence established the dream. The Bill of Rights brought it to life by protecting our personal liberties.

The Bill of Rights is the name given to the first ten amendments to the United States Constitution. Four of those amendments deal with asserting or retaining our affirmative rights (e.g., the right to freedom of speech), while six protect us from negative actions (e.g., protection against excessive bail and cruel and unusual punishment) that the government might take to deprive us of our individual rights.

In reviewing these rights, it becomes obvious that the Founding Fathers sought to achieve a delicate balance between individuals, states, and the federal government—a goal they achieved. Federalist and Anti-Federalist came together and compromised to add these basic pillars to the American Dream platform.

There have been 17 additional amendments to the Constitution since the original 10. As presented in the following table, six of these amendments directly expanded the American Dream for citizens or extended it to previously disenfranchised classes.

Table 3.1: American Dream-Related Constitutional Amendments		
Amendment	**Key Content**	**Year Ratified**
XIII	Abolished slavery	1865
XIV	Clarified citizenship status of persons "born or naturalized" in the U.S.	1868
XV	Gave the right to vote regardless of race or color or previous condition of servitude	1870
XIX	Gave women the right to vote	1920
XXIV	Eliminated the payment of poll tax as a requirement to vote	1964
XXVI	Gave 18-year-olds the right to vote	1971

Policies and Regulations

The dominant rules and regulations for our society are reflected in government or public policy. It shapes the terrain for the betterment of America and future achievement of the American Dream. Viewed in this manner, understanding and contributing to what is or is not enacted as policy becomes one of the most important acts of responsible citizenship. It is a fundamental obligation and civic duty.

This book is not meant as a primer on policy analysis. It is, however, intended to stress that policy matters. It matters a lot. We ignore getting involved in policy development at our own peril and that of the nation.

Government policy usually takes one of three forms: executive orders, legislation, and judicial rulings. A central element of policy also includes the extent to which something is regulated or deregulated. To grasp the significance of each of these aspects of policy, consider the following:

The first executive orders President George W. Bush signed as president in 2001 related to establishing a White House Office and Agency for Faith-based and Community Initiatives. Other executive orders President Bush signed during his first year included one establishing the Department of Homeland Security (DHS) and a series of orders establishing succession plans at all the major government agencies.

The first orders that President Barack Obama signed as president in 2009 related to presidential records and ethics commitments by Executive Branch personnel. Other orders that Obama signed early on included one focused on Guantanamo Bay and another on the establishment of a White House Economic Advisory Board.

On the legislative front, one need only look at the endless health-care debate and the American Reinvestment and Recovery Act of 2009 to see not only what does and does not get done, but also how money gets spent based upon policy priorities. Or, look back in time again to the Bush administration and at pieces of legislation such as No Child Left Behind or the Civil Rights Act of 1964 that outlawed racial segregation to see how policy influences the American landscape.

Taking a more historical perspective on the court's role, think about the decisions in Brown v. the Board of Education (integration of schools), Roe v. Wade (a woman's right to choose), and Title IX, which gave women equal rights for support of their athletic activities. These cases, and many more, have a tremendous impact on the nature and thrust of our democratic society. Established law is one of the most difficult things in the United States to change.

Finally, there's the issue of whether and what to regulate. This is one of the areas where conservatives and liberals differ and tangle the most. Conservatives accuse liberals/progressives of wanting to regulate everything and to put it into a straightjacket. Liberals accuse conservatives of wanting to regulate nothing and to let it roam free in its birthday suit.

Birthday suit or straightjacket, the unintended consequences on either side can be disastrous. As examples, one need only look to the abolition of Glass–Steagall in 1999 and the elimination of other financial regulations which led to the financial meltdown of the past few years.

In summary, all those who tread the halls of Congress understand that making governmental policy is not a meaningless or a leisure-time activity. As citizens, we need to have that same understanding and appreciation. If we do not, and policy development becomes the exclusive province and battlefield of those on Capitol Hill or in state houses and city halls, the nation and the dream will pay a very high price.

Programs and Initiatives

Governmental policies are most visible through the programs and initiatives that are implemented because of them. These programs reflect the country's values and over time, have enabled, advanced, and sustained the American Dream. For example, Social Security, Medicare, and the GI Bill were all programs established by the government to aid citizens.

Think about it—education, homes, jobs, social insurance. That's the stuff of the American Dream brought to you in part or enabled by federal government programs. Where would the country be without these and countless other programs that help to provide the springboards and the foundations for economic security for our citizens and businesses?

One of the mistakes commonly made is to discount or underestimate the positive significance and contributions of government programs and initiatives in all of our lives. Stephanie Coontz corrects this view in her book, *The Way We Never Were*, where she goes to great lengths to point out the role that government played in creating the post-World War II era of the 1950s and helping establish the basis for economic advancement and development of the middle class.[3]

Christopher Howard comes at it from a different perspective in his book, *The Welfare State Nobody Knows: Debunking Myths about U.S. Social Policy*.[4] Based upon a rigorous and thorough statistical analysis of data from the 1990s and early 2000s, Howard's conclusion is that when it comes to welfare, we are all on it and the affluent and middle class benefit more than those in the lower income brackets.

Howard's calculation of "welfare" for the middle class and affluent includes subsidized fringe benefits such as health insurance and retirement pensions; home mortgage deductions; charitable deductions; child tax credits; and capital gains tax breaks. He observed, "The American welfare state is larger and more popular than commonly believed. . . . The American welfare state does not do much to lift people out of poverty or to close the gap between rich and poor. What redistribution there is occurs more across age lines than income lines."[5]

Is it any wonder that such a large number of people at the healthcare town halls were older citizens? Think about that for 1 minute.

What would the economic collapse of 2008 and 2009 have looked like if there had been no Social Security or Medicare? That's a frightening thought, both for the future of the country and the American Dream.

THE AMERICAN DREAM PROCESS

While sound policies and programs establish the platform or floor for the American Dream, they do not set the ceiling for it. Creating that ceiling is everyone's business. It's not just the government setting policy, business creating jobs, and nonprofits and community organizations providing the social glue. Most importantly, it is not being satisfied with the status quo. The status quo is what got us to where we are today.

Renewing the American Dream with all of its forms of capital will depend on translating plans into action and implementing them effectively. This can only be accomplished through a process focused on transformation and not on incremental adjustments or tinkering around the edges. The key components of that transformational process are:

- Leadership, organizational, and individual renewal
- Preparation, involvement, and execution
- Twenty-first-century citizenship

Leadership, Organizational, and Individual Renewal

These are the three essential ingredients for launching the renewal of the American Dream:

- **Leadership Renewal:** It has been said, "managers do things right; leaders do the right things." In this era of the new normal for the United States, leadership is more important than ever. As citizens, consumers, and employees, we have lost confidence. We are looking for leaders with the "right stuff" to do the right things to help restore that confidence and reboot Enterprise USA.

- **Organizational Renewal:** Organizations of all types are the building blocks of a developed and democratic society. In the same way that highways and electrical grids define and constitute the country's physical infrastructure, organizations define our economic, social, and cultural infrastructure. In combination, they generate capital of all forms. Virtually all American organizations have been challenged by the economic crisis and recession. Many have disappeared while some have already reinvented themselves. All will have to do some form of renewal to succeed going forward and to contribute to the reinvigoration of America and the American Dream.

- **Individual Renewal:** Americans value individualism and independence. But, as noted, our confidence has been shaken by recent events. Whether you are wealthy or poor, you have felt the strain. The strain has increased for many of us as we realize that recovery may be to a new "normal." Given this, each of us will have to find our own "true north" on the compass and chart our own personal path to individual renewal.

These three interlocking ingredients work individually and in combination to create the Renewal Model. (We present and explain this model in detail in Chapter 14 of the book.)

Preparation, Involvement, and Execution
For America to be renewed, its organizations in all sectors—private, public, and nonprofit—must be renewed. This will not be accomplished through quick fixes or "ax murders." It requires a focused and sustained effort in an implementation cycle comprised of three components:

- **Preparation:** planning, organizing, and ensuring the level of competence to perform professionally and properly.
- **Involvement:** securing the engagement of the appropriate stakeholder groups and individual citizens to ensure participation and ownership.
- **Execution:** putting the proper procedures and processes in place to manage performance and to take corrective actions as necessary.

Call it the P-I-E Cycle. (We present and explain the cycle in detail in Chapter 15 of the book.)

An excellent example of putting the P-I-E Cycle to work in the public sector comes from Pennsylvania. The State of Pennsylvania got $235 million in weatherization funding as part of the federal government's stimulus bill. The money did not flow to the state until July of 2009.

The state's Weatherization Providers Task Force, chaired by Gene Brady, Executive Director of the Commission on Economic Opportunity of Luzerne County used the period from November 2008 until July 2009 to "ramp up" for the expansion by surveying the agencies and organizations involved, meeting to discuss the results, prioritizing projects, and making recommendations. By the time the funding came through, they were ready to implement their plans. (Sadly, because of a deadlock over the Pennsylvania state budget, the Pennsylvania weatherization agencies were barely able to begin to implement their plans by the end of the year.)

In contrast, an example of the P-I-E Cycle not at work was provided by the national security breakdown which allowed a Nigerian terrorist to attempt to bring down a commercial jetliner headed from Amsterdam to Detroit on Christmas Day, 2009. President Obama commented at length on the failure, noting that intelligence officials had "failed to connect the dots." Thomas Kean, cochair of the 9/11 Commission, observed, "We still haven't fixed the systemic flaws in U.S. intelligence."[6]

The P-I-E Cycle could be thought of as just good management practice. And, it is. In fact, because of the way that the American democracy works, implementing the cycle here is much more difficult and daunting than it would be in centrally controlled economies like China, Japan, and South Korea. Yet, that is absolutely what will be necessary to renew the American Dream.

Twenty-First-Century Citizenship

The final component of the American Dream process is twenty-first-century citizenship. The overarching role for the twenty-first-century citizen is to be a "capital creator." The fundamental responsibility for each of us to fulfill that role is to build our own *individual capital* by becoming a peak performer—to use marine terminology, "to be the best that you can be."

We can then engage and contribute fully to the seven other areas of capital formation—social, economic, intellectual, organization, community, spiritual, and institutional. To maximize our contributions in those areas, we will need to be:

- **Interested**—concerned about the common good and the American community as opposed to purely pecuniary or personal concerns

- **Issues-oriented**—focused on areas of civic and social concern as opposed to rigid ideologies

- **Informed**—dedicated to gathering and analyzing objective data as the basis for civic and social engagement

- **Independent**—committed to exercising personal judgment as opposed to taking totally partisan positions, and

- **Involved**—engaged actively in addressing those issues that are of paramount concern to our community and nation

The circumstances, interests, and capacity of each twenty-first-century citizen will vary. Therefore, each of us will have to determine where, when, and how to be involved.

Being on the sidelines or being a spectator, however, is not an option. We must recognize that as Americans, we have the broadest set of rights in the world and that along with those rights come responsibilities. We must commit ourselves to our own courses of action based upon that understanding and recognition.

You might be reading this and saying to yourself that a single person or a small group can't make a difference. However, from the establishment of the nation to this day, individual citizens have been leaders in bringing about the reforms and changes required in our society and in governmental policies and programs.

Senator Bob Graham describes 10 of these citizens, such as Candy Lightner, the founder of Mothers Against Drunk Driving (MADD), in his new book, *America, the Owner's Manual: Making Government Work for You*. He also sets out a systematic methodology that can be employed to "make government work for you."[7] Graham's book, along with various material available from Public Agenda, a nonprofit organization that has been working around the country since 1975 to promote greater community engagement and a more citizen-centered approach to politics, are excellent "how-to" references that we, as citizens, can employ to initiate and work on changes in the governmental arena.[8]

America is the world's grandest experiment. America is, and always will be, a work in progress. When someone says something can't be done, we do it. When someone says our best days are behind us, we prove them wrong. When someone says we can't get along, we unite. When someone asks where do we start, the twenty-first-century citizen responds, "Let the renewal begin with me."

Renewing America and creating Enterprise USA requires transformation in all sectors of society. In the next section of this book, we present our analysis and recommendations for beginning that transformational process.

Section II

Reviving the Dream

One of our fundamental responsibilities as citizens is to provide input and feedback to help shape the policies and an agenda that can be used to create a competitive advantage that will renew America and the American Dream.

We address the areas that we believe are most critical for establishing that advantage in the six chapters in this section of the book:

- Chapter 4: Jobs Matter
- Chapter 5: The Middle Class Matters
- Chapter 6: Manufacturing Matters
- Chapter 7: Small Business and Entrepreneurs Matter
- Chapter 8: The Media Matters
- Chapter 9: The World Matters

There are undoubtedly other areas that are of importance for competitive advantage. We selected these because, in our opinion, they are the bedrock for it.

There has been erosion in all of these areas for almost a quarter of a century that accelerated during America's **decade of decline**. If these areas are not addressed in an adequate and timely manner in this **decisive decade**, it will be virtually impossible to create the essential environment for establishing and sustaining a competitive advantage.

4 | Jobs Matter

A lot of fellows nowadays have a B.A., M.D., or Ph.D.
Unfortunately, they don't have a J.O.B.

Fats Domino

By August of 2009, the American economy had begun to recover. Unfortunately, that recovery didn't include jobs. To add insult to injury, the unemployed and underemployment numbers continued to go up.

The Treasury Department conducted a stress test on several Wall Street financial institutions in early 2009. If a stress test had been administered to the American working public in August or later in 2009, the pressure reading would have been off the charts. Americans were, and still are, in a state of high anger and anxiety.

The anger was fueled by a number of factors, including the Wall Street bailouts, the automotive industry bailout, the failure to hold anyone accountable for the economic collapse, and the increasing national deficit. The anxiety stemmed from a substantial loss in the value of homes and retirement accounts, coupled with almost complete uncertainty about the future.

The fear factor was coming to the forefront for a larger and larger segment of the public as unemployment stood at 10.2 percent in November from a starting point of 7.2 percent at the beginning of 2009. Predictions were that it would be in the 10 percent range throughout 2010. The American economy lost 3.5 million jobs in 2009 and a total of 7.2 million jobs in the past 2 years. Given our country's population growth, it is estimated that the economy is 10 to 11 million jobs short going into 2010.[1]

When Bill Clinton ran for president in 1992, his mantra for the campaign was "It's the Economy, Stupid." The mantra for those in government at the beginning of 2009 should have been "It's Jobs, Stupid." Jobs should have been job one from the outset of the year. As the year ended and 2010 began, a jobs bill was being drafted by the Congress. Our concern is that it is 1 year late and could be several billion dollars short.

THE HUMAN COSTS OF JOBLESSNESS

A person who is without a job is classified as unemployed. It seems to us that "unemployed" is a much cooler term than "jobless." It turns the individual without work into a statistic. Behind each statistic, however, is a human story—a story that tells the true tale of being without work. The person who loses a job loses part of his or her sense of self-worth. The person who loses a job is knocked down a couple of rungs on Maslow's hierarchy. The person who loses a job loses part of the social network. The person who loses a job is less able to provide for those he or she supports. That's just for starters.

If that person stays jobless for an extended period of time, the psychological and economic costs can be enormous. There's more time to fill with less things to do. Stress can increase and abuse of self and others is possible. Self-doubt and hatred is possible. Debt can increase. A home can be lost. A marriage can be broken, or a family torn apart.

Years ago, renowned industrial/organizational psychologist Charles Hulin advised ". . . the loss of a job has fundamental consequences for our lives." That's because work provides so much to our lives. Given all that work provides, Hulin says the ultimate consequence of the loss of a job could be the loss of life. His research shows that suicides in the U.S. tend to increase significantly during times of high unemployment.[2]

Work is important to each of us, but its significance varies. As a result, the impact of the loss of a job will vary considerably from person to person, but there will be some amount of impact for all. Unlike unemployment numbers, the full impact of the loss of a job on a person's life is neither measured directly nor reported publicly. In the final analysis, it is what counts the most, but it cannot be counted.

It's not only about the jobless. It's also about those who are substantially underemployed or in fear of losing their job. In some instances, the toll here can be just as great as for those who have no job at all. FEAR is an acronym for False Events Appearing Real. Fear can become debilitating or immobilizing—especially when the events may not be all that false.

A jobless community has a way of affecting the outlook of its children. When George Muñoz served as president of the Chicago Board of Education in the 1980s, he discovered that one way to reduce the number of school dropouts was to work with the business community to assure employment to those who graduated. When inner-city minority children see their adult relatives with no jobs, regardless of their schooling, they grow up to think that schooling is irrelevant in their lives. We have worked too hard to reverse the school dropout problem in many of our inner cities. We cannot afford a relapse.

What we are really grappling with here is our sense of confidence about the future. That confidence cannot and will not be addressed by stabilizing the financial system, regulating economic transactions, or expanding and improving healthcare. It will only be restored by getting the nation back to work in as rapid a manner as humanly possible.

How difficult will that be? Here's where the statistics help tell the story.

THE TRUE NATURE OF THE EMPLOYMENT MARKET

In May 2009, the Bureau of Labor Statistics (BLS) announced that official unemployment stood at 9.4 percent. That meant that 14.5 million American workers were jobless. By November, that number had risen to 10.2 percent, and 15.7 million Americans were officially unemployed.

Those sound like big numbers, and they are, but they only tell half the story. The "effective unemployment" rate in May actually stood at 18.7 percent according to Leo Hindery, chairman of the New America Foundation Smart Globalization Initiative.[3] By November, Hindery reported that the rate had grown to 19.2 percent. (Effective unemployment includes farm and self-employed workers and accounts for unemployed workers not included in BLS's official announcement.)[4]

That means in actuality, 30.6 million people, or approximately 1 out of every 5 American workers, was un- or underemployed. That's an amazingly high number. However, even it does not tell the full story about the true nature of today's employment market in the United States.

There is another category of employee that does not appear in the BLS statistics or in the New America Foundation calculations—a category of workers in what we call *undernourished jobs*. Undernourished jobs are those in which employees' hours have been cut back or the salary and wages have been reduced by some across-the-board percentage.

These jobs exist in the public and private sectors and in all industry sectors from construction and real estate to manufacturing and hospitality. In 2009, *The New York Times* reported that "private wages and salaries have fallen for each of the last ten months as businesses trimmed costs by freezing pay, imposing salary cuts and reducing the work week. Personal income has dropped by a seasonally adjusted $372 billion since September."

To our knowledge, there's been no study done to quantify the number or percentage of undernourished jobs. However, Dean Baker, codirector of the Center for Economic Policy and Research stated, "We are talking the equivalent of adding back four to five million jobs just by restoring hours lost in this recession."[5]

Based upon Mr. Baker's estimate, anecdotal evidence, and selected newspaper stories that we have seen, we think that realistically, the percentage of undernourished jobs could be anywhere from a low of 5 percent of the total number of jobs in the U.S. to more than 10 percent. Using those figures, the un- and underemployment rate jumps to somewhere in the 25 percent–30 percent range.

The most disturbing trend underlying all of these statistics is the growth in the temporary workforce. In December 2009, temporary jobs grew for the fifth consecutive month in a row, adding 48,000 short-term positions. Some saw that as an indication that employers might be getting ready to hire full-time workers.

We don't see it that way. *BusinessWeek's* cover article for its January 18, 2010, issue was titled "The Permanent Temporary Workforce." The article reports that "by one broad measure about 26 percent of working Americans have 'non-standard' jobs." In the main, these are jobs with low pay, few benefits, and no security.[6] Unfortunately, these jobs look like the wave of the future for many members of the American workforce and not an interim phenomenon.

NO COMPANY FOR OLD MEN—OR MILLENNIALS

These startling statistics become sad ones when you look at who is jobless as well as the prospects for job recovery. Every group is hurting, some groups more than others.

The top-line statistics released by the BLS for the third quarter of 2009 showed that the most disadvantaged in terms of unemployment were: teenagers (25.1 percent), African Americans (15.0 percent), and Hispanics (12.7 percent). These figures concealed as much as they revealed. Other available data points from 2009 showed that:

- Workers aged 45 to 64 had lower unemployment rates, but a higher proportion of those unemployed had been out of work for more than 6 months, and even those who get new jobs earn less in them than in their prior positions. As Jim Dauner, an ex-business colleague of Ed Crego, put it, "In this economy, most professionals, particularly those over 45, have a better chance of winning the lottery than finding a job or even appropriate contract work."

- There were 6.4 million high school and college graduates looking to enter or reenter the workforce.

- By May of 2009, there were 800,000 more workers over 55 in the workforce than in December 2007.

- Job seekers in certain states, such as Florida, California, Nevada, and Arizona, were having much more difficulty in finding employment than those in other states.

By the end of the year, almost 6 million individuals—2 out of every 5 people unemployed—had been without work for more than 6 months.

All in all, no matter what color you paint it, it's not a pretty picture. The jobless picture gets even bleaker when you look at the consequences of massive un- and underemployment across the board.

THE CONSEQUENCES OF JOBLESSNESS AND JOB CONCERNS

When the Federal Reserve announced in August of 2009 that the recession was ending, it also added a cautionary note that the recovery would be slow and that unemployment was likely to remain high for the next year. The Fed observed that "consumer spending, financial markets and inventory building by corporations all continued to stabilize."

The day after the Fed made its announcement, the Department of Commerce released its retail sales report for the month of July. The report showed that overall, sales had fallen by 0.1 percent in spite of a large spike in auto sales caused by the Cash for Clunkers rebate program during the month. Sales fell at gas stations, department stores, electronics outlets, and furniture stores.

This trend in lack of consumer spending carried through to Black Friday spending on the day after the Thanksgiving holiday. Customers turned out in much greater numbers, but sales were up by only 0.5 percent compared to 2008—and the 2008 numbers were disastrous.

How significant is this? The American consumer accounts for approximately 70 percent of the economic activity in the United States. If their wallets and purses stay shut, the recovery could stall or be so immaterial that you would need a micrometer to measure it.

Given the current situation in terms of the "true" nature of the country's employment, it is very difficult to foresee anything other than an extremely sluggish recovery that will be significantly impeded, if not negated, by economic conditions in 2010. That's because you can't spend what you don't have and won't spend if what you have is worth a lot less than it was before. That's common sense, and it's also behavioral economics at work.

To borrow a phrase from the economist Jared Bernstein, the American consumer has been "crunched."[7] Their homes and retirement accounts are worth less, healthcare costs have gone up, and credit card rates have risen. Traditionally, America has been a highly mobile society. If there were economic problems in one part of the country, workers moved to an area that was doing better—but that's no longer an option for most of us.

In April of 2009, the Census Bureau released a report revealing that "the number of people who changed residences declined to 35.2 million from March 2007 to March 2008, the lowest number since 1962 when the nation had a 120 million fewer people." With no or few economic resources remaining, the jobless American is both strapped and trapped.

So, what we have is a downward spiral. No job means less money to spend. Less money to spend means businesses close. Businesses closing mean fewer jobs. Fewer jobs mean consumers lose confidence. Consumers losing confidence means they spend less. Less money spent means less jobs. It is a vicious cycle.

By the middle of 2009, it had become painfully obvious to even the most casual observer that the job market was dismal on all fronts and the country was in a jobless recovery. Unfortunately, those casual observers didn't appear to include many of the elected officials inside the Beltway.

THE CHANGING STRUCTURE OF THE JOB MARKET

The American economy lost nearly 6.5 million jobs from December 2007 through June 2009. That's a 4.7 percent decline in nonfarm jobs. Not all sectors shrank. Some grew, and some declined.

Not all jobs are created equal. With the exception of oil and gas extraction and coal mining, the job gains were in the service sector where wages tend to be lower. In contrast, with the exception of temporary help and employment services, the job losses were in the manufacturing or production sector where wages tend to be higher.

The trade-off between jobs gained and jobs lost provides an indicator for the future of the American economy and the potential pace of a recovery. See the jobs balance sheet that follows for an indication of that future.

Table 4.1: Job Gains/Losses by Category in the First Two Quarters of 2009[8]			
Jobs Gained %		**Jobs Lost %**	
Home healthcare	(+8.6)	Motor vehicles and parts	(−35.0)
Oil and gas extraction	(+8.6)	Temporary help services	(−32.8)
Federal Government	(+6.5)	Employment services	(−28.6)
Ambulatory healthcare services	(+4.8)	Furniture and related products	(−25.0)
Offices of physicians	(+4.1)	Textile Mills	(−24.4)
Educational services	(+4.0)	Residential building	(−21.9)
Healthcare	(+3.7)	All construction	(−17.1)
Outpatient care services	(+3.6)	Semiconductor/ electronics	(−15.3)
Coal mining	(+3.6)	Plastics and rubber products	(−15.3)
Hospitals	(+3.4)	Furniture/home furnishing stores	(−15.2)
State government education	(+3.0)	All manufacturing	(−14.0)

While there was evidence at the end of the year that an economic recovery was underway, it was most assuredly a jobless one. The presenting questions were for how long and why.

THE JOBLESS RECOVERY

In the minutes from an April 2009 Federal Open Markets Committee meeting, the Federal Reserve opined that "unemployment is unlikely to settle at the desired 'normal' level for another five to six years." Later in the year, the Federal Reserve reiterated this position but expanded those parameters to 5 to 7 years.

Robert Reich, former secretary of Labor in the Clinton administration, predicted that most lost jobs are not coming back. Roger Lowenstein and the New America Foundation provide extremely useful insights on what is creating this condition and the impact that it will have. Lowenstein attributes the jobless recovery to a variety of factors, including: a marked absence of "labor hoarding" (businesses keeping employees on the payroll to be prepared for the rebound), companies' significantly reduced appetite for hiring, and businesses' lack of confidence regarding the recovery.[9]

The New America Foundation points out that two of the most recent recessions, 1990–1991 and 2001, were followed by jobless recoveries in which "the labor market remained weak and relatively high unemployment persisted, well after the 18 months that it usually takes such indicators to rebalance themselves after downturns." The foundation predicted a jobless recovery this time as well because: so many jobs were lost so quickly, productivity due to technological progress and operational efficiencies remained high, and many industries have experienced structural downsizing.

The problem with a jobless recovery of any extended length is that it feeds upon itself and inhibits the potential for meaningful economic recovery because a typical recovery is driven by consumer consumption and residential investment—both, of which, we predict will continue to be absent from this recovery. Instead, there will be considerable deleveraging as consumers save and change purchasing habits.

This time around, there is an unprecedented level of un- and under-employment, coupled with an employed workforce that has a diminished capacity to consume due to high debt and/or reduced wages. To add insult to injury, "wages and family incomes have been essentially stagnant for the past 10 years: the real median age for males has actually decreased since 1999, by 1.1 percent . . . In recent years, inflation has outstripped wage growth resulting in negative real wage growth and less real purchasing power for American workers."

Finally, it's not just about the quantity of jobs lost; it's also about quality. Those jobs that create higher wages and greater benefits have more of a multiplier effect on consumption, the economy in general, and a recovery. As the New America Foundation points out, "The industry with the highest total number of unemployed persons in the United States right now is (in addition to construction) manufacturing—precisely the sector that must be expanded if production is to compensate for the fall-off in consumer spending."[10]

At the beginning of 2010, the BLS announced that the economy had lost 85,000 jobs in December. On the same day, this depressing news was matched by announcements of major layoffs from UPS and Lockheed Martin—grim news to end the old year and start the new.

What was—and still is—needed are jobs.

THE EFFECT OF THE STIMULUS BILL

Instead, what we got in 2009 was a stimulus bill. Those who supported passage of the stimulus bill knew there was a need for government intervention to try to maintain some equilibrium in the economy at the beginning of 2009. But no one in power saw how problematic the economy was going to become. Unemployment was projected to peak at 8.6 percent around year-end from the starting point of 7.2 percent. Underemployment was not even a major topic of discussion.

As a result, a modest stimulus package of more than $780 billion was put together. Saving or creating jobs was a central element of the bill, but not a driving force. The Obama administration projected that the bill would create or save 3.6 million jobs within a 3-year time frame.

Conservative critics accused the bill of being just a series of earmarks or pork. Liberal critics labeled the bill as being far too small in scope and funding to make a difference and called for a much-larger stimulus.

By the end of the year, there was a general consensus that overall the stimulus had a positive effect on the economy and jobs. There were arguments about how many jobs the stimulus bill had really created or saved.[11] But there was universal agreement on one thing—we were in a jobless recovery. A jobless recovery is a joyless recovery. A jobless and joyless recovery is not sustainable, and as a result, neither will be the recovery in any meaningful sense.

What we had with the stimulus package was a "trickle out," or indirect approach, to job creation. It was not sufficient to address the full scope and nature of the jobs problem which was far, far worse than most professional observers and analysts imagined or predicted.

What we need now is a "flood" approach to job creation where jobs become the cause and stimulus becomes the effect. People with jobs and decent wages can, and will, consume. Consumption and consumer confidence will drive the American economy and its recovery. It must not just be about Wall Street and Main Street. It must also be about blue highways and city alleys.

The program for coming out of a jobless recovery must be concentrated and comprehensive. A "recovering economy" cannot be an acceptable condition for the United States. The goal must be a recovered economy as soon as it is fiscally feasible and humanly possible. This demands passion and a sense of urgency. It also demands a clear purpose and priorities.

RENEWING JOBS RECOMMENDATIONS

In midyear, there was much discussion among the cognoscenti in Washington about whether there was a need for another stimulus bill. By the third quarter, the discussion had shifted from a second stimulus bill to a jobs bill.

As 2009 ended and 2010 began, jobs appeared to have become job one in Washington, D.C. In December, President Obama held a jobs summit, and the House of Representatives passed a jobs bill of $150 billion-plus. In January 2010, the president's FY 2011 budget proposed almost $100 billion for jobs. By early February, the Senate appeared to have the makings of a jobs bill in the $80 billion range brokered through a bipartisan "compromise." Harry Reid, Senate Majority leader, pushed back and declared this potential compromise should be stripped down to only its specific job creation component, which was about $15 billion dollars.

The Council of Economic Advisors (CEA) released the Economic Report of the President which projected that in 2010, the economy would grow at approximately 95,000 jobs per month. This would generate a total of approximately 1.1 million new jobs during the year. The report also projected that the unemployment rate would stay at around 10 percent throughout 2010 and come down to 8.2 percent by the end of 2012.

We think there is something incredibly fuzzy and wrong with this math and logic if the economists and politicians are really trying to make job creation a priority and a driver of full economic recovery instead of just growing GDP. The reason for this is simple. The economy needs to create around 1.5 million jobs just to stay apace of new entrants to the job marketplace annually and to create another 2 to 3 million jobs to begin to make a dent in the unemployment.

The New York Times agrees with our perspective on the inadequacy of the proposed approaches. It ran an editorial right after the Senate announced its potential jobs bill titled, "How Not to Write a Jobs Bill." That editorial noted that the so-called jobs bill contained over $30 billion in tax cuts for businesses with no guarantee of jobs being created because of them and another $10 billion to be spent to renew an expiring Medicare payment formula so that doctors wouldn't incur a pay cut. (Can you say, "earmark"?) The editorial also observed that the $15 billion that Senator Reid was calling for "with 14.8 million Americans unemployed—more than 40 percent of them for more than 6 months—is so puny as to be meaningless."[12]

Neither of the congressional bills or the Economic Report of the President indicated an attempt to do anything to deal with the real unemployment rate or the conditions of underemployment that existed in 2009 and carried over with a vengeance into 2010. These are the canaries in the coal mine. They are the warning signs that the job problems are much more serious and endemic than many want to discuss or acknowledge.

Please note that we have used the word "appear" frequently in this discussion of the attempts to do some problem solving regarding the "jobless recovery" dilemma. Appearances can be deceiving and rhetoric is not reality. Our conclusion, unfortunately, must be that even though the issue of jobs was put on the governmental front burner, little was put into the pot and the burner was turned to low. What is still needed is a meaningful and measurable jobs bill along the lines recommended here—one that is focused on true job creation, rather than legislating and pork barreling in the usual manner.[13]

As business owners who have created thousands of jobs, there is no question in our minds that a jobs bill is essential. There is no piece of legislation that is more important to America's future. There is no better investment of taxpayer dollars.

Therefore, we strongly recommend that Congress should implement an authentic jobs bill. To have maximum impact, the bill must be structured and designed correctly. It cannot look like the stimulus bill and must not look like what became the healthcare reform bill. Much like a strong strategic plan, the bill must be targeted and designed for speed of implementation and impact. The bill should be structured to:

- Generate the largest number of "high-quality" jobs in the shortest period of time
- Focus on jobs that will have the greatest multiplier effects on local economies as well as consumer spending and confidence
- Ensure the federal government disperses funds according to an established timeline
- Ensure that state governments and other recipients use the funds to create new or replacement jobs instead of protecting existing jobs or to cover operating costs

The primary focus of the jobs bill should be to put *job-ready and skilled workers back to work* and *new, well educated entry-level workers to work in as short a time frame as possible.* The bill should have four primary components

1. **Small Business Component:** Major appropriation for direct and guaranteed loans to small businesses; targeted jobs tax credits; tax incentives, such as payroll tax credit with Social Security match; reduced and accelerated depreciation for capital investments for creating jobs that meet established criteria.

2. **Public Service Employment Component:** Major appropriation for job creation at state and local levels to restore government services and for the establishment of WPA and CCC-type programs focused on "shovel-ready projects" addressing the needs of America's crumbling infrastructure.

3. **Community Service Component:** Major appropriation for employees to work in nonprofit, community-based, and other service organizations to restore and increase social safety net services.

4. **Manufacturing for Export Component:** Major appropriation that uses the Golden Rule to our advantage—whoever has the gold sets the rules. Increase funding for manufacturers of products for exports, and increase funding of the U.S. Export-Import Bank so that it can finance American exports.

The bill should be targeted in terms of the priority groups to be reached and the priority industries/sectors in which jobs should be created. At a minimum, the priority groups should include: 45- to 65-year-old age groups; millennial age groups; highly skilled and educated professionals and white-collar workers; entry-level workers with college degrees and high school diplomas; and disadvantaged minorities. At a minimum, priority industries should include: manufacturing; construction; infrastructure development and modernization; information technology; and education. The bill should also carve out additional funds for those states with the highest un- and underemployment rates.

If you're thinking this is a substantial bill, you're correct. Mark Zandi of Moody's was advocating for a bill of $125 billion at the beginning of 2010. We won't put a dollar amount on the bill we recommend, but it should help create 300,000 or more jobs per month if it is going to be sufficient to convert an extremely fragile macroeconomic recovery into one that has the capacity to make a difference at the microeconomic level in consumers' pocketbooks and spending patterns. As noted earlier, we need to create between 100,000–150,000 jobs a month just to keep up with new workers entering the workplace. We need the additional jobs created and not just saved to start reducing the unemployment rate.

The jobs bill should have a time limitation and not be considered permanent. It should be in place long enough to jump-start the economy and to move it back to "normal," but no longer. Given the current estimates for a jobless recovery, we anticipate this to be 3 years.

The bill should have a strong performance management framework to ensure its proper rollout through appropriate planning, involvement, and execution. This does not require a performance officer to audit what has happened—it requires a performance management team to make it happen. We recommend that the performance management team be established in the Employment and Training Administration at the U.S. Department of Labor. Many of the members of this team could be drawn from the unemployment and underemployment pool.

The jobs bill should be thought of as an employment benefits bill and an alternative to unemployment benefits. Unemployment benefits certainly have their place. They do not, however, create jobs, nor do they restore the dignity that only a job can provide. Moreover, unemployment benefits are insufficient to stimulate the increased consumer spending needed for an economic recovery.

Unemployment benefits unintentionally create a sense of dependence and personal helplessness. Employment benefits, in contrast, promote a sense of independence and self-sufficiency. Unemployment benefits are static. Employment benefits are designed to be dynamic.

Consideration should be given to developing a new program that leverages unemployment insurance dollars to create new jobs. An example of how we envision the program working is an employer agreeing to match or supplement the unemployment payment made to a worker to be hired. This would do three things: (1) give the unemployment recipient more dollars to spend and meaningful work to do, (2) give the employer an expanded and enhanced workforce at a lower cost, and (3) address the need to get more money circulating in the economy.

In addition to the foregoing, we offer the following ideas for consideration as part of the government's job creation efforts:

- Establish a jobs bond program in which both individuals and institutions can invest. This can help bring the private funds from the sidelines and get the private sector vested in this job-creation venture. The U.S. government would guarantee a modest but certain return to these "U.S. Jobs Bonds." Congress has approved war bonds to be used to support the conflicts in Afghanistan and Iraq. It seems to us that the majority of U.S. citizens would be much more likely to invest in this domestic program than one related to unpopular wars.

- Launch a national demonstration project related to the U.S. Census that will be conducted in 2010. That census taking will create 1.2 million temporary jobs. The demonstration project should be directed at developing a certain number of those jobs in the private and nonprofit sectors and converting them to full-time positions with career ladders. A national competition should be held, and grants and awards should be made to enable this.

- Implement a national demonstration project around weatherization of entire communities. Many have been advocating a "cash for caulkers" program. While this idea has some tactical merit to put workers to work in the short term, the real opportunity from a strategic standpoint would be to leverage this employment by creating "whole community green sustainability plans." These plans could be used to drive long-term activities and employment directed at reducing a community's energy consumption and improving its environmental quality.

- Take advantage of the "reset" mentality and fund jobs that are dedicated to building a new infrastructure for delivery of alternative energy sources (solar, wind, biofuels, etc.), rather than petroleum-based. This will help cut the ties to Middle East oil and help the environment.

- Provide tax incentives for "Entrepreneur Funds" focused on technology advances and job creation/preservation. This can help bring the U.S. out of its doldrums and encourage the small business persons and inventors to work on reversing our economic slide. We have seen this work. When Frank Islam started his business with one employee, he received a government contract through the Small Business Administration. It took him less than 10 years to grow the business to 2,000 employees.

We are in precipitous times. Unlike past recessions, many of those unemployed today are highly skilled with advanced degrees and substantial experience. Those in the 45–65 age cohort who should be in the prime earning years have been dislocated and disadvantaged. At the same time, the new high school and college graduate can't access the first rung on the career ladder.

We are dealing with these problems in the most incremental of fashions by passing small jobs bills and related legislation that may generate tens of thousands of jobs at best. This is inadequate and inexcusable.

As we have noted, this is a problem that can't be solved by fixing the financial system or reforming healthcare. It is a transcendent problem that affects our individual and national livelihoods and future. Unlike healthcare, there is only one option. That is the jobs option. We must exercise it now.

5 | The Middle Class Matters

"Upper classes are a nation's past, the middle class is its future."
Ayn Rand

THE AMERICAN MIDDLE CLASS MAY SOON GO THE WAY OF THE dinosaur. But it will not disappear completely or become extinct.

As the lizard is the survivor and descendant of the mighty dinosaur, there will be a few stick figures that remain as a reminder of what once was. However, they will bear only a scant resemblance to the massive middle class that existed in earlier and better times.

There was a time when dinosaurs roamed and ruled the world. There was a time when the middle class mattered. Both those times appear to have disappeared. It may not be too late to salvage one of them, however.

INVENTING THE MIDDLE CLASS

It's hard to imagine the United States without the middle class. In fact, it's impossible. The concept of the middle class did not originate in the United States. But the middle class as we have come to know it was invented here. America is not only the land of the free and the home of the brave; it is the homeland of the middle class.

In many ways, the middle class is the American Dream. The middle class represents the chance for those born here to work hard to earn a decent living and lead a good life. It's also the reason many immigrants come here—to have an opportunity to move up rungs of the ladder in a way that would have been impossible in their native lands.

The phenomenon of the American middle class is a product of the last century. The nascent beginnings of the middle class can be traced back to Henry Ford, America's industrialization, and to unions that organized for better pay and benefits. The middle class really came into its own in the period following World War II.

The 1944 GI Bill gave returning veterans money for college, businesses, and home mortgages. The country went on a building spree. Residential construction units went from 114,000 in 1944 to 1.7 million in 1950. Subdivisions were created. New job opportunities were created. Wages went up. Spirits soared. Expectations rose.

In the 1950s, the Eisenhower administration led the development of the nation's highway system. The middle class bought cars to travel those highways. They bought TVs to watch themselves in shows like *Ozzy and Harriet* and *My Three Sons*. They got their first credit cards.

Middle-class consumption fueled economic growth, and upward mobility fueled the middle class. Decent wages, real income going up annually, and discretionary purchasing power allowed those in the middle class to own not only a home and a car, but also a cottage in the woods, a recreational vehicle, and even a second car. That's the stereotypical picture of the American middle class from the 1950s through the 1970s.

As with most stereotypes, it's not completely accurate. But it exists because it captures part of reality. That reality is the economic condition of the middle class. What it doesn't capture is that being part of the middle class was as much a state of mind, lifestyle, personal accomplishment, and potential as it was about income level. As we now know, middle-class reality is being challenged and threatened on all fronts.

THE ERODING MIDDLE CLASS

"Even Middle Americans whose salaries put them squarely in the middle class feel they are slipping below a comfortable standard of living. The material rewards that Middle Americans had begun to take for granted—a house, vacations, college for the children—have become more difficult to obtain."[1]

Believe it or not, that's a quote from a November 3, 1986 *Time* magazine article titled, "Is the Middle Class Shrinking?" While there was some debate nearly 25 years ago on whether the middle class was shrinking, there's virtually none now. On the contrary—there's considerable evidence that no matter how you define them, the middle class *is* shrinking.

Interestingly, there is no standard definition for the middle class. The Census Bureau does not have an official definition. The Bureau does report, however, that the median household income in the United States in 2008 was $50,000-plus. In 2007, the Congressional Research Service issued a report on the middle class that covered a range of income from $19,000 to $91,000 a year.

Regardless of the bandwidth for what constitutes "middle class," there have been numerous surveys which show that the majority of Americans identify themselves as being middle class. A Tax Foundation poll in 2007 found that four out of five individual Americans consider themselves middle class.[2] A Pew Research study in 2008 found that over 50 percent of the respondents referred to themselves as middle class— nearly 40 percent of those individuals were making $100,000-plus.[3]

The conclusion you can draw from this is that being middle class is a state of mind. When you ask an average American who they think makes up the middle class, they would most likely answer "me." According to most measures, "me" is not doing nearly as well as he or she was previously.

- The 2008 Census Bureau report on income and health insurance showed that the median household income fell to $50,303. In 1998, the median income was $51,295. That's an income decline of over 3.1 percent in a 10-year span. As David Leonhardt of *The New York Times* noted, "In the four decades that the Census Bureau has been tracking household income, there has never been a full decade in which median income has failed to rise . . . it doesn't seem to have happened since at least the 1930s."[4]

- In testimony before the United States Senate Finance Committee in 2007, Professor Elizabeth Warren of Harvard Law School, based upon an analysis of median income data from

1970–2004, observed, "the typical man working full-time today, after adjusting for inflation, earns about $800 less than his father in the early 1970s . . . The shift from one income to two has had seismic implications for families across America. It means that all the growth in family income came from adding a second earner."[5]

- Using Census Bureau reports, the Pew Research Center found that in 1970, 40 percent of all adults lived in middle-income house-holds, with "middle" defined as being within 75 percent to 150 percent of the median. By 2006, only 35 percent were in the middle-income tier. Pew noted that this "hollowing out" was created by increases in both the upper- and lower-income categories.[6]

- It also appears to be getting more difficult to become middle class. Senior Fellows Isabel V. Sawhill and Ron Haskins of the Brookings Institution observe that "If you are born into a middle class family . . . you have roughly an even chance of moving up or down the ladder . . ." They continue to observe, on the other hand ". . . if you are born poor, you are likely to stay poor."[7]

Some contend that the middle class is shrinking because the upper class has been growing. There have definitely been a few more people added to the upper-income categories. What has been growing most significantly, however, is the share of income that the upper-income earners take out of the total income pie, leaving less for the middle class. Writing for *Forbes*, Thomas F. Cooley reported, "the share of income earned by the top 10 percent declined from a peak of nearly 50 percent in 1928, the height of the roaring '20s, to a plateau of around 35 percent until about 1982. After that the share of the top 10 percent took off, reaching nearly 50 percent by 2006."[8]

Cooley's analysis further disclosed that it is the top 1 percent (those with earnings above $380,600) of the top 10 percent who have taken the lion's share of the earnings since 2000. The others in the top 10 percent have stayed about the same in terms of their share of earnings. Economist Paul Rosenberg makes a similar point in a blog posting where he notes, "the bottom 99 percent of the American people, in terms of income, have barely seen any income growth since 1973."[9]

Based upon the foregoing data, we come to the following conclusions:

- The middle class is shrinking in numbers, but also in terms of real income
- The poor will always exist, but the middle class may not
- Things started going south for the middle class much earlier than expected—in the early-to-mid-1970s
- The middle class decline began to accelerate in the mid-1980s
- The very rich (the top 1 percent) have done very well since the early 1990s and most especially in the first decade of this century

The real story is about more than income redistributed from the middle class to the extremely wealthy. It is about much of the middle class being at substantial risk.

For most Americans under the age of 65, they cannot (and have not) envision a shrinking middle class—it is the antithesis of the American Dream. Yet, most of the countries of the world live in the reality of small and insignificant middle classes. Ironically, as part of the foreign policy of the U.S. government, our country has tried to increase the middle class of other countries as a way to ensure peace in the world. From the Marshall Plan to federal agencies such as the Overseas Private Investment Corporation (OPIC) and the Millennium Challenge Corporation, millions of American tax dollars have been spent to promote economic development in "emerging market countries."

Because of his experience as the president of OPIC from 1997–2001, George Muñoz knows only too well that the lack of jobs and economic security in the world lead to instability and security risks for us. When asked why the U.S. created OPIC, Muñoz would point to what President Roosevelt said toward the conclusion of World War II, "essential to peace—permanent peace—is a decent standard of living for all individual men and women and children in all nations. Freedom from fear is eternally linked with freedom from want." The "freedom from want," which most Americans have come to enjoy, is slipping for many. What we need now is an equivalent of OPIC for our economically devastated U.S. communities.

CAN YOU SEE ME NOW?

Elizabeth Warren, Jared Bernstein, and the Demos Group have been leaders in helping us see the plight and prospects of the middle class for some time. Here are some insights culled from them.

Harvard Law Professor Elizabeth Warren, who is also currently chair of the Oversight Panel created "to review the current state of financial markets and the regulatory system," summarized the nature and extent of that stress in a posting on the *Huffington Post* in December of 2009: "Today, one in five Americans is unemployed, underemployed or just plain out of work. One in nine families can't make the minimum payment on their credit cards. One in eight mortgages is in default or foreclosure. One in eight Americans is on food stamps . . . The economic crisis has wiped more than \$5 trillion from pensions and savings."[10]

Jared Bernstein is executive director of the White House's Middle Class Working Families Task Force and Economic Policy advisor to Vice President Joe Biden. In his book *Crunch*, Bernstein describes and captures the essence of the "big squeeze" as follows: "Most of the indicators that matter most to us in our everyday lives—jobs, wages, mid-level incomes, prices at the pump and the grocery store, retirement security, college tuition—are coming in at stress inducing levels . . ."[11]

It's interesting to note that Bernstein's book was published in 2008, and he was using data from 2000–2006 for his analysis. If things were at "stress inducing" levels then, by mid-2009, they had moved to the traumatic stress level.

In 2007, Demos and The Institute on Assets in Social Policy (D-IASP) at Brandeis Institute issued a report titled, "By a Thread: The New Experience of America's Middle Class," which complements the reports of Warren and Bernstein.[12]

D-IASP constructed a Middle Class Security Index. Using data from 2006 in the index, D-IASP concluded that: Only 31 percent of middle-income families matched the profile for being securely middle class. Nearly four out of five families matched the high-risk profile for financial assets. Over 50 percent of those families had no net financial assets at all.

CAN YOU HEAR ME NOW?

That's what the numbers tell us that the middle class was experiencing. How were they feeling about it? In April of 2008, Pew Research Center released a report with the telling title, "Inside the Middle Class: Bad Times Hit the Good Life." That report revealed that:

- Fewer Americans than at any time in the past half century believed they were not better off than they were 5 years ago. Thirty-one percent felt they had fallen backward. Twenty-five percent felt that had not moved forward. That's a combined 56 percent.

- Almost 80 percent indicated that it was more difficult to maintain their standard of living. Slightly more than half indicated they'd had to "tighten their belts."

- Looking forward 5 years, more than one-half felt the future would be better than today.

- Most expected that their children's standard of living would be better than their own.[13]

In December 2009, the Pew Research Center released a report that showed the attitudes of the general public regarding the decade of the 2000s. Although not focused specifically on the middle class, we think it is fair to extrapolate from this survey to them.

The survey respondents rated the decade as the worst in 50 years. Fifty percent of the participants said they had a generally negative impression of the decade as opposed to 27 percent who said they had a generally positive one. The word used most frequently to describe the decade was *downhill*. Other bleak terms used as descriptors included: *poor, decline, disaster, scary,* and *depressing*.[14]

THE NEED FOR THE MIDDLE CLASS

The decline of America's middle class and rise of its working poor is indisputable. Some assert that the middle class in America as we've come to know it is not renewable. The argument is that the middle class developed at a point in time where a confluence of events redounded to the American worker's benefit, and that as a result, Americans developed unrealistic expectations and led unrealistic lifestyles.

We do agree that the excesses of the past decade put things out of kilter. As we discuss in Chapter 2, we need to reframe the dream. But reframing it does not mean we should miniaturize it or make it accessible to a smaller pool of people.

The strategic and threshold question for us is whether America needs a vital middle class in order to sustain its competitive advantage. For us, the answer to that is simple—*yes!*

We need only look at our two major competitors on the world stage, China and India, to come to that conclusion. They are both in the process of building huge middle classes. China's middle class will be over 300,000 million people—eventually larger than the current population of the entire United States. China and India both understand that middle-class wealth and consumption is what fuels growth and drives a nation's economic success. We understood that once in the United States.

A thriving middle class makes for a thriving nation. An "at-risk" middle class puts the nation at risk. A concentration of wealth and power in too few hands is a formula for the end of the American democracy as we have known it. For us, saving America's middle class is not a matter of morality but of economic necessity. The middle class needs to be renewed for America and the American Dream to be renewed.

REINVENTING THE MIDDLE CLASS

No matter how you look at it, the middle class is in serious trouble. The presenting problem is what is going to be required to reinvent it. Bernstein, Warren, and D-IASP identify several critical areas and issues to be addressed in this regard. While we are not endorsing these recommendations, we present them here as points of reference for consideration in building a middle-class reinvention agenda.[15] They include:

- **Workforce Bargaining Power.** Pursue full employment through means such as public service jobs and unions. Establish higher minimum wages and less porous safety nets like an unemployment insurance system that covers more of those who fall out of the job market.
- **Healthcare.** Pool risk, cut costs, and provide disability coverage.

- **Immigration.** Control immigrant flows, initiate economic integration, employ a nationalized identity system, and encourage earned citizenship for those already here.

- **Education.** Offset inequalities early on and provide access to higher education with remediation for anyone motivated enough to go to school. Place an emphasis on preschool education and strengthen our public schools.

- **Globalization.** Ensure job security and quality, addressed through initiatives directed at full employment through public-private projects targeted at energy independence and public infrastructure, universal healthcare, and pensions.

- **Finances.** Reduce individual debt and build up individual assets.

RENEWING THE MIDDLE-CLASS RECOMMENDATIONS

There has been substantial analysis and an overwhelming number of ideas generated to renew the middle class. While we offer our own detailed recommendations throughout this book, in this instance, we don't believe that what is required is a blizzard of additional suggestions.

Instead, all recommendations should be reviewed, evaluated, prioritized, and put into a time-phased middle-class renewal agenda. That agenda should be established based upon the emergency medicine principle, "First stop the bleeding," and Maslow's hierarchy of needs.

Psychologist Abraham Maslow developed a hierarchy of needs construct in the early 1940s comprised of five levels of needs: (1) physiological, (2) security, (3) social, (4) self-esteem, and (5) self-actualization. Without going into a lot of theory, suffice it to say that in order to achieve our full potential (self-actualization), we need to achieve our more basic needs (physiological, security, and social) first.

During the past 2 years, a large segment of the middle class has been stuck well below the level of self-actualization. Many have lost their jobs and homes and have no health insurance. Many are fearful and concerned about the future and whether or not they will be employed. The renewal agenda for the middle class must begin with correcting these deficiencies and eliminating fear. We recommend a three-part phased approach for accomplishing this:

1. Middle-Class Survivability
2. Middle-Class Stabilization
3. Middle-Class Sustainability

Phase 1: Middle-Class Survivability

The survivability agenda should have an immediate and concentrated effect on the un- and underemployed through a three-step process:

1. **Implement a Major Jobs Program.** This program should generate at least 10 million jobs between 2010 and the end of 2012. We provide our detailed recommendations on the nature of this in Chapter 4, "Jobs Matter." Green jobs are a good start, and by most accounts, the stimulus bill will generate approximately 3 million new or replacement jobs before it expires. Both of these measures, however, will be far too insufficient to match the scope of the need.

   The rationale for a jobs program of the scale proposed is supported by a variety of sources. In September of 2009, the government announced that official unemployment had hit 9.8 percent; by November, it had jumped to 10.2 percent. A Rutgers University study released in late September of 2009 predicted that it may take until 2017 for the United States to replace the jobs lost during this recession.[16] The Obama administration's own projections for the job recovery are also bleak—having ranged from a high of 10.2 percent in 2009 to a low of 7.7 percent in 2012. That compares to a full employment figure in the 4.5 percent range. As Paul Krugman observed, "This should not be considered an acceptable outlook. For one thing it implies an enormous amount of suffering over the next few years. Moreover, unemployment that remains that high that long will cast long shadows over America's future."[17]

   We couldn't agree more. When that level of unemployment is combined with the decline in real wages for middle-income workers, you have a formula for disaster. One need only look to Japan's circumstances in the period from 1997 to 2003 when private sector wages fell an average of more than 1 percent in each year. Japan went into a period of stagnation from which it has still not fully recovered.

This should be seen as a harbinger of what might be ahead for the United States. If the United States does not move aggressively and assertively on programs for renewing middle-class jobs and income, we could suffer a similar fate.

2. **Ensuring Adequate and Affordable Healthcare.** The facts regarding healthcare reform as it relates to small businesses and the middle class should have been overwhelmingly convincing. Just take a look at a few that appeared in "Why Middle Class Americans Need Health Reform" prepared by Vice President Biden's Middle Class Working Families Task Force:

- On average, middle-class families with private health insurance spend 9 percent of their household income on health insurance premiums, deductibles, and copayments.

- From 2001 to 2006, the percentage of privately insured middle-class Americans facing a high financial burden from healthcare costs rose from 14 percent to 22 percent—more than a 36 percent increase in just 5 years.

- In 2007, 11 percent of middle-class adults reported delaying needed care, and 8 percent avoided care altogether because of the high cost.

- Over one-quarter of the uninsured are middle-class Americans.[18]

These are persuasive statistics. They should have been overwhelmingly convincing, but they weren't. Suffice it to say that one of the lessons from this should be never underestimate the status quo and people's resistance to change—especially when that resistance is stoked by those who recognize that a loss of that status quo threatens their livelihoods and profits.

Now that we have a healthcare bill, there is a split opinion on whether it will make healthcare more affordable for the middle class. One camp argues that it will impose a hardship on middle-income families who will be required to buy healthcare they can't afford.

The other camp argues that it helps to address healthcare differences caused by inequality of wealth. In our opinion, as we state in the first chapter of this book, the healthcare bill as it stands is merely a beginning. To make, healthcare adequate and affordable over the next decade for the middle class, costs must be reduced substantially and quality must be improved dramatically.

3. **Providing Home Owner Assistance.** Additional legislation should be introduced to protect the homes of middle-income families who will be facing foreclosure during 2010 to 2012. The legislation should include stronger provisions for renegotiating mortgages and revisit the possibility of using courts to facilitate that renegotiation. Consideration should be given to allowing the home owner to convert to a renter. In addition, middle-income families who rent from a home owner who is forced into foreclosure should be protected.

Foreclosure prevention legislation has been passed that helps a narrow swath of home owners. Coverage needs to be expanded to protect the many more that will become at risk over the next 2 years as the jobless recovery continues. In addition, actions must be taken to ensure that those who are ostensibly protected benefit from this coverage. In late March 2010, the administration rolled out a new and expanded foreclosure package. The success of the package, however, will be dictated by the manner in which it is executed and not the quality of its design.

The rule here should be to anticipate and prepare. If a person's home is his or her castle, we need to reinforce the moat surrounding it.

Phase 2: Middle-Class Stabilization

The stabilization agenda needs to be focused on the near- and mid-term economic security needs of all middle-income earners. It should overlap with phase one in terms of the timing for its implementation. Measures that should be considered for inclusion in this part include asset-building assistance, enhanced credit safety, training for job placement, affordable college loans, retirement security, and workplace security.

Phase 3: Middle-Class Sustainability

The sustainability agenda needs to be focused on the longer term and the future of the middle class and include measures such as preschool education, higher education and remediation, and immigration management.

Senator John Kerry (D-MA) is sensitive to the plight of the middle class. He states, "We are squeezing the middle class, we are losing the middle class, and the gap between the haves and have not is growing wider and wider." This situation must be corrected.

As the Ayn Rand quote at the beginning of this chapter notes, for a nation, "the middle class is its future." For America's middle class, the future must be now. A renewal agenda for the middle class renews the United States and guarantees its future—lack of one guarantees that its future will have passed.

6 | Manufacturing Matters

"The American consumer is also the American worker, and if we don't do something to protect our manufacturing base here at home, it is going to be hard to buy any retail goods."
Senator Lindsey Graham (R-SC)

AMERICA IS A COUNTRY WITH DEGENERATIVE DISC DISEASE. IN THE human body, the spine allows us to stand upright and to walk. As people age, a certain amount of degeneration to the discs in the spine is normal. If there is a trauma, a person's degenerated disc can lead to a chronic, debilitating condition and have a serious negative impact on the quality of life.

In America, manufacturing was the backbone on which the nation was built. The discs in that backbone began to degenerate over 2 decades ago and are degenerating at an accelerating and alarming rate today. A trauma has occurred.

Just as a human being cannot function fully with degenerative disc disease, a nation cannot function fully without a strong manufacturing base. Manufacturing's degenerative disease must be treated and cured—if not, America will never walk upright again.

MANUFACTURING AMERICA

America was built on manufacturing, and it is a still a major contributor to our economy. In 2007, it accounted for approximately 13 percent of the country's GDP. Manufacturing-produced goods were valued at a record $1.6 trillion in that year—nearly double the $811 billion produced a decade earlier.

That $1.6 trillion alone would have made the United States the eighth-largest economy in the world. The 2009 Economic Report of the President noted that in 2007 (the last full year for which data were available), manufacturing output was at its highest point ever. It was 8 percent higher than it was in 2000, 81percent higher than in 1987, and 213 percent higher than in 1967.[1]

Maybe it's not as bad as it seems. Those statistics indicate that the United States still makes things. However, when you take a closer look, you get a much different and considerably more worrisome picture of what's going on. Or, stated more correctly, what's *not* going on.

Manufacturing has taken a precipitous dip as a percentage of total United States GDP. In 1987, manufacturing was more than 20 percent of GDP. By August of 2009, it had fallen to 11.7 percent. The most disconcerting part of this decline was that it has remained a continuous one, with a drop off the cliff after the economic collapse triggered in September 2008.

During its first term in office, the Bush administration saw the handwriting on the wall regarding American manufacturing's plight and tried to take corrective action. In 2003, then U.S. Secretary of Commerce Donald Evans initiated and led a manufacturing initiative that culminated in a report issued in January of 2004 titled, "Manufacturing in America: A Comprehensive Strategy to Address the Challenges to U.S. Manufacturers."[2]

The report made excellent recommendations in six areas, including "Promoting Open Markets and a Level Playing Field." Other priorities, however, took sway, including the Iraq War and the housing construction bubble. Consequently, as with most governmental reports, the report gathered more dust than attention. The result is that manufacturing today is a soft underbelly instead of a solid backbone for rebuilding the American economy.

Since 2000, manufacturing has been losing large segments of whole industries due to the closing of factories and off-shoring of American jobs in a wide variety of industries, including furniture, technology, steel, and machine tools. The collapse of these industries and the subsequent loss of jobs impacted entire communities, causing them to disintegrate into ghost towns.

Elkhart, Indiana, the once-proud home of the recreational vehicle, has not disappeared, but it definitely falls into the at-risk category because the vehicle manufacturers that were located there have closed their doors. Elkhart is a recent example, but these seismic job losses destroying the economic fabric of entire communities have been going on for more than decades.

Ed Crego grew up in Streator, Illinois. During the summers of the mid-1960s, he worked at Owens Illinois Glass to earn money to go to college. At that time, there was a sign on the road leading into town that read, "Welcome to Streator—Glass Container Capitol of the World." In the mid-1960s, more than 5,000 workers were employed in Streator's glass manufacturing plants. Today, there are fewer than 500 workers making glass containers there.

The decline of manufacturing diminishes the potential of the nation to have a vital and vibrant economy. Robust economies are diversified. To our knowledge, there is no hard and firm figure for what percent manufacturing should be of a country's GDP. But common sense and our experience tell us that GDP of approximately 12 percent is far too low and a number closer to 20 percent should be the minimum.

Why? In general, manufacturing jobs pay more than nonmanufacturing jobs and provide better benefits, especially for workers without 4-year college degrees. They also generate more additional jobs for suppliers than nonmanufacturing jobs. Finally, manufacturing jobs lead the way to the development of entirely new industries driven by product innovation and emerging technologies (more on that later).[3]

A very important but frequently ignored point is that a diminished manufacturing capability in the United States threatens the country's security. U.S. Senator Brian Dorgan (D-SD) pointed out that Stalin said that the Allies would not have been victorious without America's substantial manufacturing supremacy during World War II. He noted, "When we outsource the manufacturing of components critical to our military technology, we not only lose jobs, we weaken our national security and preparedness. But when we take steps to keep that manufacturing at home, we keep our jobs here and invest in security."[4]

At the beginning of 2010, Senator Dorgan announced he was not going to seek reelection. With his departure, the manufacturing sector and the American worker will lose a strong ally. We hope for the sake of America and the American Dream that his influence and perspective remain after his departure. Our belief is that Senator Sherrod Brown (D) from the manufacturing state of Ohio will assume Dorgan's mantle. He's already demonstrated significant leadership in this area based upon his collaboration with the New America Foundation.

TAKING/GIVING IT ALL AWAY

Just a few short decades ago, the United States manufacturing sector excelled at making and exporting goods and creating jobs stateside. Over the past 10 to 15 years, this situation has reversed. The United States has become expert at exporting jobs and importing goods from abroad. That doesn't strike us as the type of expertise that creates long-term competitive advantage for the nation.

This exporting of jobs is typically called *outsourcing*, or when it's taking jobs from one country to another, *offshoring*. Over a 20-year period from 1982 to 2002, employment in the American manufacturing sector was relatively stable, ranging from 16–18 million with the bottom of the range occurring during recessionary periods. With the recession that came at the start of this century, manufacturing employment went down the gurgler in a big way—first to 15 million, then to approximately 14 million by the end of 2007, the lowest level of employment in this sector since 1950. The manufacturing sector then lost an additional 1.960 million jobs in the period from December 2007 through July 2009, approximately 30 percent of all of the jobs lost in the United States during that time frame.

Some of those manufacturing job losses were undoubtedly due to factors such as production cutbacks, inventory freezes, and productivity increases. Some, and maybe many, of those jobs were shipped around the world to lower-cost manufacturing locations. Many of those jobs won't be coming back. They are gone forever.

In 2009, the National Association for Manufacturing (NAM) projected that "over 40 percent of the manufacturing jobs lost during the recession may be regained."[5] That may sound like good news—but there's a catch. Those jobs won't be regained in total until 2014. That means around 5 years from now the number of manufacturing employees in the United States will limp back up to the new bottom rung of 12.7 million jobs. That's 1 million less than the number of workers employed in the manufacturing sector since before 1950 when manufacturing jobs constituted 35 percent of the jobs in America.

The bottom line for the bottom rung of the jobs ladder is that offshoring has cost the United States jobs for both the short term and long term. Businesses have shipped millions of jobs to other countries primarily to lower their costs of goods sold. Businesses are driven by profit and their actions are understandable and logical within that context.

What is not as well understood is that there are other factors that have contributed to or aided and abetted this mass exodus of jobs including:

- The trend toward the paper-intensive economic sectors of Finance, Insurance, and Real Estate (the so-called FIRE economy)
- A bias toward multinational corporation trade policy
- A bias against manufacturing
- The value-added assembler trap
- The blind belief that "comparative advantage" benefits all.

The FIRE Economy

In the early to mid-1980s, manufacturing lost its dominating clout in the halls of Congress. Wall Street and Washington, D.C., became joined at the hip and the FIRE sector (Finance, Insurance and Real Estate) became the new locus of power.

We believe that the FIRE sector term was first coined by Eric Janszen, president of iTulip and a former venture capitalist and CEO of technology start-ups. He noted that, "for nearly 25 years, our economy has been dominated by asset bubbles in the FIRE Sector. But now the FIRE-economy is over."[6]

We don't think it's over. It is too seductive, and too tied to Washington. The FIRE economy led to the Wall Street bailouts and the propping up of the financial institutions and to fire sales for many more legitimate businesses that were making money the old-fashioned way—by making and selling things.

Somehow, Washington was led to believe that Main Street America needed to bail out Wall Street. Maybe that was true. But Washington needs to understand that a shrinking middle class and manufacturing base can also spell disaster for everyone—including Wall Street.

While there have been proposals made to reign in some of the more egregious behavior through financial regulations, until early 2010, there was little to no evidence of behavioral change in the FIRE sector that bears primary responsibility for the economic meltdown and the current recession. As a matter of a fact, Wall Street had begun to bundle individual insurance policies into complex derivatives to find new ways of making money by doing nothing. We think John Bogle, founder of The Vanguard Group, summed this situation up nicely in his recent book:

> *"On balance, the financial system subtracts value from our society. We have moved to a world where far too many of us seemingly no longer make anything; we're merely trading pieces of paper, swapping stocks and bonds back and forth with one another, and paying our financial croupiers a veritable fortune. In the process, we have inevitably added even more costs by creating ever more complex financial derivatives in which huge and unfathomable risks have been built into our financial system."[7]*

Bogle's book should be required reading for all of the members of Congress and employees of the Federal Reserve and FDIC. The FIRE sector sucks the oxygen out of the room. The manufacturing sector breathes new life into it. It is the most value-added sector in a vibrant economy. We can't have a vibrant economy long term without a vibrant manufacturing sector.

A Bias toward Multinational Corporation Trade Policy

That's not to say that manufacturing companies don't have some influence on Capitol Hill; they still do. But the bulk of that influence is rendered by the large manufacturers who want the world to be their factory and not to be encumbered by the boundaries of any nation in terms of the goods they import or export. While free trade may be the words that multinational corporations employ, their true desire is "freewheeling" around the world.

NAM notes that more than 99 percent of manufacturers are small businesses and that these businesses employ more than 9 million in the U.S. If that number is accurate, it's about 75 percent of the manufacturing jobs in the U.S. today. Because of this, the government needs to ensure that the trade policies it adapts are fair and balanced and that it provides opportunity for the small business manufacturers. That is why we are advocating that we assure access to capital to the small business manufacturer of products for exports and increase funding of the U.S. Export-Import Bank with a direction focused on financing exports of products from our small business manufacturers. This will be Frank Islam's mantra as a member of the advisory committee of the Bank.

A Bias against Manufacturing

America's higher educational system has been central to the success of the United States. It is unrivalled in the world. As America became a "post-industrial society," the higher educational system—especially at the graduate-school level—started to turn out more and more M.B.A.s skilled in financial analysis and fewer and fewer individuals focused on managing and leading businesses that had blue-collar workers and smokestacks.

Our best and brightest were dissuaded from entering manufacturing careers either because they weren't "the future" or salaries weren't high enough. No one was advised to get into plastics unless that plastic was for credit cards.

It wasn't just the academic community. The entire country seemed to revel in the new service economy. Others would do the dirty work for us in some far-off land. We would keep our hands clean and clean up in the market while we got our goods cheaper because some underage or underpaid worker was producing them for us.

The tenor needs to change, and it is, both in higher education and throughout the land. Making things doesn't seem all that bad again. Manufacturing may still be dirty work, but it is no longer a dirty word. Industry leads to industriousness. Without industriousness, there is no future.

The Value-Added Assembly Trap

One of the key concepts that manufacturers have employed for decades as part of outsourcing pieces of the supply chain is value-added assembly. Simply put, the concept is that the company that assembles the miscellaneous pieces into the final good or product (think cell phone, car, or airplane) creates the most value and can thus generate the largest share of profit.

This concept makes good business sense with two caveats. First, the manufacturer needs to protect its "core competence" at all costs, meaning, it should not outsource the design or manufacture of a piece or part that is central to its value chain. Second, it needs to be able to ensure the timely and quality delivery of pieces and parts to produce the final good effectively and efficiently in order to generate the desired level of sales and profits.

Over the past few decades, as the supply chain has become global, businesses have outsourced more and more to suppliers in order to gain a cost and/or expertise advantage. This has frequently paid off. Other times, it has not worked exactly as planned, as evidenced by Boeing's experience with its 787 Dreamliner.

The Dreamliner will be the most revolutionary plane in the world when it is brought to market. It has been built with light carbon fiber-reinforced plastic and other composites. At the end of 2009, however, the Dreamliner was 2½ years behind its original production schedule.

It was originally thought that pieces of the wings and fuselage for the Dreamliner (which were outsourced) would be delivered fully fitted and then snapped together, like Lego blocks. That didn't work. The supplied pieces were not delivered on time and did not live up to required standards. As a result, Boeing implemented a rigorous program to retrofit them, acquired some of the companies that it had used as outsourcers, and regained control of an outsourcing program that had been too broad and not well managed.

Boeing's takeover worked. In December 2009, the company took the Dreamliner on its first test flight in the Seattle area. The Dreamliner soared as did the spirits of Boeing employees and many Americans who saw the American Dream aloft once again with the maiden flight for this new plane.

Boeing has learned its lesson—protect your core competencies and manage execution. It is a lesson that should be studied by all manufacturing companies as they look at future outsourcing initiatives as part of their approach to value-added assembly. It is a lesson that could save countless American jobs and businesses.

Blue-Collar Baloney

The $73-per-hour Detroit automobile worker became the poster child for anyone who wanted to beat up on American unions and the supposedly outrageous compensation paid to an assembly line worker. Never mind that the $73-per-hour worker never existed.

As the Economic Policy Institute (EPI) reported in early 2009, the Detroit autoworker was actually being paid approximately $55 per hour in 2006. This $55 per hour was a fully loaded figure that includes benefits, vacation days, etc. When all of these fringes are taken out, the actual take-home wage is roughly $30 per hour—still, not a bad wage.

As EPI points out, this wage is comparable to that paid to Japanese, German, and Canadian autoworkers. EPI also observed that the average wage for American workers is actually similar to that paid in the 20 richest countries tracked by the Bureau of Labor Statistics (BLS). American workers rank 17 out of 20 among these countries in terms of compensation, and they post higher productivity levels than many of the United States' most important trading partners.

American workers' wages are far higher than those paid in countries like Brazil, China, and Mexico.[8] We don't assume that anyone would assert that American workers should cut their wages to the level paid in those locales to keep jobs in the United States. At the same time, we don't believe it is productive to assume or assert that the American blue-collar worker is an overpaid and lazy lout.

MANUFACTURING UNDER THE MICROSCOPE

There are three major factors that will contribute to building a stronger and more competitive manufacturing base and creating new jobs:

1. The right industries
2. The right skill mix
3. The right policies and investments

The Right Industries

The right manufacturing industries for the future will be those design-ing and creating high-tech products. Many of those industries are still emerging. Some will be completely new. Others have yet to emerge.

Harvard Professors Gary Pisano and Willy Shih wrote that "many high-tech products can no longer be manufactured in the United States because critical knowledge, skills, and suppliers of advanced materials, tools, production equipment, and components have been lost through outsourcing." Pisano and Shih looked at a number of product catego-ries and identified products that are already lost because of outsourcing as well as those that are at risk. These include: semiconductors, light-ing, electronic displays, energy storage, green energy production, com-puting and communications, and advanced materials.[9]

Based upon this analysis, it's obvious that the United States has not only been outsourcing jobs and manufacturing to other coun-tries, it has also been shipping core competencies and competitive advantage around the world. For America to remain a superpower in manufacturing—and we use that term advisedly—it needs to regain its high-tech edge.

From many accounts, it appears that America is losing the high-tech product and industry race. The race for manufacturing advan-tage is a race that America cannot afford to lose. If it does, "Made in America" will become an anachronistic phrase and a reminder of "the good old days."

The Right Skill Mix

Professors Pisano and Shih documented that outsourcing has cost us knowledge and skill sets in certain high-tech areas. Another question is, "What is the skill set and competence of the American manufactur-ing workforce in general today?" The answer is mixed.

On the one hand, the blue-collar workforce is the most educated it has ever been. In 2007, *IndustryWeek* reported that "nearly 50 percent of production workers graduated from high school, and approximately 25 percent have attended college (fewer than 10 percent have degrees). On the other hand, research shows that almost all manufacturers (80 percent) expect a shortage of skilled workers, while more than a third (35 percent) believe there will also be a shortage of scientists and engineers."[10]

Because this research is a few years old, these shortages may have been alleviated by the recession of 2008–09. There are still manufacturing jobs for skilled positions, however, such as CNC operators that go unfilled because of a lack of appropriate training and preparation. Steve Mandes, executive director of the National Institute for Metalworking Skills, relates, "As I go around the country, business owner after business owner tells me about job postings that they can't find qualified people for."

NAM blames this shortage on knowledge and skills deficiencies on the nation's educational system.[11] In *Manufacturing a Better Future for America*, James Jacobs sees it differently. He identifies a number of culprits, including:

- A manufacturing industry that started to invest in training overseas instead of in the United States

- A shift in governmental policies under the Workforce Investment Act of 1998 that "de-emphasized training in favor of immediate job placement"

- The slashing of expenditures in all federal programs aimed at developing a skilled workforce during the Bush administration[12]

Although they look at the issues differently, NAM and Jacobs agree on two things: (1) there is a skill set problem and (2) much more attention needs to be paid to equipping the American manufacturing worker with the right competencies. We think the real issue is how to make American manufacturing a winner in the twenty-first century. One of the requirements for that to happen is to ensure the American manufacturing worker is properly prepared.

The Right Policies and Investments

Policies, or the lack of them, matter immensely for the future of manufacturing in the United States. We present our recommendations on these policies at the end of this chapter. Suffice it to say here that we need policies in the following areas: industry and innovation, taxes, jobs, education, fair trade, and healthcare. In addition to those policies, the appropriate investments need to be made and encouraged to ensure that these are not unfunded mandates, and restructuring needs to be done to the existing delivery systems that impact manufacturing in order to produce the desired results.

MANUFACTURING MAELSTROM

In August of 2009, The Institute for Supply Management (ISM) reported that the manufacturing sector had begun to recover after 18 months of poor performance. Its manufacturing index rose to 52.9 from 48.9 in July (a reading above 50 indicates economic growth, while a reading below 50 indicates economic contraction).

President Obama called these results "a sign that we're on the path to economic recovery." The problem was that as in other sectors of the economy, the recovery was a jobless one. In spite of the uptick in manufacturing in general, ISM's manufacturing employment index contracted again in August with four industry groups saying their payrolls were growing and nine indicating they were declining. In addition, NAM reported that there was "a legitimate concern about the possibility of a jobless recovery . . . the projections estimate a return of 913,000 manufacturing jobs by 2014."[13] That's 913,000 out of a total of almost 2 million manufacturing jobs lost during the recession that began in December 2007. So, while it might not be called a jobless recovery if NAM's projections are accurate, the recovery will be one in which fewer jobs are recovered—a lot fewer.

NAM tracks 19 major manufacturing industries. Based upon an analysis of NAM's projections, when you look at the industries that are projected for only modest gains and employment declines, you can see that the majority of the jobs shipped offshore are never coming back.[14]

Those industries that have stayed closest to the American homeland will recover the quickest and strongest. That's why we need to ensure that there are policies and practices to stimulate manufacturing growth and job creation in the United States.

RENEWING MANUFACTURING RECOMMENDATIONS

The United States has not had a comprehensive and coordinated industrial policy in place since World War II. While the country is not in a worldwide military war, it is in an economic one. We need to implement a comprehensive and consistent set of policies and practices that put manufacturing front and center on the nation's radar screen as the basis for creating the American economy of the future.

Excellent recommendations for creating this future have been advanced by groups such as the New America Foundation, the Alliance for American Manufacturing, the National Association for Manufacturers, the U.S. Business and Industry Council, and numerous others, including academics and industry practitioners. Our specific recommendations parallel and reinforce many of them.

We offer the following four primary recommendations and seven subsidiary recommendations for renewing manufacturing:

Manufacturing Primary Recommendations

1. Develop and fund an industrial and innovation policy focused on driving research and development (R&D) and the rapid growth and restoration of manufacturing in targeted sectors.

2. Reform corporate tax policies and create strong incentives for American manufacturers to establish plants and manufacture products domestically.

3. Create vehicles for public–private financial support for targeted R&D and manufacturing/industrial initiatives. (Incentives and financing for an "Entrepreneurs Funds" should be established as part of this innovation and restoration of manufacturing leadership.)

4. Continue to expand funding and heighten public awareness of the importance of STEM (Science, Technology, Engineering, and Math) and how basic workforce competencies and cutting-edge expertise in these areas can make our manufacturing sector second to none in the world.

Manufacturing Subsidiary Recommendations

5. Implement a major jobs program focused on creating manufacturing and construction jobs related to rebuilding America's crumbling and critically important infrastructure, including a new infrastructure for delivery of alternative forms of energy—solar, wind, biofuels, etc.

6. Develop an integrated education and training plan that rational-izes the nation's approach for developing a skilled manufacturing workforce.

7. Ensure the manufacturing, technical training, and support capa-bilities of America's community college network.

8. Ensure the level of financial and technical assistance required to make small businesses leaders in manufacturing.

9. Provide assistance to small manufacturing companies to help them reduce their healthcare costs.

10. Establish a trade agreement with China that is based on the prin-ciple of reciprocity.

11. Heighten public awareness of the importance of manufacturing and manufacturing careers.

We present and discuss our primary recommendations in this chapter. The subsidiary recommendations are detailed in the Appendix to the book.

1. Develop and fund an industrial and innovation policy focused on driving research and development and the rapid growth and restoration of manufacturing in targeted sectors.

The United States Industrial and Innovation Policy should be developed as a formal plan. That plan should be prepared by the administration and appropriate governmental agencies in collaboration with Congress and with input from representative industry groups.

The most logical owner of the plan is the Department of Commerce. An office should be established at Commerce to oversee the implemen-tation of the plan. An advisory board comprised of representative stake-holders from industry, labor, education, academia, and government should be established to review the plan. (We should note that initial steps have been taken to enhance the focus on innovation by creating an office of Innovation and Entrepreneurship within the Department of Commerce. By making this recommendation, we are advocating an order of magnitude increase in the resources and attention devoted to this area and an intensified focus on manufacturing and technology.)

The plan should set an objective to increase U.S. GDP from manu-facturing to at least 17 percent within 10 years. It should be focused on targeted areas such as high-tech manufacturing, green technologies, and infrastructure renovation and restoration. It should provide funding for basic and applied research and build a bridge to commercial R&D. The plan should also include projections for jobs to be created in targeted industries, areas, and products.

Free traders might argue that development of an industrial and innovation policy by government represents an unnecessary intrusion into private sector affairs. The fact is that the United States currently has an implicit industrial and innovation policy and has throughout the majority of the last century. Unfortunately, it is a patchwork quilt.

That quilt has covered initiatives such as the development of the TVA, Hoover Dam, the nation's highway system, the Internet, global positioning systems, and countless defense projects. More recently, through the automotive industry bailout, emphasis on the development of electric cars, and the provision of $2 billion in grants for the manufacturing of advanced batteries and other components for those cars, the Obama administration has unofficially articulated part of its industrial and innovation policy.

Is there a reason to take it any further and to formalize a policy? Absolutely, for the following three reasons:

1. Without a focus on manufacturing, it is impossible to make manufacturing the key driver it needs to be.

2. The evidence is overwhelming that the United States is, and has been, losing its competitive edge in manufacturing for some time.

3. Other nations, such as China, Japan, South Korea, Taiwan, and Germany, have more centralized approaches to state capitalism and are outperforming us as a result.

The time for an industrial policy is now. As for the need for reestablishing the United States as the industrial power, Jeff Immelt, CEO of General Electric, has not only gotten the message—he's become one of the messengers. He's calling for the United States to manufacture much more domestically and to have at least 20 percent of its jobs in manufacturing—nearly twice what it is today.

Immelt is putting GE's money behind his rhetoric. GE is building a 350-employee plant in Schenectady, New York, to make high-density batteries that will turn many locomotives into diesel-electric hybrids. It's also putting a plant in Louisville, Kentucky, that will employ 420 workers producing hybrid electric water heaters there that are currently manufactured in China.[15]

Alan Tonelson, Research Fellow at the United States Business and Industry Council Education Foundation, points out Immelt is a recent convert to the "Build in the USA" bandwagon. Tonelson blames Immelt and others for the deterioration of American manufacturing and advocating too timid an agenda to revive it.[16] Tonelson may be correct.

We're just happy, however, that Immelt has gotten some of that old-time American manufacturing religion again. We do agree with Tonelson that there is absolutely a need for a trade policy overhaul, and that is why our tenth recommendation in this section is "To establish a trade agreement with China based on the principle of reciprocity."[17]

2. Reform corporate tax policies and create strong incentives for American manufacturers to establish plants and manufacture products domestically.

The U.S. needs to develop tax policies and incentives that are "manufacturing friendly" and that convert hundreds and thousands of business owners to Immelt's pro-American manufacturing stance. Today, the U.S. places far too high a tax burden on its manufacturers and does little to motivate them to build plants stateside. The result is that after research and development is done and a new product is designed here, the actual production takes place outside the United States. In order to reverse that, we suggest the following actions:

- Reduce the corporate income and payroll tax of manufacturers.
- Revise the tax structure to eliminate current incentives that cause manufacturers to go offshore and create advantages and possible financial assistance for manufacturers to create jobs and build or maintain factories in the United States.
- Implement an on-going "Buy American" program for federal procurement.

- Establish and make permanent an R&D tax credit that encourages American manufacturers to do the applied and commercial research necessary in the areas of high-tech manufacturing.

- Conduct a comprehensive study of existing tax policies and tax credits and their impact to determine if there are other "revenue-neutral" actions that can be taken to improve the competitiveness of the American manufacturer.

Nations in Asia and Europe actively court high-tech manufacturing with tax breaks and all types of special incentives while we continue to have the highest corporate taxes in the industrialized world. Several organizations, including NAM and the New America Foundation, have called for lower tax rates for manufacturing organizations. The New America Foundation also observed that the United States appears to be the only major developed nation without a significant "buy domestic" procurement program.

The administration is providing tax credits and loans to help companies build factories dedicated to making solar cells and lithium ion car batteries, and it has upped the ante on research and development. It's a start, but it's time to go all the way in a systematic and structured way by reviewing and realigning the tax and incentive system to square with a fully articulated industrial and innovation policy.

3. Create vehicles for public-private financial support for targeted R&D and manufacturing/industrial initiatives.

Our recommendations for renewing manufacturing come with a fairly heavy price tag. Fortunately, some of these recommendations will result in revenue generation—either through product commercialization or by generating interest and returns on investments. Private sector money can be combined with or piggybacked on public sector money to support industrialization- and manufacturing-related initiatives.

Recognizing this, the government needs to create shared investment opportunities in areas such as R&D, infrastructure development, and high-tech manufacturing facility development. This can be accomplished by creating vehicles such as tax credits, twenty-first-century manufacturing industrial revenue bonds, and jointly owned public–private manufacturing partnerships. We like several ideas that have come from Eric Janszen, Adrian Slywotsky, and Pete Engardio.

Janszen advocates a public–private partnership (PPP) in which the government "envisions infrastructure projects we need and then arranges their funding by private investors as well as by public money." He proposes a competitive process in which PPPs would compete against each other for large-scale public works projects. The winning PPP could then sell bonds to citizen investors over the Internet.[18]

Slywotsky, a management consultant, takes a somewhat similar route. He recommends jump-starting R&D by establishing a national network comprised of three large industrial research labs and five small ones that would cost approximately $20 billion. Slywotsky sees these being paid for by "leading companies devoting a small percentage of their R&D budgets to pure research in exchange for a tax credit."[19] Engardio suggests low-cost loans for factories to be built in the U.S., establishment of industrial zones for specific industries, and accelerating tax write-offs for development of new factories.[20]

These are all innovative ideas to stimulate American innovation and ingenuity. They, and others, should be examined carefully to determine what actions to take to rekindle the American Dream machine.

4. Continue to expand funding and heighten public awareness of the importance of STEM (Science, Technology, Engineering, and Math) and how basic workforce competencies and cutting-edge expertise in these areas can make American manufacturing second to none in the world.

Basic competencies and cutting-edge expertise in STEM are central to creating and maintaining leadership in the manufacturing sector. Unfortunately, today, the United States lags significantly in the STEM areas.

In 2008, the Congressional Research Services reported to Congress that a large majority of secondary-school students fail to reach proficiency in math and science and many are taught by teachers lacking adequate subject matter knowledge. The report noted that studies have shown that 15-year-old students in the U.S. ranked twenty-eighth in math literacy and twenty-fourth in science literacy in an international assessment, and the U.S. ranked twentieth among all nations in the proportion of 24-year-olds who earn a degree in natural science or engineering.[21]

Congress has not been oblivious to the critical needs in this area. In FY 2004, it dedicated $3 billion to fund federal STEM education programs. A Government Accountability Office (GAO) study found that almost three-quarters of this funding went to the National Institutes of Health and the National Science Foundation, but concluded that the programs were too decentralized and required better coordination.[22] Based upon these studies, the Bush administration and Congress passed bills in 2006 and 2007 to expand STEM education programs and establish new ones in agencies such as the Department of Energy and the Education Department.

The Obama administration has intensified the STEM focus. In November 2009, it launched the "Educate to Innovate" campaign and dedicated $250 million directed to moving "American students from the middle to the top of the pack in science by the end of the decade." In January 2010, the administration announced the expansion of this program and five new public–private partnerships that will spend more than $250 million to help prepare over 10,000 new math and science teachers and train over 100,000 existing teachers.[23]

We applaud the administration and Congress for raising STEM higher on the flagpole and its emphasis on teachers and classroom training. The more exciting part of the new agenda for us, however, is bringing the private sector to the table to "serve as champions for STEM" and a proposed "annual science fair" for students to be held at the White House. Given the critical need to enhance America's manufacturing capabilities, we recommend that a wide range of manufacturing leaders be included among those "champions" and that a specific section of the White House science fair be dedicated to manufacturing innovations. Consideration should also be given to having students from different manufacturing disciplines invited to compete in a national "manufacturing fair" to demonstrate their STEM knowledge in applied settings.

Finally, we suggest that the administration consider initiating a national campaign in association with organizations of manufacturers and representatives of labor to help make "manufacturing" a top-of-mind consideration for students and their parents. The campaign should be similar to the race for the space campaign initiated during the Kennedy years. It should give students a sense of learning for a purpose and a part of that purpose would be to keep America great and a leader in manufacturing. We firmly believe that if American students are challenged in this way to accomplish something specific that is explicitly patriotic, they will do so, and America will be better off because of it.

7 | Small Business and Entrepreneurs Matter

"Some people dream of success . . . while others wake up and work hard at it."

Anonymous

Many politicians in the United States pay lip service to small businesses and entrepreneurs. But they must not believe what they say because they do very little for them.

Historically, when it comes to policy and resources in general, small businesses and entrepreneurs have gotten the rhetoric while big business has gotten the reality. The bailouts of 2008 and 2009 demonstrated that bias. There have been recent initiatives directed at making small businesses matter more, but they pale in comparison to the money directed at large businesses and Wall Street.

Small businesses are located in every nook and cranny across this nation; they come in all shapes and sizes. Small businesses are job creators. Small businesses are the lubricant for society. Like grains of sand, they look insignificant standing alone next to a big business. But when you multiply their numbers by millions, small businesses become a larger contributor to our society than all big businesses put together.

That is the reality. Unfortunately, it is a reality often ignored by Washington and banks. Entrepreneurs create small businesses and build them into big businesses. America needs to recognize this. America needs to think small to win big.

SMALL BUSINESS SCORECARD

The United States has always prided itself when it comes to creating and supporting small businesses and entrepreneurs. That revelry was caught short in August of 2009 when John Schmitt and Nathan Lane of the Center for Economic and Policy Research disputed that status.[1]

Schmitt and Lane reported that the U.S. ranked second to last out of 22 countries in the proportion of the total workforce that is self-employed. They also asserted that the U.S. was near the bottom in workers employed in small manufacturing companies and computer-related services.

Small business constitutes more than 99 percent of the total number of businesses in the United States, and they make a tremendous contribution to the overall American economy. Consider the following from the Small Business Administration (SBA):

- As of 2008, there were 6.1 million employer and 23.1 million non-employer firms in the United States.

- Small businesses with fewer than 500 workers account for half of the nation's private nonfarm real GDP; half of all Americans are employed by a small firm.

- Small firms have a higher percentage of patents per employee than large ones, and younger firms are more likely to have a higher percentage of patents than older ones.

- Since the mid-1990s, small businesses have generally created 60 to 80 percent of the net new employment.

- "Gazelles"—fast-growing, high-impact firms—accounted for almost all of the growth in private sector employment in 2008.

- The start rate for new businesses is similar in both rural and urban areas.

- Immigrant entrepreneurs generate nearly 12 percent of all business income in the United States.[2]

The SBA observed that, as was the case for most American businesses, 2008 was a very difficult year for small businesses:

- Unincorporated self-employment fell from 10.4 million in 2007 to 10.1 million.
- In the first three quarters of the year, the United States lost 1,695,000 jobs—60 percent of those jobs were in small businesses.
- There were 627,000 start-ups and 595,600 shutdowns.

The SBA reported that small businesses' major challenges included difficulty accessing capital, healthcare expenditures, attracting a quality workforce, and meeting global competition.[3]

In contrast to the SBA's findings on capital in the fall of 2009, the National Federation of Independent Businesses (NFIB) stated that only 14 percent of business owners reported that getting a loan was harder and a mere 4 percent identified "financing" as their number-one business problem. As the NFIB noted, however, "loan demand is down due to widespread postponement in inventories and historically low plans for capital spending."

While the NFIB reported that there were positive signs in the marketplace, it also stated that those signs were modest. Most importantly, they reported that job creation was still in a negative position and expected to remain that way through the end of 2009.[4] They were correct.

SMALL BUSINESS AND ENTREPRENEURIAL JOB CREATION

It is important to recognize the role of the small business and the entrepreneur as a job engine and to address significantly more resources to assist them in the job creation process. Not only do small businesses and entrepreneurs create most of the new jobs in the economy during "good times," there is overwhelming evidence that they have been the job creators following the past two recessions.

The Ewing Marion Kauffman Foundation, a foundation devoted to entrepreneurship and small business, looked at the start-ups during recessions and bear markets and reached several interesting conclusions:

- Recessions and bear markets do not appear to have a significant impact on the formation or survival of businesses.
- Well over half of the companies on the 2009 Fortune 500 list, and just under half of the 2008 Inc. list, were started during a recession or bear market.
- Job creation from start-ups is much less volatile and sensitive to downturns than job creation in the economy as a whole.[5]

As entrepreneurs and small business owners, we're not surprised by these findings. Tough times stimulate entrepreneurs and small businesses. That's because entrepreneurs are tough people. They see opportunity where others see only challenges. They know that when the going gets tough, the tough get going.

THE SOUL OF THE SMALL BUSINESS: THE ENTREPRENEUR

There's been a lot of quantitative research done and much written about entrepreneurs—who they are and what characteristics they share. We think the best way to understand entrepreneurs, though, and why they succeed is up close and personal through case studies. Here are three such studies for small business owners we know well: Frank Islam, Burt Cabanas, and Allan Boscacci.

We introduced Frank in the preface and talked about how he successfully built his information technology firm, QSS Group, Inc., from less than a $100,000 to almost $300 million in just 13 years. Frank was able to do this because he adhered rigorously to his set of core management principles which included:

- ***Distinctive Core Competence:*** Integrate a blend of engineering, science, and information technology skills in the firm. IT firms in D.C. were a dime a dozen. Frank knew that his firm would stand out with the right skill set and by emphasizing the engineering and science qualifications as its differentiators.

- *Laser-Beam Customer Focus*: Get one key client. Treat the client extremely well and use that as the basis for building the business. From 1994 to 1999, NASA was QSS's only client. QSS got the first assignment with NASA because of Frank's scientific background and the experience he gained in working as an executive at Raytheon.

- *Niche Differentiation*: Expand outward from the core client business to those with similar characteristics and needs. QSS's first work outside NASA was with NOAA (National Oceanic and Atmospheric Administration) and the FDIC. After that, QSS added the Department of Defense, HUD, and other agencies.

- *Perfection in Performance*: Past performance is critical in getting governmental contracts. Frank knew that many IT firms were late on deliverables and sometimes did poor project management and shoddy technical work. He vowed that his firm would stand apart from other firms in his competitive arena and established "Performance as Promised" as QSS's corporate motto. It was more than a motto. It was the way QSS did business and a springboard for getting additional business.

Frank also placed a strong emphasis on top team recruitment and selection and sharing the wealth as part of his formula for success. Finally, unlike many entrepreneurs, Frank wasn't a control freak involved in every detail of the business. He trusted the key decision-makers he had recruited to run the business while he concentrated on marketing and sales and financial management. As Frank put it, "I hired the very best. I knew my role was to hold them accountable and get out of the way and let them do their jobs."

Burt Cabanas is the chair and CEO of Benchmark Hospitality International, a conference center hotel management company headquartered in Houston, Texas. Burt started in the hospitality business at the age of 14 when he was hired as a lifeguard and clean-up boy at the Shelborne Hotel in Miami Beach. He immediately fell in love with the industry and knew it was what he wanted to do for the rest of his life.

Burt started his entrepreneurial career in 1986 with the purchase of Benchmark. When Burt acquired Benchmark, it had only a single contract at the Woodlands Resort and Conference Center outside

Houston, Texas. He has built the company into the premier independent conference center operator with properties in the United States and around the world.

Burt and his team accomplished this because, like Frank Islam, he had a strong vision, a concentrated and differentiated focus—in this case, on conference center management, and a commitment to superior customer service. Burt developed a trademarked philosophy of what makes a great conference center, hotel, or conference resort, which is a balance on living, learning, and leisure. He and his associates at Benchmark emphasized the living and leisure elements as value-adds along with a predictable package pricing to deliver an exceptional experience and value to his conference center meeting planner customers.

There have been three major recessions since Burt has been at the helm of Benchmark. Benchmark has not only survived them all, it has thrived, growing business as it went through each downturn.

Part of the reason for this is Burt's positive mental attitude, which is contagious, and the fact that as a former marine, he always looks forward and never backward. Where others may shrink in the face of adversity, Burt advances. He's done the same with Benchmark during this current recession. As a result, Benchmark has significant growth plans for 2010 and beyond. According to Burt, "We used 2009 to become more disciplined in execution and to plan strategically for the future. As a result, we are perfectly positioned to take Benchmark to the next level—both domestically and internationally."

While Allan Boscacci is not an ex-marine, he rivals Burt Cabanas in terms of his mental toughness and positive attitude. He is the former president and chair of the board of AB&I Foundry, a 100-plus-year-old soil pipe foundry located in Oakland, California.

Allan was the third-generation family owner of AB&I. When he came into the business in 1967, there were 23 soil pipe foundries in the United States, 10 of which were on the West Coast. Today, there are only three soil pipe foundries in the United States, and AB&I is the last foundry standing on the West Coast where it has fought China imports to a draw. As a result, where thousands of foundry jobs have disappeared or gone overseas, Allan and his AB&I team members kept 200 jobs stateside.

They accomplished this with a combination of investment, ingenuity, and inspiration. Allan's philosophy from the time he took over AB&I was to purchase cutting-edge equipment and then to use and reengineer it to increase productivity and make AB&I a low-cost producer. The company accomplished this on a continuous basis.

But the true accomplishment was forging a virtually unrivalled alliance with the foundry workforce that was unionized. This was driven by Allan's belief that AB&I could not continue in this competitive business unless union and management and salaried and hourly could find a way to work together.

Under Allan's direction and in collaboration with the union rep, they did. Time clocks were taken down. Everybody became a "team member." Financials were shared with the team, and 23 percent of after-tax profits were distributed among the total team (salaried and hourly). In some years, as much as 2 months' wages were shared at the end of the year.

Allan personally met in one-on-one meetings with all 200 team members twice a year for at least 30 minutes to understand their personal and business goals. The plant supervisors met with team members three times a year to keep them up to speed and to ensure that they knew where they had to do to improve.

This philosophy and approach kept the company from going bankrupt during the recession of the early 1990s. Because of the bond that had been built, the entire team took a 10 percent wage cut, worked overtime for straight time, and was furloughed as much as a week a month. AB&I survived that recession and paid everyone back the wages they had given up and came out stronger than ever.

As Allan explains, "We were able to do this because our team members looked at AB&I as their company. We treated them as managers of their job. I'd frequently flip the organization chart upside down and let the line guys know they were the ones making the money and our role as managers and supervisors was to remove roadblocks so they could perform at the highest level."

THE MIND OF THE ENTREPRENEUR

The stories of Frank Islam, Burt Cabanas, and Allan Boscacci are illustrative. They demonstrate that entrepreneurs think and act differently. The Kauffman Foundation has done a good job of looking into the traits and thoughts of the entrepreneur. Studies conducted by the foundation revealed that:

- The founders of technology-based companies tended to be middle-aged and well educated. The vast majority came from middle- and upper-lower-class backgrounds. Most had significant industry experience before starting their companies.

- The primary motivators for starting a company in rank order were: desire to build wealth; capitalizing on a business idea; always wanting to have their own company; appeal of a start-up culture; being independent.

- Entrepreneurs are confident and want to control their own destinies.[6]

The Kauffman Foundation has launched "Build a Stronger America," a movement to unite entrepreneurs and help give them a stronger voice in the public discussion about the country's economic future.[7] Why do entrepreneurs feel a need for a stronger voice? Why do they, along with small businesses, feel like voices in the wilderness when they're responsible for so much growth in the economy? By looking at the federal government's practices and performance as it relates to small business, we can find the answer.

THE FEDERAL GOVERNMENT AND SMALL BUSINESS

Question: When is a small business not a small business? *Answer*: When it's the recipient of federal government set-asides targeted by the SBA for small businesses. In fact, given the contracting performance of the SBA during the period 2000–2008, the agency might have been more appropriately named the Big Business Administration.

The SBA sets an annual goal for a percentage of prime contractor dollars to be awarded to small businesses. Based upon a variety of sources, including the SBA's own Office of Advocacy and Inspector

General, it appears that the SBA was giving credit to small businesses for contracts actually awarded to large ones.

In a 2005 report, the SBA Inspector General stated, "One of the most important challenges facing the Small Business Administration today and the entire federal government today is that large businesses are receiving small business procurement awards and the agencies are receiving credit for these awards." That year, the Office of Advocacy found that 44 of the top thousand small businesses were actually major corporations.[8]

Fast-forward to 2008 to see how the SBA and the federal government have done in meeting that challenge—the SBA prime contractor dollar goal for 2008 was 23 percent. Commenting on his blog in 2009, Robb Mandelbaum noted, "In 2008 small business contracts accounted for just 21.5 percent. Not only is that below the goal, it's worse than in 2007 . . . The federal government as a whole hasn't met this goal since 2005."[9]

The Kauffman Foundation reported that the SBA's budget was cut 28 percent between 2000 to 2008. According to Senator Mary Landrieu (D-LA), "The agency's funding was cut more than any other agency in the last 8 years."

How did things go in 2009? The stimulus package provided $730 million to the SBA. The total stimulus package was $787 billion. That meant only approximately 1 percent was earmarked for small businesses. This might seem like "chump change" given the total bill, but the administration assumed the SBA funds would leverage tens of billions in private sector financing for small businesses.

There were three major elements in the SBA portion of the stimulus bill for small businesses: (1) expansion of the 7(a) lending program "to accommodate the most diverse range of business financing needs," (2) expansion of the 504 lending program for "long-term financing for major fixed assets," and (3) establishment of Business Stabilization (ARC) loans for "short-term relief for viable small businesses facing immediate financial hardship." Together, these components accounted for 86.3 percent of the money directed at small businesses.

SBA's initial rollout of the small business stimulus was slow. In addition, a number of apparently qualified loan applicants were rejected by lenders. Thanks to the continuous push from Congresswoman

Nydia M. Velazquez, chairperson of the U.S. House Committee on Small Business, the SBA has had its positive moments. By September 2009, for example, the SBA reported that it had accomplished the following:

- Increased loan volume by 60 percent
- Made loans to more than 1,100 lenders that it had not made loans to since October 2008
- Made more than 2,200 ARC loans totaling over $72 million

There were some hiccups along the way that slowed things down. For example, the SBA announced a cap on the loan guarantee it was willing to extend on "goodwill" financing for purchase of small businesses to $250,000—there had been no cap prior to that. After considerable pushback from the business community and Chairperson Velazquez, the SBA eventually increased the guarantee to $500,000.

In September 2009, Commerce Secretary Gary Locke announced the establishment of an Office of Innovation and Entrepreneurship and a National Advisory Council on Innovation and Entrepreneurship. The office reports directly to Secretary Locke and works with the White House and other federal agencies to encourage entrepreneurship, including training, access to capital, and policy incentives. The council will advise the Commerce Department on policy related to small businesses and help the department engage in an on-going dialogue with the entrepreneurial and small business communities.[10]

In addition, there were bipartisan efforts in Congress directed at small businesses. In July 2009, the Senate passed the Financial Services Appropriation Bill, which included a $22 million increase for SBA over the president's budget request. The final funding of $697 million for SBA was a $150 million increase from the prior year. In July, the Senate also unanimously reauthorized the Small Business Innovation Research (SBIR) and Small Business Technology Transfer (STTR) programs for 8 years. The House Committee on Small Business submitted recommendations for the Fiscal Year Budget for 2010 of $1.43 billion, doubling previous budgets. This would restore SBA funding to levels similar to those in the last year of the Clinton administration.

While 2009 was not a banner year for small businesses, there was definitely a much-stronger focus and greater activity generated to support small business and entrepreneurship in the federal government arena than in the prior 8 years. The question is whether it is sufficient and proportionate to the needs of entrepreneurs and to the leadership role and contributions that they can make to turn this fragile and jobless recovery into a robust and job-filled one.

In our opinion, not yet. We believe we've come a long way—but there's still a long way to go. The Kauffman Foundation research indicates that since 1980, all net job growth has come from businesses less than 5 years old. The foundation's Index of Entrepreneurial Activity also shows that more than half a million people every year launch a new business.[11]

The evidence and data are overwhelming. Small businesses and entrepreneurs who create jobs have, and will continue to be, the leaders in bringing the United States out of the recession. Recognizing this, it's time to invest much more of the government's money where it counts and where it will get the best return on investment.

RENEWING SMALL BUSINESS AND ENTREPRENEURSHIP RECOMMENDATIONS

It appears that is what President Obama intended to do at the beginning of 2010. In his State of the Union address, the president announced a $30 billion commitment to community banks which they could use to make loans to small businesses. He planned to fund this commitment from TARP monies that were unused or returned by larger financial institutions.

The president got immediate pushback from those on the Republican side of the aisle as well as fiscal conservatives who said the funds were not appropriated and should not be used for those purposes. Even those on the Democratic side of the aisle and small business owners were a little skeptical regarding this proposed new initiative. Rep. Nydia Vasquez (D-NY), chairwoman of the House Committee on Small Business, proclaimed, "All of the efforts so far have focused on helping banks, and yet, small businesses still can't find affordable loans."

We agree with the dedication of this money to support small business loans—with two stipulated conditions. First, if the money is given to banks, there should be restrictions that state it can only be used for making loans and not to improve the banks' balance sheets, as was the case with the large banks. As we note elsewhere in this book, the large banks used the initial influx of their TARP dollars as follows: 43 percent went to bolster bank capital; 31 percent went to other investments; 14 percent went to repaying debt; and 4 percent went to acquisitions.

Second, the loans need to be large enough to make a difference for small businesses. They should be used to either increase employment or cut operational expenses. They should not be used by the bank to help a business pay down or off a loan that is owed to that bank. This is important because that is how some of the current money provided under the stimulus bill and SBA loans is being used. It doesn't address the underlying need, but instead, exacerbates existing problems related to cash flow and capitalization.

As reported in *The New York Times*, Barbara Wright, who owns a small uniform company in Chicago, got a $35,000 loan from her bank. She thought it could be used for operations, but she was wrong. It could only be used to help pay off a previous loan of $50,000. Based upon this, *The Times* observed, "Federal officials and Congress structured the loan program to help banks as much as their customers."[12]

Is it any wonder that American small business owners are becoming increasingly more frustrated and pessimistic? In December of 2009, the National Federation of Independent Businesses' monthly small business optimism index stood at 88. It had been below 90 for 15 months. A number below 100 reflects a lack of optimism.[13] If steps aren't taken along the lines proposed here in 2010 to unfreeze bank lending, that index will become frozen permanently and the only index that will exist is a pessimism one.

Given the foregoing, it is obvious that there is clearly renewed support for entrepreneurs and small business owners. In spite of this support, the money does not seem to be flowing as intended. There is still not the appropriate alignment or allocation of resources and action. Our recommendations which follow are designed to help bring about that alignment, allocation, and action. We offer three primary and six subsidiary recommendations for accomplishing this.

Small Business/Entrepreneurship Primary Recommendations

1. Increase funding and expand the current direct and guaranteed loan program for start-ups
2. Implement small business-friendly tax policies and incentives
3. Merge the SBA into the Department of Commerce

Small Business/Entrepreneurship Subsidiary Recommendations

4. Implement a targeted jobs program for entrepreneurs and small businesses
5. Enforce and increase the federal government goal for small business contracts
6. Increase the funding for the SBIR and STTR initiatives
7. Ensure the effective implementation of target group initiatives
8. Listen to and incorporate the voices of small businesses and entrepreneurs
9. Implement small business-friendly healthcare programs

1. Increase funding and expand the current direct and guaranteed loan program for start-ups.

The federal funding to support small businesses' growth, development, and establishment is woefully inadequate. There should be an order of magnitude increase for funding support of these entities. SBA is irrelevant for most of America's small businesses. That needs to change, because banks are not providing the capital that these businesses need. Those "small businesses" that are bigger than microbusinesses but smaller than major corporations are left without an advocate or support system. The SBA needs to grow up with them. There should be a substantial increase in direct loans now that banks have reduced their lending.

Less than 1 percent of the total dollars appropriated in the stimulus package was allocated to start-up entrepreneurs. Given their role, historically, in growing the U.S. economy, there needs to be a substantial increase in microloans for new businesses and entrepreneurial start-ups.

We are concerned about the whole guaranteed loan concept—especially when you are protecting up to 90 percent of the lender's exposure. We know how it benefits and protects the lender. We're not certain what it does in terms of adding value for the new business or borrower.

As noted earlier in this chapter, small businesses constitute more than 99 percent of the businesses in the country, employing more than one-half of the citizens and accounting for more than half of the nation's GDP. That's why it's hard to comprehend why so little money is dedicated to them or when special arrangements are made to provide funding, the money runs out before the end of a fiscal year.

2. Implement small business-friendly tax policies and incentives.

Tax policies and governmental regulations are ordinarily the single biggest issue of concern of small businesses. In Chapter 7, we provided recommendations on tax policies and incentives for manufacturers. There are several recommendations from that chapter that can be applied to small businesses and entrepreneurs:

- Corporate income and payroll taxes of small businesses should be reduced for a period of time.
- An on-going "Buy American" program for federal procurement should be established.
- An R&D tax credit that encourages small businesses to invest in applied and commercial research to create new products and services should be established permanently.
- A comprehensive study of existing tax policies and tax credits should be conducted to determine if there are other "revenue neutral" actions that can be taken to improve the competitiveness of small businesses.

In addition, we recommend the following:

- Ensure that the process of starting and launching a business is as simple and inexpensive as possible.
- Ensure that there is flexibility in new regulations as they apply to small businesses.
- Ensure that the small business owner or entrepreneur is protected and not unduly penalized if the business venture fails.

Finally, at the federal level, the special tax provisions of 2001 and 2003 are set to expire in FY 2010 and the alternative minimum tax becomes a bigger issue each year. This needs to be properly addressed. If not, we might unwittingly kill the small business geese that lay the golden eggs that become the jobs in our economy.

3. Merge the SBA into the Department of Commerce.

We recommend merging the SBA into the Department of Commerce and renaming the merged entity the Department of Commerce and Entrepreneurship. This new department would intensify the nation's focus on small business and entrepreneurship and achieve a much more effective and efficient allocation and utilization of resources.

This merger would elevate the status of the small business to a cabinet-level position. It would also provide the potential for the reconsideration of the mission and functions for the merged entity and a "wall-to-wall" reexamination of the role that the Department of Commerce should be playing for the United States.

The department's proposed discretionary budget for FY 2010 was over $15 billion with full-time equivalent employment of close to 142,000. More than 80 percent of that budget was for the National Oceanic & Atmospheric Agency (NOAA) and the Census Bureau. In past years, the combined percentages for these units was about 75 percent. The percentage went up because 2010 is a census year and the Census Bureau will have a number of temporary employees. In normal years, NOAA accounts for more than 50 percent of Commerce's budget.

The point here is that based upon its budget allocation, the department doesn't appear to have business, commerce, or entrepreneurship of any type at the top of its agenda. That's why bringing SBA into Commerce makes sense. It helps to legitimize Commerce's existence.

The SBA was created in 1953 with the mission "to aid, counsel, assist, and protect the interests of small business concerns, to preserve free competitive enterprise, and to maintain and strengthen the overall economy of our nation." Sounds like something the Department of Commerce should be interested in, too, wouldn't you think?

The SBA has a portfolio of more than $90 billion dollars in loan guarantees, over 2,000 employees, and 14,000 affiliated counselors nationwide who work with resource partners, such as the Service Corps of Retired Executives (SCORE) and Small Business Development Corporations (SBDC), to assist small businesses. The major services that SBA provides include financial assistance, technical assistance, contracting assistance, disaster assistance, special interest programs, and advocacy.

The SBA's proposed budget for FY 2010 was for $799 million in new budget authority. Of this amount, the SBA requested $83 million of credit subsidy, or a little more than 10 percent for loan guarantees. The SBA budget proposal estimated that this would generate more than $28 billion in small business financing.

The SBA's budget is significantly lower than both NOAA and the Census. However, it is much larger than any of the other organizational units in Commerce except for the National Institute of Standards and Technology (which, historically, has been about 5 to 10 percent larger than SBA's).[14]

The SBA would be a meaningful entity and a big fish within Commerce—no more swimming upstream. It would be positioned to increase both its overall budget and the amount available for credit subsidies in future years—good for Commerce, the SBA, small businesses, entrepreneurs, and the nation.

We're sure you're seeing that there is a theme that emerges from this chapter and these recommendations—small business and entrepreneurs need to drive our new economy. If manufacturing is our backbone for the economy, small business is the heart.

We find it ironic that at the same time the federal government bailed out the automobile manufacturers in Detroit, they inadvertently contributed to the closing of thousands of automobile dealerships across the country. Those were the small businesses that helped to give many small communities their heartbeats. They employed dozens of people, put their names on the Little League jerseys, and supported local charities. In many instances, they were second- and third-generation family businesses started by an entrepreneur with a dream who passed that dream on to the next generation.

We are quite certain that the intent behind the bailout was not to extinguish those dreams. But sometimes policies can be wrongheaded and create unintended consequences. This can be especially true if the interests of those who are too large to fail prevail over those who are too small to help. It's time to let small businesses and entrepreneurs know that help is on the way by putting a much higher priority on them.

8 | The Media Matters

"Objective journalism and an opinion column are about as similar as the Bible *and* Playboy *magazine."*
                                                      Walter Cronkite

THE BOTTOM OF THE BANNER FOR THE *CHICAGO TRIBUNE* USED TO read, "The World's Greatest Newspaper." Today, The World's Greatest Newspaper is bankrupt—as is its last remaining major Chicago competitor, the *Chicago Sun Times.*

Several decades ago, Chicago had four "great" newspapers: *Chicago Tribune, Chicago Sun Times, Chicago Daily News,* and *Chicago Daily American.* Each of these papers had their own devoted audience and writers who won Pulitzer Prizes. Today, the two survivors are shadows of their former selves.

The headline has become the deadline. Some say good-bye and good riddance—that's yesterday's news. The future belongs to the electronic media and the bloggers. Others say America needs a multifaceted news media with distinctive capacities and capabilities.

We say that this is not a theoretical argument. How it is resolved will make a major difference in the future of the American democracy and the American Dream.

NOT NECESSARILY THE NEWS

The electronic media used to be dominated by the broadcast news: CBS, NBC, and ABC were kings of the hill. Now they're at the bottom of it. They have been replaced at the top by cable news and a new brand of reporting.

Frankly, we feel that "reporting" is a strong term to use because much of what is done is carping and criticizing those with ideas or ideals different from the commentators. If you've watched any cable TV, you know who these folks are.

On the left, there's Keith Olbermann, Rachel Maddow, and Ed Schultz. On the right, there's Glenn Beck, Sean Hannity, and Bill O'Reilly. In addition, there are others who don't wear their political stripes on their shoulders: Lou Dobbs, who referred to himself as "Mr. Independent," and Jon Stewart and Steven Colbert, who take a no-holds-barred comedic approach in going after both sides. Also there's Bill Maher, who leans libertarian and agnostic while also swinging from the comedian's side of the plate.

What do we call this group? Some have suggested using the label "entertainer." In our opinion, Colbert, Stewart, and Maher would probably accept the "entertainer" label with some type of modifier. We're not certain that the others who are working the cable news circuit would classify themselves in this way. Reporters, broadcast journalists, commentators, perhaps?

The job title doesn't matter. These individuals are in point of fact *opinionators*. They get paid a lot of money for stating their opinion in an assertive and sometimes aggressive manner so that it has the strongest appeal to the market segment that they have been targeted to reach. They're in the business of market ratings and market share. If they don't keep or grow their share, they could lose their job or customer base.

These individuals are also opinion leaders and role models. This is where things become more problematic. If opinionators act in a manner that is destructive or dismissive of others, their message is that full frontal assault is okay to those who watch or listen to them. They establish a behavioral norm and code of conduct that is then acceptable for their followers to adapt and employ in everyday life.

Words and language are powerful conditioners and persuaders. They have the ability to incite or inspire. They can be used for good or for bad. They can liberate or repress.

We live in an increasingly uncivil era. When cable news show opinionators pump up the volume and fire up the rhetoric unnecessarily, they are not only setting a bad example, they are contributing to the decline in civility and reducing the potential for any meaningful dialogue or discussion on issues and matters where positions differ.

We are focused on cable news because research shows clearly and convincingly that an increasing majority of us now get our news on cable TV or over the Internet (more on that later). Cable news definitely influences individual perspectives and opinions. It can either report facts or reinforce stereotypes. Much of the time it appears to do the latter.

This has led to what Robert J. Burgess, "the focus group guy," calls the "Cable News Effect." Burgess defines this effect as "an approach to debate and discussion which accentuates differences, and does little, if anything, to promote a common understanding or solve problems." Burgess goes on to say that this effect is "one of the primary drivers of divisiveness which now plagues our country."[1]

We're not so sure it's a primary driver, but we are sure it's a contributor. The more we think about it—given much of what passes for news on cable TV—the more we might be better off calling it "not necessarily the news." Cable news is like jumbo shrimp—an oxymoron.

It's not just the disputative nature of much of what's on cable; it's the fact that the coverage is there 24/7. This means shows get repeated over and over and the public is subjected to depressing and diminishing spectacles of political posturing and grandstanding—à la the Bill Clinton impeachment inquisition, the Florida recount, and the Sotomayor confirmation hearings.

Ex-Supreme Court Justice Sandra Day O'Connor commented on this when she was on the *Morning Joe* show on June 30, 2009, being interviewed by Mika Brzezinski and Joe Scarborough. She was asked who created the circus-like atmosphere surrounding Supreme Court confirmation hearings.

She replied, "You did." Joe and Mika looked startled. Justice O'Connor continued to clarify that by "you," she meant cable news that had to cover things from gavel to gavel to fill up time and air space. Justice O'Connor further observed that up until 1978, there were not even hearings held for appointees to the Supreme Court.[2] Those were kinder and gentler times.

In looking back to that time period, it was also when the news was the news. Nationally, it was anchors like Dan Rather, Tom Brokaw,

Walter Cronkite, and Edward R. Murrow. In Chicago, it was Floyd Kalber, Bill Kurtis, Fahey Flynn, and Joel Daley. Fill in the blanks for your own city and state.

When Cronkite, after considerable soul-searching and personal agony, asserted that he thought it was time for the U.S. to withdraw from Vietnam, and when Murrow took on the establishment, and Senator Joe McCarthy's calculated deceit of a witch hunt for Communists, it wasn't because they were saying the politically correct thing from the right or the left. As Americans, citizens, and journalists, they were speaking truth to power.

Today, there are still some calmer and cooler heads on broadcast TV: Diane Sawyer, Brian Williams, Chuck Todd, David Gregory. They don't, however, have much of an audience, and the evening news hour has shrunk to half an hour—take out the ads and you only get about 26 minutes, if you're lucky.

The PBS NewsHour is still an hour and is presented without commercial interruption. During that hour, Jim Lehrer and his colleagues (Ifill, Brown, Warner, Suarez, and Woodruff) cover the news in-depth and with dignity and distinction—no hostile questions, no prisoners taken. The show provides an example of what excellence in news coverage looks like.

In 2008, TV lost Tim Russert, another exemplar of excellence in reporting and listening. As host of *Meet the Press*, Tim could ask the tough question without being rude or condescending. He could disagree without being disagreeable. He held all of his guests to a higher standard.

Tim was a uniter, not a divider. He understood that there were, and are, divides that separate us, and that the best way to move the nation forward was not debating those divides in heated terms but discussing them rationally and without malice.

AMERICAN DEMOCRACY AND THE NEWS MEDIA

American democracy does not exist because of the media, but it could not exist without it. Indeed, the media made a major contribution to the establishment of the United States of America. In 1735, a printer named John Peter Zenger was taken to trial for libel for articles that he had published in the *New York Weekly Journal* that were critical of the British government. Zenger was tried and acquitted. The first die was cast in the media's role in helping to fan the flames of revolution.[3]

Then in the run-up to the Revolutionary War in the 1760s and 1770s, patriots sponsored, or subsidized, newspapers so that they could build popular support for separating from England. Paid circulation was low. These four-page papers were passed from hand to hand and read aloud in communities.

It is estimated that a paper's total audience was probably 20 times its circulation during that revolutionary period and that Thomas Paine's *Common Sense* reached more than 500,000 people when the total population of the United States was a mere 2,500,000.[4] The flames for revolution and establishment of the American democracy grew higher and were definitely fueled by newsprint.

Given this pivotal role of the news, is it any wonder that the First Amendment to the Constitution states, "Congress shall make no law abridging freedom of speech or of the press"? Or, that Thomas Jefferson wrote in 1787, "The basis of our government being the opinion of the people, the very first object should be to keep that right; and were it left to me to decide whether we should have a government without newspapers or newspapers without a government, I should say I would not hesitate a moment to prefer the latter."[5]

The free press has been a cornerstone of American democracy from the outset. It remains a differentiator today. In her book, *Mass Media and American Politics*, political science Professor Doris Graber notes that only 18 percent of the countries in the world have "full press freedom." The United States is among that 18 percent, ranking 21 out of 195 countries.[6] Professor Michael Schudson, a sociologist, rates the United States much higher. In his new book, *Why Democracies Need an Unlovable Press*, he asserts, "The press is more free of government restriction in the United States than in any other nation on earth."[7]

We're not concerned about the ratings, however. What matters is the key functions the news media should play in a representative democracy like the United States and how well they are fulfilling them.

KEY FUNCTIONS OF THE NEWS MEDIA

A good starting point for thinking about those functions is the Pulitzer Prizes for Journalism. In 2009, prizes were awarded in the following categories: Public Service, Breaking News Reporting, Investigative Reporting, Explanatory Reporting, Local Reporting, National Reporting, International Reporting, Feature Writing, Commentary, Criticism, Editorial Writing, Editorial Cartooning, Breaking News Photography, and Feature Photography. That's a broad spectrum and virtually everything a newspaper does.

Professor Schudson narrows the perspective by identifying six specific key functions that journalism has assumed to a greater or lesser degree for citizens in democratic societies:

- Information: provided fairly and fully

- Investigation: into concentrated sources of power

- Analysis: furnishing in-depth and coherent frameworks to help explain complex topics or issues

- Social Empathy: describing the conditions and situations of others in society and the world, especially the disadvantaged

- Public Forum: being a centralized communications vehicle for dialogue and discourse on issues and matters of importance

- Mobilization: advocating for particular positions, programs, or actions[8]

The next question is how well is the news media performing those functions?

THE CITIZEN'S ATTITUDE TOWARD THE NEWS MEDIA

In September 2009, the Pew Research Center released a report with the disturbing headline, "Press Accuracy Rating Hits Two-Decade

Low: Public Evaluations of the News Media 1985–2009." While the lead for the report was negative, there were a few positives in the report regarding the news media in general:

- The majority of respondents continued to express favorable opinions of local TV news (73 percent), daily newspapers with which they are most familiar (65 percent), and network TV news (64 percent). Ratings for all three of these sources were above 80 percent in 1985.

- Most of the respondents supported a "watchdog role" for the press (62 percent). Since 1985, this rating has always been over 50 percent. As would be expected, Democrats are most in favor of the watchdog role when a Republican is president and vice versa.

- Most of the respondents said losses of current news outlets would be important. They rated the loss of local news the highest (82 percent) and large national outlets the lowest (68 percent). Losses of the other sources including network TV evening news, cable news, and local newspapers were rated in the mid-70s.

On the flip side, here are some of the more negative highlights from the report:

- Only 29 percent of those surveyed said that news organizations "get their facts straight" compared to 55 percent in 1985.

- A mere 18 percent felt that news organizations "deal fairly with issues" compared to 34 percent in 1985 and a high of 36 percent in 1989.

- Approximately 63 percent felt that news organizations' "stories were often inaccurate" compared to 34 percent in 1985.

- Nearly 60 percent thought that the press was politically biased with 78 percent of the Republicans responding this way and 50 percent of the Democrats.

- Almost 60 percent of Republicans indicated that they thought the press was "too critical of America" compared to only 33 percent of Democrats.[9]

In summary, the Pew Report shows citizens much more distrustful of the media than they were 25 years ago with a significant difference in attitudes along party lines.

CHARTING THE STATE OF THE TRADITIONAL NEWS MEDIA

As citizens' attitudes toward traditional news media (newspapers and TV news) have soured, the media has fallen on hard times. It's not due to the changing feelings of readers, however, but because of a failing business model.

Historically, both newspapers and TV have depended on paid advertising to be the primary source of their revenue. The last half of the twentieth century was the golden era and growth years for them. During that time period, the reliance paid off handsomely. Due to the emergence of the Internet and its explosive growth since 2004, the payoff has diminished significantly, and with it, the fame and fortunes of the traditional media. Combined print and digital ad revenue in 2008 was down 16.6 percent, the worst drop since the Great Depression.

This decline pales in comparison to that experienced in the first three quarters of 2009. The combined revenue fell 28.3 percent in quarter one and 29 percent in quarter two. In spite of a slight rebound in the third quarter, as Richard Pérez-Peña wrote in a *New York Times* article, "people who monitor the newspaper business for a living say it has not hit bottom yet."[10] PricewaterhouseCoopers predicted that by 2013, combined print and digital ad revenues would be less than print-only ad revenues in 2008.

The consequences of this dramatic loss of revenue are captured fully in an important report issued by the Columbia University Graduate School of Journalism titled, "The Reconstruction of American Journalism" (Reconstruction Report). The second sentence of the report sums up the current state of the newspaper industry: "As almost everyone knows, the economic foundation of the nation's newspapers long supported by advertising is collapsing, and newspapers themselves, which have been the country's chief source of independent reporting, are shrinking— literally."[11] They are shrinking in two ways—size and substance.

Newspaper editorial employees, which had grown from about 40,000 in 1971 to more than 60,000 in 1992, dropped back to approximately 40,000 in 2009. The number of newspaper reporters covering state capitals full-time fell from 524 in 2003 to 355 at the beginning of 2009. Most large newspapers eliminated foreign and Washington correspondents. In 2008 and 2009, metropolitan dailies such as Denver's *Rocky Mountain News* and the *Seattle Post Intelligencer* stopped printing newspapers, and several smaller chains and individually owned newspapers either filed for bankruptcy or went out of business.

The two key fatalities on the substantive side were the loss of local independent reporting and accountability journalism. Accountability journalism is the "watchdog" function of the press. It ensures scrutiny of those in positions of power and influence in a free society. One of the roles of independent reporting is educating citizens so they can make informed decisions about the world around them. In addition, reporting provides interpretation, analysis, informed opinion, and advocacy. It helps prepare us to participate in our society and life.

We believe that independent reporting and accountability journalism are essential in a democracy. If the capacity and capability for these functions are significantly reduced or diminished, democracy is put at risk. We also believe that the independent press has taken significant body blows and will not be able to contribute what it did only a few short years ago.

Is the current media constellation sufficient to fill that void, and what should the role of traditional media be going forward? To answer that question, we need to look at the nature of the media in America today and what it will look like in the foreseeable future.

CHANNELING THE FUTURE OF THE NEWS MEDIA

The Columbia University Reconstruction Report acknowledges the dramatic changes in the news media since the dawning of the Internet age. It points out that the Internet has enabled news to be gathered and distributed in new ways, such as "online news organizations, nonprofit investigative reporting projects, public broadcasting stations, university-run news service services, community news sites with citizen participation, and bloggers." Add to that, data available in this era of increased transparency from all government agency Web sites and through sites such as congresspedia.org or factcheck.org for politics, and you have a virtual cornucopia of information that can be searched, captured, arrayed, analyzed, and reported by anyone with an Internet connection and an inquiring mind. In this new era for the news media, each and every one of us has the potential to be, as Arianna Huffington labels them, "citizen journalists: online Paul Reveres."[12]

The times are a-changin' at warp speed. Think about the world before or without YouTube, Google, and the iPhone. It's hard to imagine, isn't it? In the future, the limits for the news media will only be limited by an individual's imagination.

The news media will not belong to the individual completely. But the individual who wants to participate will have much greater access to shape and influence journalism and the nature of democracy. The individual citizen's voice will probably not dominate, but it will definitely be a stronger part of the celestial choir.

What will the other parts of the news media look like going out to 2020, a decade from now? It would be foolish to think that one could paint a comprehensive picture—a decade ago, who could have foreseen the rise and ascent of infomediaries like Google or the decline and fall of newspaper giants like the *Tribune* chain. However, some leading indicators are provided by what is happening currently with emerging news media entities and the repositioning by members of the traditional media.

On the emerging side in the Internet today are a number of operations focused on politics like the Huffington Post, Politico, Salon, the Daily Kos, and the Daily Beast. There are also some local online news-only sites supported by local community foundations or individuals such as the Voice of San Diego, started up by local businessman Buzz Woolley because of his frustration with his local paper. In addition, there are small shops such as John Marshall of Talking Points Memo who did the research and analysis that broke the original story about the politically motivated firings of the U.S. attorneys during the Bush presidency. The most interesting example is provided by ProPublica, which is defining a new approach to doing investigative reporting in the Web era.

ProPublica is a New York-based nonprofit and nonpartisan organization with an investigative and news staff of 32. It was established in 2008 with funding from philanthropists—most notably the Sandler Foundation—for approximately $30 million. One of the things that ProPublica does is research and write stories for coauthorship and distribution through the traditional news media. In October 2009, Paul Steiger, editor-in-chief of ProPublica, reported that his staff had already worked on over two dozen stories and more than half a dozen stories with *The Los Angeles Times.* ProPublica has also put together a team of more than 2,200 volunteers at the local level to provide reporting from the field on topics of political and social interest, such as the use of stimulus money.[13]

In the electronic media space, cable news for targeted audiences such as businesspeople and those interested in politics and government continues to trump TV news. However, as the Pew Report results show, TV evening news still has a somewhat special place in the public's heart and minds.

Moving from the emerging to the traditional side of news reporting, what can be seen is that the few remaining giants such as *The New York Times* and *The Washington Post* are restructuring themselves to look more and more like their competitors. They've added blogging columnists, streaming videos, and established more collaborative ventures with volunteer reporters and more independent sources not aligned with the newsroom staff. The primarily business publications for targeted audiences such as *The Wall Street Journal,* the *Financial Times,* and *The Economist* are growing and commanding advertising and subscription premiums. Other niche publications such as *Mother Jones, Atlantic, Nation, National Review,* and *American Spectator,* which were never dependent on advertising, are holding their own.

In contrast, many of the mainstream news magazines are having significant difficulty because of lost revenue and difficulty reinventing themselves. In May of 2009, *Newsweek* announced that it was restructuring itself and would no longer re-report the news that had already been covered by TV, cable news, and the Internet. Instead, it would go to a new format that would be designed to include "reported narratives that rely on intellectual scoops and pair them with essayistic arguments." Jon Meacham, publisher of *Newsweek*, said that this format was designed to appeal to "'virtual Beltway,' people who do not live in those confines but 'are part of that sensibility.'"[14]

We don't think there are enough of those virtual Beltway readers to pull this game out. We hope we're wrong, however, because *Newsweek* is a well written and edited magazine that has contributed much to its readers in its more than three quarters of a century's existence.

Back to newspapers. Many smaller local newspapers and newspapers in locations where there is no major competition continue to do well. Those in metropolitan areas where there is significant competition of all types are doomed to an existence that is, and will be, significantly different than it was on the ride up for the past 50 years or so.

To paraphrase Mark Twain, reports of the death of the newspaper or the press as we know it are indeed premature. Reports of the decline of newspapers and television news, however, are real and not exaggerated.

The news media constellation in the future will be significantly different from what it is today. There are significant opportunities that need to be exploited and serious threats to be avoided in order to ensure that the media is restructured and reshaped in a way that makes American democracy stronger.

The opportunities include: greater transparency and access to information of all types, an enhanced role for citizens and smaller organizations to participate in the news-making process, either individually or collectively, more collaboration among media organizations, both traditional and emerging, development of new models for reporting based upon exchanges between the Internet media and the traditional media, and ventures where professional news organizations enlist the support of volunteers.

The threats include: a loss of capacity in investigative and accountability reporting, a diminution of local and community news coverage, advocacy journalism swamping and displacing straight information reporting and analysis, a loss of quality in what is reported as the news due to a lack of any uniform journalistic standards, and just plain false information being promulgated deliberately and broadly with mischievous intent (for example, the rumors that claimed Sarah Palin was the mother of her daughter's baby).

RENEWING THE NEWS MEDIA RECOMMENDATIONS

We offer two selected recommendations to address these opportunities and threats and to respond to our analysis of the media's situation presented in this chapter. They build off and complement recommendations made in a report from the Knight Commission on the Information Needs of Communities in a Democracy titled, "Informing Communities: Sustaining Democracy in the Digital Age," that was issued in early October 2009, and the aforementioned Columbia University Reconstruction Report.[15] These reports provide bookends for sustaining democracy by addressing communities and the information they need and the news media and the information it provides.

Reconstruction Report Recommendation

The Columbia University Reconstruction Report made six recommendations:

1. Any independent news organization substantially devoted to reporting on public affairs should be allowed to become a non-profit. Philanthropic organizations should be allowed to make program-related investments in these organizations and for-profit news organizations.

2. Philanthropists, foundations, and community foundations should substantially increase their support for news organizations that have demonstrated a substantial commitment to public affairs and accountability reporting.

3. Public radio and television should be substantially reoriented to provide significant local news reporting in every community served by public stations and their Web sites.

4. Universities should operate their own news organizations and become on-going sources of local, state, specialized subject, and accountability news reporting as part of their educational missions.

5. A national Fund for Local News should be created with money the Federal Communications Commission now collects or could impose on telecom users, television, and radio broadcast licensees. This fund should be administered in open competition.

6. More should be done by journalists, nonprofit organizations, and governments to increase the accessibility of public information.[16]

These recommendations immediately kicked off a firestorm of reaction within the journalistic community upon their release and will no doubt be debated and reconstructed throughout 2010 and until the reconstruction of journalism takes place.

We have no specific substantive recommendations to add to those in the Reconstruction Report, but we do have a process recommendation:

Convene a national journalism reconstruction commission similar to the Knight Commission comprised of a mixed group of industry experts, allies, and informed consumers to conduct a comprehensive study on the current and projected future state of journalism (both broadcast and print). The commission should use the Reconstruction Report and its recommendations as a starting and reference point. The commission staff should develop an action research study designed to address areas that were ignored or slighted in the report and to explore and evaluate the proposals that have been advanced in the report and by others in response to the report. The commission should implement that design and come up with its own analysis and recommendations to be presented in Reconstruction Report 2.0.

It might be possible to get a foundation like the Knight Foundation and some local community foundations with newspaper connections to fund this follow-on study. This study focused on journalism would dovetail nicely with the work of the Knight Commission on community information needs and align with its interests. As the commission notes, "While the Knight Commission did not set out to 'save' journalism . . . there is a clear understanding that we must find sustainable models that will support the kind of journalism that has informed Americans. The fair, accurate, contextual search for the truth is a value worth preserving." It is, and that is why we make our recommendation to convene a commission.

We recognized the need for a commission of this type based upon our own reaction to the report and a review of the reactions of some of the first responders to it. We thought that the report was very much inside-out and heavily focused on newspapers and the print medium. It didn't bring the consumer's perspective to bear. This is critical because the Pew Report shows the public has become increasingly disenchanted with the media. So, it's not just the loss of advertising revenue that is hurting the traditional media sources. It's also the loss of viewers and readership. Finally, we also had concerns on the desirability and workability of the recommendation for establishing a Federal Fund for Local News and the recommendation for the "substantial reorientation" of public TV and radio to cover local news.

We agree that public TV and radio should have more local coverage, and it is our understanding that this is in the works. The need for a "substantial reorientation" is questionable. Public TV and radio have their niche audiences (we are among them), and they are devoted and generally satisfied with much of the current programming. It is possible that any substantial reorientation could cause a loss of those customers and financial supporters. In terms of federal funding, even though this is not a bailout, it's pretty close and seems very difficult to administer—especially if the money were to be used for investigative or accountability reporting projects into the government that provided the funds.

These considerations in conjunction with our own cause us to make this process recommendation. The handwriting is on the wall. Journalism and newspapers as we have known them will never be the same again.

The solution in the long term may not be reconstruction but deconstruction. We are definitely in the midst of what economist Joseph Schumpeter labeled "creative destruction"—the process whereby older and more hidebound companies disappear and are replaced by new companies with new business models and old companies that can adapt and become part of the new breed. A commission with a well structured research methodology would help us understand this and ensure that as this transformation occurs, we develop integrated solutions that put the interests of the community and citizens first.

Informing Communities Report Recommendation

The Knight Commission Informing Communities Report focused on communities as opposed to the media. It concentrated on information that citizens need to participate in the life of their communities. The commission was comprised not of a panel of experts but of a group of 15 "thoughtful Americans." It was cochaired by Marissa Mayer, Google Vice President, Search Products and User Experience who leads the company's product management efforts on search products and Theodore B. Olson, a partner in Gibson, Dunn & Crutcher and former solicitor general of the United States. The report presented three ambitious objectives and 15 recommendations summarized below:

1. *Maximize the availability of relevant and credible **information** to all Americans and their communities by*: directing media policy toward innovation; increasing support for public service media, higher education, and nonprofit organizations; requiring government to operate with transparency; and developing systemic measures of community information ecologies.

2. *Strengthen the **capacity** of individuals to engage with information by*: integrating digital and media literacy as critical elements for education at all levels, funding and supporting public libraries as centers for digital and media training, setting ambitious standards for nationwide broadband availability, maintaining the national commitment to open networks as a core objective of Internet policy, and supporting the activities of information providers to reach local audiences with quality content through all appropriate media.

3. *Promote individual **engagement** with information and the public life of the community by*: expanding local media initiatives to reflect the full reality of the communities they represent, engaging young people in developing the digital information and communication capacities of local communities, empowering all citizens to participate actively in community self-governance, emphasizing community information flow in the design and enhancement of local community's public spaces, and ensuring that every local community has at least one high-quality online hub.[17]

The Knight Commission stated, "Nothing in this report is meant to be prescriptive. Everything in this report is meant to propose and encourage debate." We believe that the proposals in the report are squarely on target. We wholeheartedly embrace the three objectives and 15 recommendations and recommend them as part of the renewal agenda.

We would add, however, an additional recommendation for civic engagement competency building:

Implement a national civic engagement competency-building program for youths and adults that equips them with the basic competencies to make informed decisions and participate fully in the democratic process and their communities.

The program should have two components: (1) a knowledge component addressing the rights and responsibilities of citizenship, and (2) a skill-building component developing data gathering and analytical abilities and critical thinking skills. The program should be implemented for youth beginning in middle school and reinforced in high school and college for older youth and young adults. It should be conducted for out-of-school adults of any age through organizations such as community colleges, high schools, and community-based organizations (CBOs).

As we have noted at other points in this book, the nation suffers from a substantial civic literacy gap—"chasm" might be a better word given its severity. Part of that gap is a lack of understanding—the other part is a "literacy gap," which impedes productive participation in community debate and dialogue.

The literacy gap is extremely serious. According to the National Center for Education Statistics, in a 2003 survey, 43 percent of adults did not meet the standard for "intermediate" prose competence. That means they were unable to read and understand moderately dense text. They were not able to meet the standards for summarizing, making simple inferences, determining cause and effect, and recognizing an author's purpose.

The Knight Commission's recommendations do an excellent job of providing proposals for bridging the digital and media divide. However, they do not address the literacy gap at all. If that gap is not addressed, the participation gap cannot be closed. In addition, the participation that occurs may be misinformed and possibly contrary to the best interests of the individual or of democratic society itself.

Current governmental educational policy places a high premium on basic literacy and teaching to the test in math and science. Math and science alone do not build the critical thinking and reasoning skills that are required to maintain a democratic and civil society, nor does broadband access.

Broadband will not matter much if the person who has the access has a narrow bandwidth. Remember: desktop, laptop, shoulder top. At the end of the day, it will be the power of the shoulder top that will enable the individual citizen to contribute and all of those citizens' shoulder tops united (our collective intelligence and IQ) that enable the community and the nation to prosper. That is why we feel so strongly about the need to add this recommendation to the original 15 crafted by the Knight Commission.

9 | The World Matters

*"What we in America want to pass on to the rest of the world, we
must first find in our own hearts."*

Dwight Eisenhower

I⟨T HAS BEEN SAID THAT THE⟩ U⟨NITED⟩ S⟨TATES IS THE WORLD'S LAST⟩
best hope. The new reality is that the world is the United States' last
best hope.

Over the past half century, the world has been the stage for the
United States, and we have played the leading role on it for at least the
last quarter of the twentieth century. The world will also be the stage for
the United States in the twenty-first century. With only 5 percent of the
world's population, however, we will have to earn our role on that stage
on a continuing and evolving basis.

In the future, our role on the stage will most probably change from
star to costar in terms of economic might. The chance for the United
States to play the preeminent role as the international leader in terms
of caring and concern for citizens around the globe and the globe itself,
however, will be unrivalled. We can use this leadership role as a source
for enhancing the nation's competitive advantage.

AMERICA IN THE WORLD'S EYE

Before sharing our thoughts on America's role in the world, we should
look at how the world sees us. The Pew Global Attitudes Project
released a report in July of 2009 that provided this perspective. The
report presented the results of a survey of nearly 27,000 people located
in 25 countries worldwide.[1]

The key finding from the survey is that our image improved greatly in most parts of the world in 2009. The most recent surveys showed improvement in favorability ratings everywhere with the exceptions of Israel (–7 percent from 2007), Pakistan (–3 percent from 2008), Russia (–2 percent from 2008), and Poland (–1 percent from 2008). The U.S.'s ratings shot up most significantly in the European Union (EU) countries, as well as in Latin America. While the ratings went up slightly in most of the Muslim countries, they still were anemic (10–20 percent) compared to the EU and Latin America.

Stunning increases were seen in the percentages of respondents who felt that President Obama "will do the right thing in world affairs" as opposed to the ratings given to his predecessor. The ratings in most of the EU countries went up by over 70 percent and ranged between 13 and 64 percent better in other countries with the exception of Pakistan (+6 percent) and Israel (–1 percent).

Interestingly, "for the first time over the course of Pew's surveys, there is more confidence in the American president than in Osama bin Laden in a number of countries with predominantly Muslim citizens including: Turkey, Egypt, Jordan, Nigeria and Indonesia." Bin Laden, however, still held a significant lead in ratings over Obama in the Palestinian Territory and Pakistan.

The approval ratings for some of Obama's expressed international policies, such as closing Guantanamo and troop withdrawal from Iraq, were very high in most countries. The disapproval ratings for sending more troops to Afghanistan, however, were also high—ranging from 55 percent to 84 percent.

Other findings from the survey that help to shed light on America's global presence include:

- The majorities of Western Europeans and Canadians once again approved of our antiterrorist efforts. For the first time, there was increased support apparent in Poland, Russia, Brazil, and Mexico.

- Global warming was viewed as a serious problem by the survey respondents from all countries. Majorities or pluralities in almost every country expect the U.S. to take significant measures to control climate change.

- Overwhelming numbers of people around the world continued to see the U.S. as having too big an influence over their country.

In summary, the survey showed a much more favorable view of the United States worldwide. On the other hand, the needle moved only a modest amount in the primarily Muslim countries.

Surveys are snapshots in time. Responses can vary greatly from sample period to sample period based upon events and results achieved, as demonstrated by the swings from low popularity for President Bill Clinton at the beginning of his presidency to high popularity at the end and vice versa for President George W. Bush.

It seems logical that President Obama's decision to commit 30,000 more troops to Afghanistan will not enhance his image or that of the United States in the world. Similarly, the lackluster results from the Copenhagen climate warming summit will most probably not reflect well on the Obama presidency.

Polls should not be used to define policies or to decide what role we play in the world. Those are strategic decisions that must be driven by data, independent analysis, and values. Polls do indicate, however, context and potential consequences in terms of the level of support that there will be for a position or approach that we, as a nation, take.

UNITED STATES GLOBAL LEADERSHIP ROLE SET

Recognizing this dynamic, we propose the following six key roles for the United States as a global leader in the twenty-first century:

- Land of opportunity
- Partner
- Peacekeeper
- Problem solver
- Role model
- Economic nation-state

Land of Opportunity

Frank Islam left his homeland of India at the age of 15 to pursue the American Dream. On the day he departed, Frank's father said to him, "Now you will have the opportunity that I never had."

Frank came to America and through education, hard work, and initiative, captured the American Dream. Because of his business success and commitment to his new homeland, he now lives the dream. Not a day goes by that Frank does not think about his father's words and how the "norm" in other countries is to live with masses of unemployment and underemployment and poverty.

As it has for millions of other immigrants, the United States gave Frank the opportunity his father predicted. People from around the world have all come to America in search of that same opportunity, and the majority have achieved their goals.

That's what the Economic Mobility Project discussed in its 2007 report, "Economic Mobility of Immigrants in the United States."[2] The project was a nonpartisan collaborative effort of the Pew Charitable Trusts and was led by Pew staff, a Principals' Group from The American Enterprise Institute, the Brookings Institution, The Heritage Foundation, and The Urban Institute.

Ron Haskins of the Brookings Institution and author of the project said, "The great story of America is that it still offers a job to first generation immigrants and better jobs to their children."[3] The report revealed, however, that the climb up the economic ladder is becoming more difficult for some immigrants. In 2000, first-generation immigrants earned 20 percent less than the typical nonimmigrant worker (versus 6 percent less in 1940 and 1.4 percent less in 1970). There has also been a narrowing in the gains in the difference between the average wage increases between first-generation immigrants and second-generation immigrants (5 percent comparing 1970 to 2000 as opposed to an increase of 9 percent comparing 1940 to 1970).

These shifts can be attributed to two factors: (1) A substantial increase in immigrants—more than a million a year from 1990 through 2005 versus 300,000 a year during the 1960s. (2) In absolute numbers, many more immigrants with low skills and low education were in the immigration pool.

The report found, however, that education makes a difference and can have a significant moderating effect for second-generation immigrants. Those immigrants with high-school and college degrees were capable of earning much higher wages on average than those without a degree. It also found that the children of immigrants achieved much higher educational levels than their parents. In fact, they were more likely to attain college degrees and advanced degrees than nonimmigrants.

At the same time that there were many more first-generation immigrants with low education levels, there were also a much larger percentage of these immigrants (10 percent) with advanced degrees than those in the nonimmigrant population. According to a 2003 National Science Foundation study, 3,352,000 U.S. scientists and engineers were immigrants.

Immigrants have made—and will continue to make—major contributions to the United States in all fields. This was highlighted again in 2009 when the Nobel Prize for Physiology or Medicine was awarded to Elizabeth H. Blackburn of the University of California San Francisco, Carol W. Greider of Johns Hopkins University School of Medicine, and Jack W. Szostak of Massachusetts General Hospital and Harvard Medical School. Blackburn and Szostak are immigrants whose common bond is that they are Americans and Nobel Prize winners. The United States needs to remain the land of opportunity for those who wish to bring their talent and aspirations to our shores. As Waldo Proffitt, former editor of the *Sarasota Herald Tribune* noted, "Szostak . . . points out the rest of the world is rapidly catching up in science, so the U.S. needs to work harder to attract smart people and make sure they stay here."[4]

We need smart people. There are still major issues that need to be dealt with regarding illegal immigration. We also need to ensure the appropriate education for children of low-level education first-generation immigrants to facilitate their education, economic mobility, and contribution to the country. These issues need to be balanced with supporting the vital flow of highly skilled and educated first-generation immigrants.

Partner

We believe that no one was more stunned by the award of the Nobel Prize for Peace to Barack Obama than President Obama himself. We don't know if he was more stunned by this unexpected victory or the unexpected defeat and dashing of Chicago's hopes to host the Olympics.

We do know that President Obama did not declare mission accomplished after learning of his nomination. In fact, he did just the opposite. At a press conference held shortly after learning of the award, President Obama proclaimed, "I am both surprised and deeply humbled by the decision of the Nobel Committee. Let me be clear, I do not view it as recognition of my own accomplishments, but rather as an affirmation of American leadership on behalf of aspirations held by all nations . . . To be honest, I do not feel that I deserve to be in the company of so many of the transformative figures who've been honored by this prize . . ."[5]

In spite of these disclaimers, the president's selection was viewed as extremely controversial and questioned by many, including Ross Douthat and Thomas Friedman, columnists for *The New York Times* (we'll get to their responses in a moment).

First, let's look at the Nobel Committee's rationale for awarding the prize. They declared that the prize was for "extraordinary efforts to strengthen international diplomacy and cooperation between peoples . . . Obama has, as president, created a new climate in international politics. Multilateral politics has regained a central position. . . . Dialogue and negotiations are preferred as instruments for resolving even the most difficult international politics."

So, in essence, the committee was saying the prize was being given for facilitating change—the promotion of stronger multilateral collaboration and partnerships among the nations of the world. In spite of the committee's justification, it didn't sit well with many critics.

Ross Douthat recommended that the president turn down the prize. He argued that ". . . the prize leaves Obama more open to ridicule. It confirms as a defining narrative of his presidency the gap between his supporters' cloud-cuckoo-land expectations and the inevitable disappointments of reality."[6]

After stating that "it dismays me that the most important prize in the world has been devalued in this way," Thomas Friedman did not suggest turning it down. Instead, he recommended that it be accepted "on behalf of the most important peacekeepers in the world for the last century—the men and women of the U.S. Army, Navy, Air Force, and Marines."[7]

We think both Douthat and Friedman were wrong. We also think they were engaged in insular thinking.

If Obama had turned down the prize as Douthat suggested, it would have said to the committee and the world this focus of working together to achieve greater collaboration and cooperation was not worth attempting. On the other hand, if Obama had used his speech to celebrate the peacekeepers (in this instance, the military), he would have been contradicting the very reason for the award—multilateral politics, dialogue, and negotiations.

What President Obama did in accepting the award, as he does in many instances, was to find a nuanced position. He used the award to talk about a dangerous world, the unique role that the United States has played by using its military to maintain world peace, and to make the case for "just wars." We believe his speech played much better here than it did internationally.

We would have liked for the president to have acknowledged in his speech that as there are "just wars," there are also "just people," and that overall, the citizens of the United States are such a group. That's because, based upon our review of the Pew Global Attitudes survey findings, we believe that there may have been a subliminal reason that the prize was given to Barack Obama—that was to acknowledge America for electing him president. The Pew research disclosed that "In most countries where opinions of the U.S. have improved, many say that Obama's election led them to have a more favorable view of the U.S. . . . even in countries where there was little or no upswing in the U.S's ratings, many people say that Obama's election led them to think more favorably of the U.S."[8]

The election demonstrated, once again, the uniqueness of the American experiment. It renewed the hope that America and its citizens bring to an increasingly complex and challenging world.

Peacekeeper

Unfortunately, not everyone wants to, or knows how to, collaborate. Today's world is more dangerous and problematic than ever, and as the United States works diligently on collaboration, it must also be prepared for conflict.

Having the ability to be a peacekeeper is essential to the future of the human race. The capacity to create a safer and saner world will not come through military might alone. There are three requisites for effective peacekeeping:

1. Superior U.S. foreign policy and civilian agency capabilities
2. Superior U.S. defense policy and military capabilities
3. Superior alliances and partnerships with other nation-states

In the words of Teddy Roosevelt, effective peacekeeping demands the ability "to speak softly but carry a big stick." Speak first. Try to make peace. Stick second. Do what is required to keep peace.

We are not strategists or experts in the area of foreign and defense policy. Fortunately, there are plenty of those who are, including the Institute for the Study of Diplomacy (ISD) at Georgetown University, Robert Gates (U.S. Secretary of Defense), and Dr. Andrew Krepinevich (executive director of the Center for Strategic and Budgetary Assessments, Twenty-First Century Force Posture). We draw upon their expertise here.

The ISD prepared a Working Group Report during the 2008 election cycle, "America's Role in the World: Foreign Policy Choices for the Next President."⁹ The report set out 13 choices for the incoming president. The first choice was on "Foreign Policy Tools and American Capacity."

The report noted that one of the "unintended consequences of the Iraq War has been to underscore and in some respects to reinforce the comparative strengths of the U.S. military instruments of power and the glaring weaknesses of U.S. civilian foreign affairs." It went on to note there are only about 6,500 Foreign Service Officers for the State Department's mission, that USAID has lost much of its capacity, and that roughly 22 percent of American foreign assistance flows through the Pentagon.

Secretary Gates also commented on the decline of USAID during the 1990s from a high of 15,000 permanent staff to 3,000 today and the diminution of the role of the U.S. Information Agency and noted that: "The military and civilian elements of the United States' national security apparatus have responded unevenly and have grown increasingly out of balance."[10]

In his 2009 *Foreign Affairs* article, Gates went on to state, "the defining principle of the United States Defense Strategy is balance." According to Gates, the strategy is to strive for balance in three areas: (1) prevailing in current conflicts and preparing for other contingencies, (2) institutionalizing capabilities such as counterinsurgency and foreign military assistance, and maintaining the existing conventional, strategic, and technological edge, and (3) retaining those cultural traits that make U.S. armed forces successful and shedding those that don't.

While Gates called for balance, he noted that things are substantially out of balance now: "Support for conventional modernization programs are deeply embedded in the Defense Department's budget in its bureaucracy, in the defense industry, and in Congress." Gates is in favor of institutionalizing counterinsurgency skills and the ability to conduct stability and support operations. He noted, however, that "there has been no strong, deeply rooted constituency inside the Pentagon or elsewhere for institutionalizing the capabilities to wage asymmetric or irregular conflict."

Dr. Krepinevich also is concerned with asymmetry as part of what he calls the changes and challenges presented by the three A's: Asymmetry, Asia, and Allies.[11] He points out that in the twentieth century, wars were symmetrical, with many nations having the same force structure: carriers, subs, tanks, and then nuclear weapons and missiles. Today, it's totally different—the new enemy is not the nation-state but the terrorist or fanatic with a bomb or a plane.

For that reason—and the emergence of Asia as a primary focus of U.S. relationships—we need allies now more than ever before. Krepinevich notes that where in the past the United States could call others to the table, it now has to forge working relations with allies on both multilateral and selected regional bases for purposes of peacekeeping.

The operative word here is "balance," and there is consensus among the experts that achieving that delicate balance is critical to both national and international security. There is virtual agreement that things are out of balance now, and because of institutional factors, bringing them into balance will be difficult and will take time.

Secretary Gates has said the two things he has learned in his 42 years in national security are limits and a sense of humility. Recognizing this, he acknowledges that the United States is the "strongest and greatest nation on earth" but also warns that "we should be modest about what military force can accomplish and what technology can accomplish." He cautions that, "We should look askance at idealistic, triumphalist, or ethnocentric notions of future conflict that aspire to transcend the immutable principles and ugly realities of war, that imagine it is possible to cow, shock, or awe any enemy into submission instead of tracking enemies down hilltop by hilltop, house by house, and block by bloody block."

Peacekeeping is sometimes a very bloody business. But, the more there is a balance, the more likely it is that it becomes the mission of many instead of a few—and less bloody than it might have been otherwise.

Problem Solver

Just as much of the world expects the United States to be a force and ally militarily, it also looks to the U.S. for leadership in helping forge cooperative efforts to address the critical issues and problems confronting the planet, such as climate change, human rights, poverty, hunger, and economic development.

We know that, because no less of an authority than Bono, lead singer for the rock group U-2, told us so. In a 2009 op-ed column for *The New York Times* written after Obama won the Nobel Prize, Bono stated, "The world wants to believe in America again because the world needs to believe in America again. We need your ideas—your idea—at a time when the rest of the world is running out of them."[12]

Bono tied the Nobel Prize to President Obama's endorsement of the Millennium Development Goals in his speech at the United Nations. The Millennium Goals were a set of commitments made near the beginning of this century to reduce extreme poverty in the world by half by 2015. In his column, Bono noted that President Obama took it further by calling for not only halving it, but ending it.

Like Bono, the ISD at Georgetown also saw regaining global leadership and seeking the initiative abroad as key opportunity areas for the United States. The group felt, for a variety of reasons, that the United States had forfeited its leadership position over the past 8 years. The institute outlined what it felt could be done to restore that position in several areas:

- Institutions, Alliance, and Coalitions: Redirect American policies toward the building of international organizational capacity, including rebuilding alliance relationships with countries such as Turkey, reviving the International Atomic Energy Agency, and building UN capacity.

- Nuclear Proliferation: Revisit all the choices that have been made, including dropping the plan for ground-based interceptors in Europe and diminishing the role that nuclear weapons play in U.S. national security policies.

- Environmental Challenges: Be an active leader in securing U.S. and global commitments to reduce greenhouse gas emissions.[13]

The actions of the Obama administration in its first year indicate that it is advancing a choice agenda that aligns with the institute's recommendations.

Role Model

Much of the United States' influence in the world comes not from international problem solving, foreign policy, or military strength but from what the country stands for. In his book *Ark of the Liberties*, Ted Widmer, director of the John Carter Brown Library at Brown University, tells us that individuals as diverse as Mohandas Gandhi, Ho Chi Minh, and the student protestors at Tiananmen Square in China were all motivated by American ideals.[14]

The ISD noted, "We have been leaders because we have been builders of things many nations want and because of our values." The institute stated that the leadership position of the U.S. has been compromised because of the war in Iraq and the incarcerations and torture of some prisoners at Guantanamo Bay. The results of the latest Pew Global Attitudes survey support that perspective.

So, too, did the Chatham House, an independent group in London that studies international issues. In a 2009 report titled, "Ready to Lead? Rethinking America's Role in a Changed World," Chatham House noted "Barack Obama has taken on the U.S. presidency at a time when many pillars of America's international leadership have been weakened." The report cites factors such as the invasion of Iraq, the chaos caused by the U.S. financial collapse, and the U.S. as a major contributor of the greenhouse effect as reasons for the weakening. Chatham House observed ". . . the U.S. is seen by many across the world as a source of global problems rather than part of their solution."[15]

That viewpoint may be alleviating, but it's still there—and that's a problem. There has been—and still is—a continuing debate in the United States about whether the Iraq War was a war of choice or one of necessity, and whether all of the incarcerations and some of the tortures at Guantanamo Bay were justified.

In the court of world opinion, those debates are irrelevant and immaterial. The jury has provided its verdict, and that verdict is that our actions have diminished our global position of moral leadership and champion for democracy and human rights. If we feel we can go it alone or with small "coalitions of the willing," we can choose to ignore this feedback. If, on the other hand, the world matters, then we need to become the role model that we have been in the past and lead by example.

As with most things in life, we make judgments based on actions, not words. We learn through observation, not conversation. In 2009, there appeared to be a window of opportunity for the United States to be a role model in the world again. It will be interesting to see how the actions taken influence world reactions going forward in 2010 and beyond.

Economic Nation-State

This role might seem odd. Isn't the United States already a nation-state? Yes, but the question really is one of relevance. Until the financial crisis, the nation-state seemed to be increasingly less relevant to the economic world order.

The multinational corporation may trace its office or corporate headquarters to one nation, but it owes its allegiance to none—unless, of course, the corporation has a state-related investment in China. Or, they were bailed out like AIG or the Wall Street banks and we as taxpayers are now the owners. Oops—our mistake, the sizes of the bonuses that the bailout recipients handed out or proposed to give themselves proved that the phrase "national allegiance" is not part of their vocabulary. Instead, their twin mantras are "God is money" and "In money we trust."

Why is this issue of the capacity and role of the United States as nation-state so important? Consider the fact that 63 of the 100 largest economic entities in the world are multinational corporations.

Because of their size and international presence, these are really global corporations. They are able to arbitrage and play off nation-state against nation-state to create an advantage for themselves in international trade.

When the G-20 and the G-8 convene, they address these issues and their impact on the global community. However, as part of their discussion and decision making, they need to address how to work collaboratively to establish a new working balance with the most powerful players not at the tables—the global corporations.

This change needs to start with the United States making the nation-state relevant in economic terms once again. Over the past several decades, we have been able to assert a leadership position internationally because of the superior power of American values, the American military, and the American economy. We still have an overwhelming lead in terms of our military might to conduct conventional wars (although we've only fought one in the past 50 years or so).

We appear to be on the way to reclaiming the moral high ground in the area of values again. We are, however, on a very slippery slope when it comes to economic power. That slope has been greased by rampant outsourcing and by entering into trade agreements that benefited other nation-states more than our own.

The United States needs to reverse this trend by becoming an economic nation-state again. We believe that much of this can be accomplished by creating a twenty-first-century competitive advantage plan for the country and implementing the recommendations in this book. In addition, we like what Barry Lynn of the New America Foundation recommends in his 2005 book, *End of the Line: The Rise and Fall of the Global Corporation*:

- Use antitrust power to ensure that no global lead firm controls more than one-quarter of the American market
- Limit how much of any key input any industry, as a whole, can source from capacity located in a single foreign nation to no more than one-quarter of the amount consumed in the United States
- Require firms to double- or even triple-source all components and all business process services, in real time, from suppliers in two or more different nations.[16]

Lynn's recommendations are even more relevant today as we stare a jobless recovery in the face for as many as 5 years. They should be revisited.

RENEWING OUR ROLE IN THE WORLD RECOMMENDATIONS

The world matters. Our role in the world matters even more. The U.S. can reclaim its rightful place in world leadership by embracing the roles and following the suggestions of the experts cited in this chapter.

There is a tension between and among the leadership roles America must play: problem solver versus peacekeeper; nation-state versus partner. There will have to be trade-offs and choices.

Fareed Zakaria highlights this point in his book, *The Post-American World*, where he sets out six new rules for a new age for America. The first and overarching rule is *Choose*. Don't think you are omnipotent.

Set priorities and be disciplined about where to get engaged and involved. Zakaria's other five rules are:

1. *Build broad rules, not narrow interests.* Work to create general rules the world will work by, rather than acting independently and unilaterally.

2. *Be Bismarck, not Britain.* Engage with all great powers—don't cut off communications and relationships.

3. *Order à la carte.* Don't think one nation, institute, or organization can control the world's agenda or menu selection. Work with the UN on one matter and the OAS on another. Create new organizations as required.

4. *Think asymmetrically.* There may not be a new world order yet—but there is most certainly a disorder.

5. *Legitimacy.* Be the authoritative source for what constitutes a crisis, problem, or issue. This credibility comes from sharing a worldview that is documented and believable.[17]

Making the necessary choices will not be easy. Making the changes necessary to implement the choices will be even harder. As the Georgetown University Report noted, the resistance, or constraints, to change in the past have come from a variety of sources, including: "ideologically driven leadership," "the inability or unwillingness of the agencies of the U.S. government to cooperate with one another," and "Congress has been complicit in creating rather solving problems."

We would add to that list of potential constraints or resistance the relative lack of knowledge or understanding of a large part of the American public regarding the world community and international relations. As businesspeople who have traveled around the world, we have gained an appreciation and understanding of other countries, their cultures, and insights into the need for greater collaboration in problem solving and a world community. This is an opportunity that many American citizens have not had and many will not get. Given this, our recommendation for helping the U.S. to fulfill its roles in the world is:

Establish a national educational program to be conducted by public broadcasting (National Public Radio and PBS) and via the Internet that will systematically expose the citizens of the United States to information regarding the nature of the world community, the needs confronting the world and nation-states around the world, and the role of America in the world.

This program could be thought of as a reverse U.S. Information Agency—a World Information Agency that informs those of us residing in the U.S. and helps to build world community. U.S. citizens are the most charitable in the world—both on an individual and societal level. Witness the response to the Haitian earthquake of 2010, the tsunami of 2004, and President George W. Bush's African poverty initiative. Go back to the 1960s and the Peace Corps. Because of the country's self-sufficiency and scope, however, many of us have not felt the need to learn more about the rest of the world.

The world is shrinking and changing. This demands that American citizens grow and adapt. We believe a program of the type outlined will help facilitate that.

In closing, we are devoted Americans. We bleed red, white, and blue. However, our hope is that less and less blood will have to be shed on foreign soils and little blood will be shed in the United States because of America's reenergized role as world leader.

We agree completely with Craig Ferguson, host of the *The Late Late Show* and a naturalized American citizen from Scotland, who says, "America is truly the best idea for a country that any has come up with so far. Not only because we value democracy and the rights of the individual, but because we are always our own most effective voice of dissent."[18]

Even when the world matters, some places will matter just a little bit more. That's the way of the world.

Section III

Working on the Dream

Good policies and a sound agenda are starting, not ending points. They provide the rules for engagement so that we as citizens can do the hard work and heavy lifting required to renew America and the American Dream. There are five general ways in which we can do that work:

- *Individual engagement*—getting educated and working hard to become self-reliant and to achieve our personal potential
- *Organizational engagement*—contributing to the establishment, management, and operation of "high-performing" entities
- *Civic engagement*—participating directly in the electoral and governmental process
- *Social engagement*—helping to build the social capital that provides the glue that holds us together
- *Leadership engagement*—initiating ideas and taking actions that respond to issues of societal importance

The six chapters in this section provide information that can be used to explore those methods of involvement.

- Chapter 10: Government Is Not the Problem
- Chapter 11: Business Is Not the Answer
- Chapter 12: Citizens All
- Chapter 13: Bowling Together
- Chapter 14: The Renewal Model
- Chapter 15: Implementing the Renewal Process

Based upon that exploration, we can each select the methods and construct our own personal engagement agenda. Together, our citizen agendas will provide the basis for renewing America and the American Dream.

10 | Government Is Not the Problem

"If men were angels, we wouldn't need government."
James Madison

Ronald Reagan is acknowledged by many historians as one of the greatest American presidents because he accomplished the majority of his agenda during his tenure as president.

President Reagan is also known as the great "speechifier." He delivered one of his most famous lines in his first inaugural address: "Government is not the solution to our problem; government is the problem."

The theme of government as being problematic was one that Reagan repeated before, during, and after his presidency. During his second term, he told a group from Future Farmers of America, "The 10 most dangerous words in the English language are 'Hi, I'm from the government and I'm here to help'."

President Reagan's attitude toward the government may have been appropriate at a point in time in which government had undoubtedly become too big, too dominant, and unresponsive or underresponsive to the will of the people. Unfortunately, his characterization and stereotyping of all government had unintended consequences.

It exaggerated the divide between the private and public sectors and in the discounting of government employees and underestimating government's accomplishments. It made those who dedicated their careers to government service second-class citizens and government service an occupation not worth pursuing for many of our citizens. It became a wedge that split the American public.

TEAR DOWN THIS WALL

What is most interesting is that while Reagan was criticizing government, he was inadvertently and indirectly criticizing himself. The
United States Constitution established three branches of government—
executive, legislative, and judicial. The Constitution makes no reference to the federal agencies or commissions that carry out the business
of government.

It is certainly those entities that Reagan was referring to when
he cited government as the problem. Most assuredly, his attacks were
directed at the government bureaucracy and not at elected or appointed
officials.

The bureaucracy develops the programs that are passed by Congress and signed by the president. The bureaucracy is headed and led
by executives who are appointed by the president and approved by the
Congress. The bureaucracy exists to do the people's work as enacted
and endorsed by the three branches of government.

The government bureaucracy does not operate independently or
without governance or oversight. The government bureaucracy is not
perfect—far from it. But, then again, neither are the three branches of
government.

If there is a problem today—and indeed there is, the bureaucracy
is part of it as are the branches. If there is a solution, and indeed there
must be, the branches and the bureaucracy need to be a part of it
as well.

GOVERNMENT CONTRIBUTIONS

Some would argue that government has made nominal or no contributions to ensuring the success of the nation and that the best thing that
it can do is get out of the way and let free enterprise work its magic.
This is a very misguided opinion, due to either a lack of understanding regarding the economic history of the country or an unwillingness to listen to facts which interfere with preexisting opinions and
prejudices.

Government contributions to the growth and development of the
nation that facilitate the achievement of the American Dream are all

around us. In his book, *Bold Endeavors: How Our Government Built America, and Why It Must Rebuild It Now*, Felix Rohatyn spotlights large and transformative events that have contributed to America's growth.[1] They include:

1. The Louisiana Purchase
2. The Erie Canal
3. Lincoln's support of the transcontinental railroad
4. The Morrill Act creating land grant colleges
5. The Homestead Act
6. The Panama Canal
7. Bringing electricity to rural America
8. The GI Bill
9. The interstate highway system

Although not mentioned by Rohatyn, think of America without:

- Social Security
- The WPA projects that helped build the national park system, among other important contributions
- Medicare
- NASA, its satellites used for weather forecasting, communication, and GPS
- The Internet

The government played a significant role in each of these and has also played a leadership role in problem solving in tough financial times as evidenced by the yeoman work of the Resolution Trust Corporation in cleaning up the private sector mess stemming from the savings and loan fiasco in the late 1980s and early 1990s.

For far too long a time, because of the attitudes of a few, those in government employment have fallen into the Rodney Dangerfield category of not getting any respect. We feel this is grossly unfair—and unfortunate. Even though we are businesspeople, among the three of us, we have had the opportunity and privilege to lead, work with, and consult thousands of public servants. We have found them to be as competent and dedicated as the thousands of private sector employees with whom we have been associated.

GOVERNMENT CONUNDRUMS

That's not to say that government is without fault. There have been failures of omission and commission. They run the gamut from small and trivial to large and tragic in terms of consequences:

- The virtual collapse and meltdown of Wall Street and the nation's major financial institutions due to a lack of regulation and the failure to enforce existing regulations adequately

- The handling of Hurricane Katrina

- The inability to stop the terrorists attacks of September 11, 2001

- The scandal at the Department of Interior where sexual favors and contracts were traded in exchange for dinners, drinks, and dollars

- Jack Abramoff's unscrupulous and unethical lobbying that touched and affected behavior in the legislative and executive branches and the bureaucracy as well

- The Coast Guard carrier debacle where millions were spent to retrofit boats that wouldn't float.

As with most things, governmental failures get a lot more attention than the successes. Steven Kelman, Weatherhead professor of public management at the JFK School at Harvard University, puts it this way: "Media coverage of public-sector management is not different than it was before the performance turn occurred: It continues to be dominated by the same themes traditionally characterizing it—corruption, dishonesty, and waste, fraud, and abuse."[2]

Professor Kelman's words reminded us of an old GE Theater TV show (Yes—that's the show that Ronald Reagan hosted before he went on to another somewhat more important job) in which a newspaper publisher came to an old Western town to take over the paper. Everything in the paper was negative news or yellow journalism. The publisher wrote an editorial explaining that from that point forward, he would only print good news stories and asked readers to submit them.

On the first day he got none, so he printed a blank paper. On the second day, he got one story and printed it. Slowly but surely, he got more and more stories and was able to fill up an entire edition on a daily basis. The paper was transformed.

Maybe that's what we need—a media that is truly fair and balanced. Print one good-news story for each bad-news story. Yes—maybe we're dreaming. But daydream believers can sometimes make those dreams come true. You have to start somewhere.

HOLLOWED-OUT GOVERNMENT

Over the past few decades, the federal government has been "hollowed out." This hollowing out has occurred due to workforce reductions; key employees, managers, and supervisors retiring; and the contracting of governmental work to the private sector.

In 1970, the federal workforce as a percentage of the U.S. population was over 1.0 percent. By 2005, that percentage was 0.66 percent. The most significant reductions were achieved from 1990 through 2000. At a time when we are calling upon the government and its workforce to do more because of the enormous slack in the private sector, federal government has diminished capacity. The capacity will diminish even more. A 2007 study estimated that 550,000 full-time government employees would leave employment within 5 years—most through retirement. If this were to occur, it would mean almost a 30-percent turnover in the workforce.[3]

Then the government would be confronted with an expertise and experience drain of unrivalled proportions. Fortunately, America has a pool of talent, but the federal government will be losing its best and brightest. This is a situation that cannot be ignored. It must be addressed in a systematic and methodical manner.

GOVERNMENT IS A PECULIAR ANIMAL

Even when the government workforce is fully and competently staffed, government management is an inherently complex and difficult beast.

That is true for a variety of reasons which include agency silos, the distributed network, and laissez-faire leadership.

Agency Silos

The federal government is comprised of more than 70 agencies and includes a number of commissions. Each of these entities is virtually an organization unto itself that requires coordination and communication. While there are some isolated examples of cooperation—the territorial imperative reigns.

Exhibit A is the failure of the security agencies to share information prior to 9/11. This led Congress to consolidate all of these agencies into the Department of Homeland Security. Time will tell whether this move actually results in better integration and performance in the security arena or was merely a rearrangement of the deck chairs. We have our opinion and share it later in this chapter.

The American Reinvestment and Recovery Act (stimulus bill) provides another excellent example of the "silo effect" at work. The stimulus bill was over 400 pages in length. Division A of the bill contains the appropriation provisions and has 16 titles, 12 of which provide funding to federal agencies or program areas within those agencies. For example, Title I is directed at Agriculture, Rural Development, Food and Drug Administration, and related agencies. Title IV is directed at Energy and Water Development. Title VIII is directed at the Departments of Labor, Health, and Human Services, and Education, and related agencies.

Within each title, specific funding is spelled out for units, or program units, within an agency. For example, Title I includes funding for Department of Agriculture in areas such as the Agricultural Research Service, the Farm Services Agency, and the Natural Resources Conservation Services. And so it goes from title to title to title, resulting in a stimulus bill that is basically a smorgasbord of initiatives organized around the structure of the government bureaucracy with something for everyone. Instead of a whole-cloth piece of legislation with a clear intent and design structure, we got a bill that lacked cohesiveness and a central theme and that reinforced the silo system by providing funding to silos and of silos within silos.

Distributed Network

Silos make systematic problem solving and management difficult, as does the manner in which the government gets its work done—the distributed network.

Sticking with the stimulus bill and using the weatherization program contained in Title IV under the Department of Energy as an example, here is a highly simplified description of the distributed network process in action:

1. The House drafts its version of the bill.
2. The Senate drafts its version of the bill.
3. The House and Senate meet in conference committee to draft a mutually agreed upon bill.
4. Both branches of Congress vote on and approve the bill.
5. The bill as approved establishes a Recovery Accountability and Transparency Board to oversee the use of the funds.
6. The Department of Energy drafts regulations and guidelines for use of the weatherization funds and sends them to the state agencies responsible for administering the funds.
7. State agency X develops a plan for how the weatherization funds will be used and submits it to the DOE for approval.
8. The DOE approves state agency X's plan and establishes the process to oversee the plan implementation.
9. State agency X distributes funds to the state weatherization providers in accordance with the plan and puts its system in place to oversee the plan implementation.
10. Weatherization provider Y implements its plan which may include hiring and overseeing private sector contractors to do the weatherization.
11. The weatherization work is managed by the provider and/or contractor.
12. The weatherization work gets done.

Is your head spinning? What we have here is a classic case of governmental MBO. That's *not* management-by-objective. It is *management-by-oversight*—checkers checking checkers with potentially very little value added.

If you think this seems like an inefficient process, consider as the alternative the Troubled Asset Relief Program (TARP), or the Wall Street bailout as it is more commonly known. TARP ensured that the money disappeared very quickly with almost no transparency or accountability. The other program ensured that the money trickled out with lots of eyes watching that little trickle and wondering if it would ever become a stream.

Pick your poison. It would seem that there should be a happy medium, especially for something like the stimulus bill which was supposed to create jobs quickly and prime the economic pump. Given the weatherization example above (replicated over and over again throughout government), it is a miracle that as much as 10 percent of the stimulus money got out into the system by mid-July 2009—almost 5 months after the stimulus bill was approved.

Laissez-Faire Leadership

Another factor that inhibits the implementation of sound management practices in federal agencies is that frequently the individual who is selected to head the agency is more interested in policy development and implementation than in running a large organization. That's also frequently true of those who are put into deputy or assistant positions as well. Sometimes these individuals can get caught up in the trappings of power as opposed to placing a priority on performance. In these instances, it is up to the career bureaucrats to make sure that the train runs on time. This is a task much easier said than done—especially when rewards and recognition are not aligned toward this end.

Given this structure, process, and leadership, the federal workforce should be commended for what it does get done. They may not have tamed the beast, but at least they have it in a cage.

FROM PUBLIC ADMINISTRATION TO PERFORMANCE MANAGEMENT

As noted earlier, the bureaucracy and the bureaucrat get little credit for their accomplishments. In fact, the connotation for both words is negative with *bureaucracy* frequently being preceded by the word *bloated* and *bureaucrat* being preceded by the word *petty*.

Bureaucracy can be defined as "government characterized by specialization of functions, adherence to fixed rules, and a hierarchy of authority." Doesn't sound like a bad concept, does it? No reference to red tape, fraud, or abuse there.

In fact, when the German Max Weber, one of the founders of modern public administration, wrote about the "ideal bureaucracy" in the late 1800s, he saw it as a more rational and efficient way to organize and operate activities than the approaches that had preceded it. Weber enunciated seven principles for that bureaucracy, but even he admitted that the "ideal" state would never be achieved.

That doesn't mean that we shouldn't work toward that state, however. Performance management is one of the methods that the federal government has employed in the past few decades to provide more direction and control to agency activities and programs. Performance management, as presently practiced in the federal sector, concentrates on agency and programmatic results and outcomes and not just policies and processes.

There is debate about whether performance management systems will produce better results than traditional bureaucratic controls and methods that focus on inputs and processes. The naysayers argue that agencies don't control many of the outcomes because they are delegated to others; specific performance goals and plans increase administrative constraints restricting the flexibility required to perform effectively; and the results-focus can lead to creaming and skimming in an attempt to manipulate data in response to the measurement methodology.

For us, these arguments are not very persuasive and more semantic in nature than anything else. All agencies and programs should be run to achieve the intended results and to do so in a way that demonstrates organizational and operational excellence. We are not being pollyanna-ish. We know it can be done. As discussed later in Chapter 14, George Muñoz, in a couple of highly focused years, prevented the threatened demise of a federal agency by creating a repackaged high-performance agency which *The New York Times* called "the champion of American entrepreneurs in the global economy."

To accomplish this, an agency needs an appropriate methodology. It doesn't matter whether it is called a performance management system or a bureaucratic control system, or "the tail wagging the dog." We don't really care what label it is given. What we do care about is putting that system in place and using it appropriately. We should also confess that we prefer the term "performance management" to "bureaucratic control" or "public administration" and will use that term throughout the remainder of this chapter.

TOO MUCH MEASUREMENT/NOT ENOUGH MANAGEMENT

The two primary means that have been employed in the past 2 decades to implement a performance management methodology in the federal bureaucracy are the Government Performance and Results Act (GPRA) and the Program Assessment Rating Tool (PART).

The Clinton administration pushed GPRA, and Congress passed it in 1993. GPRA required every federal agency to set strategic and annual goals in terms of outcomes and then to measure performance and report on the progress of those goals. By creating PART, the Bush administration extended the performance focus to the program level.

Much attention was devoted to GPRA and PART, and a variety of groups provided solid recommendations to the Obama administration to improve their use and utility going forward.[4] At the end of 2009, it looks like the administration has decided to move away from GPRA and PART to implement a new process for setting goals and then monitoring progress toward them.

We support the necessity for goal setting and improving the scoreboard and ensuring there is the right kind of transparency and accountability in reporting. However, as experienced businesspeople, we are much less concerned about the scoreboard and goals than we are the game plan and the way the game is played. No athlete or team ever won the game by obsessing on the scoreboard or goals. They won it by concentrating and executing on the playing field.

A better scoreboard or goals will not yield better results unless there is a process in place to promote the achievement of outcomes and improve performance if results are not achieved. Based upon our experience and the opinions of others that have studied it, a major deficiency of the government's historical performance management system is that it is long on measurement but short on management.

To realize the full promise and potential of performance management, government needs to correct this situation. A comprehensive and integrated performance management system needs to be put in place that moves the performance management concept beyond transparency and accountability to a more appropriate focus on trajectory and action. That system needs to promote making the vital shifts depicted in the table below.

Table 10.1: Government Performance Management System Vital Shifts	
From	**To**
Mission and Functions	Vision and Values
Program Administration	Problem Solving
Silo Management	Integrated Solutions
Coordination	Execution
Efficiency	Effectiveness
Measurement Focus	Management Focus
Output	Outcomes
Reporting	Continuous Improvement
Isolation	Involvement
Static	Dynamic

NEW GOVERNMENT CHALLENGES

As the foregoing discussion suggests, implementing a full-blown performance management system will require changes in perspective and practices. The twenty-first century requires additional changes and presents new challenges for the governmental sector going forward.

Al Morales and Jonathan Breul from the IBM Center for The Business of Government identified many of these challenges, five of which relate to the way that government conducts its business:

1. *Crisis of Competence.* As the current federal workforce retires, the strategic question becomes how to ensure competence of the new workforce—full-time, contracted, or delegated.

2. *Governing without Boundaries.* The current governmental bureaucratic model was adapted from the corporate sector in the mid-twentieth century. As governments are moving to more collaborative networks and organizations without boundaries, how can government plan and manage effectively in this new environment?

3. *Government by Contractors.* For a variety of reasons, the federal government currently employs more contractors than ever. What work should the government do, what should be contracted out, and how should the process be managed to ensure quality?

4. *Results Really Do Matter.* The focus on results is not going away. Given this, how does government implement a strategic and systematic approach to create high-performing organizations that are truly results-focused and driven?

5. *Expect Surprises.* Hurricane Katrina. 9/11. There will be more unanticipated events in the future. How does government respond to these asymmetric incidents in a timely and effective fashion?[5]

These and other challenges such as the current economic crisis and the significantly reduced capacity of state and local governments demand a complete strategic reexamination and rethinking of how the federal government does business and the manner in which it interacts with other levels of government.

CONGRESS IN CHAOS

There are 435 elected officials in the United States House of Representatives and 100 elected officials in the United States Senate. They represent the interests of over 300 million citizens. In the past, they were usually invisible to the majority of us as they did the people's business. In the past, they were also held in high regard.

Today, neither of these points is true. Congress is front and center on most issues as well as omnipresent because of cable news and 24-hour coverage. This presence has not made the heart grow fonder. In fact, polls conducted in early 2010 suggest that many in the public hold the Congress in contempt and feel that it is irrelevant and incapable of contributing solutions to solve the problems confronting them and the nation.

A *Washington Post*-ABC news poll released on February 10 showed that seven out of 10 Americans disapprove of the job that Congress is doing. A *New York Times*-CBS news poll released on February 12 disclosed that fewer than one in 10 Americans say that members of Congress deserve reelection.[6]

Some of this is attributable to the nation's current state of affairs and the troubles confronting us as citizens. Some of it is due to the nature of the beast. There are things about the structure, process, and participation in Congress that make it inherently unwieldy in the best of times and dysfunctional in the worst, such as:

- A large majority of the members of the House of Representatives come from districts that have been gerrymandered. As a result, after they are elected for the first time, their reelection is virtually guaranteed.

- The fact that House members run for reelection every 2 years means that they have to start campaigning for reelection virtually the day after they are elected.

- There are two senators from each state regardless of the number of citizens in the state.

- The seniority system in Congress moves those from the most entrenched and partisan areas into positions of power and influence.

- The now-infamous filibuster or threat of a filibuster gives disproportionate influence to a minority in the Senate.

- The requirement for 60 votes in the Senate to get major legislation passed makes compromise a necessity to get any bill through.

- The committee structure results in many multiple committees overseeing functional areas. For example, today, eight committees

review activities related to homeland security and a similar number examine activities related to job training.

Some of these factors have been in place forever. Some are of recent
origin. Couple them with the changing norms in which elected officials
serve longer, bipartisanship is becoming less and less common, and
the primary job of an elected official is to be a fundraiser, rather than a
legislator, and you have a formula for moving Congress toward chaos
and citizens toward outrage.

There is an old saying that Washington, D.C., is "40 square miles
surrounded by reality." While that disconnect between D.C. and the
"real world" might be acceptable in good times, it is completely intol-
erable in bad. It leads to citizen alienation and astute observers such
as David Brooks of *The New York Times* to state ". . . it's time to have
a constitutional debate. We might require amendments of one sort or
another to fix the broken political system."[7] And James Fallows, in an
Atlantic article, to comment, "Our government is old and broken and
dysfunctional, and may be broken beyond repair."[8]

We do not think that the Congress is beyond repair, but we do
believe that under its current rules, regulations, and mode of operating, it is incapable of healing itself. There are many exceptional elected
officials in Washington, D.C. Under the current system, however, they
become victims of the status quo. If the system and the legislative process are not changed, they will be unable to be full partners in the problem solving that is required to move the United States successfully into
the twenty-first century. That is why we provide a recommendation for
addressing Congress's dysfunction at the end of this chapter.

CONGRESS AND COMPETENCE

Walk around Capitol Hill—you'll think that you're on a college cam-
pus. The majority of the people there are in their 20s and 30s. Many
of them are staffers for our U.S. senators and congresspeople. These
staffers are among the best and the brightest that we have in the United
States. They are excited and eager. There's only one problem—most of
them lack expertise and experience.

These are the individuals who are called upon to help conduct the government's business and shape its policy. The knowledge and skills they bring to this task primarily come from a college classroom and time spent on the campaign trail. The staff for a congressional committee is usually a little older than the congressional staff. Many of them have years, and sometimes decades, of experience combined with distinctive expertise.

But, they have their own problems. The committee staff is usually overworked and substantially underpaid. As a result, some senior staff leave and go to work in the private sector or as lobbyists where they can normally double or triple their annual salaries. If they go to Wall Street, they can make their annual salary as a bonus. The ones who stay are true public servants dedicated to good government and willing to sacrifice their pocketbooks in the interests of the country and its citizens.

How serious is the staffing issue? Consider this vignette. One of us was at a fundraiser for a U.S. congressman who had just finished his first year on the Hill. The congressman was an accomplished businessman who had started and managed a large and highly successful business.

We asked the congressman if he could change one thing on the Hill, what would it be. He responded, "I'd like to have the money to hire two adults for my full-time staff. All of my staff is extremely motivated with high energy, but they lack the professional insights and acumen that come from time spent in the 'real world.'"

The congressman put it in a nutshell. Due to inexperience and understaffing, our legislators are outmanned and outgunned when it comes to policy development. Lobbyists of all stripes and persuasions come at them from every direction with policy proposals, position papers, and reams of data to support their requests. This input frequently determines the shape and form of legislation.

In addition to its own staff and the committees, Congress has two organizations that help influence policy direction and content: the Congressional Budget Office (CBO) and the Government Accountability Office (GAO). Although they serve the Congress, the CBO and GAO are both nonpartisan and independent organizations.

The CBO's mandate is to provide Congress with "objective, non-partisan and timely analysis to aid in economic budgetary decisions on the wide array of programs covered by the federal budget" and "the information and estimates required for the Congressional budget process." While the CBO does an exceptional job of forecasting costs, it shies away from calculating benefits. The Congress could make more informed decisions with more complete cost-benefit analyses.

The GAO is frequently called the "congressional watchdog." It is headed by the comptroller general of the United States. GAO's mission is "to help improve the performance and ensure the accountability of the federal government for the benefit of the American people." The GAO provides incisive reports, but frequently they are ignored. If a stronger direct connection could be made between recommendations and requirements for follow-up, we believe the quality of government could be improved significantly.

STATE AND LOCAL GOVERNMENTS

We concentrate on the federal government in this chapter. While the federal government may be hollowed out and has significant financial problems, it can still print money and raise funds. Most state and local governments are in far worse shape—they are not only hollowed out with insufficient staffing due to workforce reductions, they are also being pushed to the brink of bankruptcy. For brevity's sake, we present our thoughts and recommendations on the needs of these governments in the Appendix to the book.

RENEWING GOVERNMENT RECOMMENDATIONS

Over the past 2 decades, there has been much good work done and ideas generated for reforming or improving the federal government. The most expansive and intensive effort was the National Performance Review (NPR) led by Vice President Al Gore between 1993 and 1997. During that period, government was significantly downsized, customer service was improved substantially, and more than 340 "reinvention laboratories" experimented with management innovations designed to upgrade government management.

In the last report produced by the NPR, Gore declared, "I can state with complete confidence that government is better today than when we started this effort four years ago . . . We have spotlighted and praised the most successful experiments—started hundreds of fires of change and fanned the flames. Now some bonfires are raging, ready to sweep entire agencies, starting with the ones that affect the public and business most."[9]

We believe that the vice president was accurate in his assessment of progress but overly optimistic in his forecast for the future—the goal of "better government"—for a variety of reasons, it is still very much a work in progress. Following are our primary and subsidiary recommendations for facilitating that progress:

Government Primary Recommendations

1. Have each federal government agency conduct a zero-based organizational assessment and develop a strategic blueprint to become a high-performing organization.

2. Implement a government-wide operational excellence initiative with maximum feasible employee involvement.

3. Ensure on-the-job training and mentoring to transfer essential knowledge and skills to new government employees.

4. Convene a congressional hearing on the dysfunctional Congress.

Government Subsidiary Recommendations

5. Establish stronger performance management capabilities in the executive and legislative branches and government agencies.

6. Ensure appropriate performance management training for all government employees.

7. Enhance the government hiring process.

8. Identify innovative and successful governmental models that can be used to stimulate integrated economic development and problem solving.

9. Build Congress's capacity and capabilities for performance management.

10. Eliminate television coverage of Supreme Court nominee hearings.

11. Provide capacity-building assistance to state and local governments.

The primary recommendations are presented here. The subsidiary recommendations are in the Appendix.

1. Have each federal government agency conduct a zero-based organizational assessment and develop a strategic blueprint to become a high-performing organization.

On June 11, 2009, Peter Orszag, director of the Office of Management and Budget (OMB), issued a memo to the heads of all departments, the first paragraph of which included the following: "To meet all of these challenges, and the many others our Nation faces, we must transform our government to operate more effectively and efficiently."

Orszag's memo noted that "identification of agency high-priority performance goals is a first step toward developing the President's agenda for a high-performing government."[10] We agree—performance goals *are* a first step toward high-performing government and organizations. They are, however, only a small step. High-performing goals are transitional, not transformational.

High-performing organizations have the right strategy, the right structure, the right systems, and the right employees, and a laser-beam focus on the needs of their customers. That's the "right stuff" for the twenty-first century. It is the next challenge that our government agencies must confront.

For 7 years, Donald Kettl led a study conducted by the Brookings Institution to assess the results of the Clinton administration's "reinventing government" initiative. In testimony that he gave before the House Committee on Rules and the Senate Committee on Governmental Affairs in 2000, Kettl gave the initiative high marks in a number of areas and an overall grade of "B."

He observed that reinvention was "focused more on downsizing and operational improvements than on broad, systemic management problems." As a result, Kettl concluded, "The federal government is no longer organized for the job that law and the Constitution charge it to do. Devolution, contracting out, and other third-party strategies have grown significantly. The federal government's capacity to manage these programs has not grown to keep pace. Many of government's most significant management problems are a direct result of this mismatch of capacity and strategy."[11]

Fast-forward almost a decade. In spite of the reinvention efforts and the use of GPRA and PART as a means to oversee and measure performance, it seems to us that at best, the situation is the same as that which Kettl described in 2000 but most likely worse. We recommend that the president have each federal agency create its own strategic blueprint for becoming a high-performing organization.

That blueprint should be created by conducting a comprehensive analysis of the agency's current state and defining its desired state. Based upon that, the agency should do a gap analysis and define the critical path to be followed to achieve the level of transformation required to achieve its desired state.

The high-performing organization strategic blueprint should be developed with the leadership of the agency's CEO, championed by the COO, and directed by the agency's performance improvement officer. Experienced organizational personnel should be involved in creating the blueprint as part of the agency's high-performance team along with agency specialists in organizational analysis and design, human resource factors, financial analysis, and information technology. The team should also have outside experts and specialists as members.

These strategic blueprints should be created over the next 4 years according to a prioritized agenda established by the president. The agenda should begin with high-impact agencies that are customer-facing, as was done with the Clinton and Gore reinvention initiative.

We believe that these high-performing organization blueprints are central to improving government performance in a manner that is strategic, systematic, and sustainable. Anything else is just "business as usual" in an era that demands total transformation of many of our agencies. As an example, the DHS was created in a time of extreme crisis by bringing together many different organizations with different cultures and performance capabilities under one umbrella. As a result, it became a camel by committee when what we needed was a *Battlestar Galactica*.

Under DHS, the CIA became, and continues to be, everyone's favorite punching bag. FEMA went from being a widely respected independent agency in the Clinton administration to an acronym for incompetence in the Bush administration. If there is any organization that needs a careful reexamination, reimagining, and redesign from the ground up, it is DHS. There is a fundamental need to clarify its vision, mission, and strategy. DHS needs a master plan and blueprint to take it through the twenty-first century. (We wrote this recommendation well before the attempted Nigerian plane bombing in December 2009. Based upon that incident and Commissioner Thomas Kean's critique of the lack of progress since the findings of the 9/11 Commission, we feel even more strongly about the critical need for action in this area now.)

2. Implement a government-wide operational excellence initiative with the maximum feasible employee involvement.

How essential is it for the government to improve its operational performance? According to a group of eight expert organizations led by the Partnership for Public Service, it's extremely important. In a 2008 report the Partnership released, they recommended focusing on the federal workforce as part of any reform through four components: (1) the right talent, (2) an engaged workforce, (3) strong leadership, and (4) public support.[12]

We agree, but must point out that these four components are primarily addressed to the human resource part of the improvement equation. The other part of the equation that is needed is a focus on operational excellence. An organization that exhibits operational excellence has the following characteristics:

- Customer-centered
- Emphasis on quality
- Balance between efficiency and effectiveness
- Streamlined processes
- Commitment to continuous improvement
- Employees capable of and involved in problem solving
- Effective measurement and management systems

- Management decisions that are data-driven and evidence-based
- Commitment to on-going innovation and organizational renewal

Many years ago, quality guru Ed Deming noted that up to 80 percent of the performance problems in the manufacturing environment were due to defective or imperfect processes and systems, rather than people. An organization that is committed to excellence understands this and focuses as much attention on those processes and the manner in which the work gets done as it does to defining, developing, and implementing policies and programs. As Mies van der Rohe put it, "God is in the details."

The National Performance Review (NPR) was unquestionably the biggest and boldest intervention ever attempted in the federal government. The intervention, however, was not all-encompassing. The reinvention labs were for "experiments" or "skunk works"-type operations and many of the agency plans were at the 10,000 foot, or strategic, level. As a result, the majority of mid-level managers and line-level employees didn't participate or didn't buy into the reinvention. As Professor Kettl reported in his testimony on NPR before Congress, more than 3 years after the launch of NPR, only 37 percent of federal employees felt that reinvention had been a top priority for their organization, and a mere 20 percent said that NPR had brought about positive change to government.[13]

A government-wide focus on operational excellence can facilitate that buy-in. This approach can be implemented in each agency from the top-down, bottom-up, and managed in the middle. It can build on the successes and address the failures of NPR, GPRA, and PART. Instead of throwing the baby out with the bathwater, we recommend inviting everyone into the tub to play a role in discovering how the government can do more and better with less.

3. Ensure on-the-job training and mentoring to transfer essential knowledge and skills to new government employees.

It has been estimated that somewhere between 500,000 and 600,000 employees will leave the federal workforce within the next 4 to 5 years. Many of those departing will be the middle managers and front-line supervisors who will be retiring.

These are the folks who currently make the governmental machine run. When they leave, they will take with them approximately 10,000,000 years of experience. More importantly, they will be taking their collective understanding and organizational knowledge—immeasurable and virtually irreplaceable. The government needs to launch a major strategic initiative to address this critical issue by training these imminent retirees to be effective on-the-job trainers and mentors so that they can transfer their knowledge and skill sets to their successors. The chief human capital officer of each agency should be required to prepare a strategic human capital training and succession plan and submit it to The Office of Personnel Management (OPM) and OMB as part of the annual budgeting and performance improvement process.

As with performance management, there are a multitude of resources available. They should be inventoried and an approved list developed following a process similar to the one we just recommended for performance management. In addition, OPM should look for best practices models that can be easily adapted and made available to the agencies for their use.

One such model is the Structured O-J-T (on-the-job) System created by the National Institute for Metalworking Skills (NIMS). NIMS created the system through a grant from the Department of Labor and with contributions and direction from an expert panel of industry stakeholders. The system provides a systematic and rigorous framework for implementing an O-J-T process. It is competency-based and has three components that address three different audiences: O-J-T Trainer; O-J-T Senior Trainer, and Training Coordinator. A candidate who completes a component receives a NIMS certificate.

Enhancing formal training and on-the-job development, implementing strategic human capital planning, and fixing the federal hiring process were all identified in the Partnership for Public Services "Roadmap to Reform." All of these are items have been talked about and bandied about for almost a decade. It is now time for action.

4. Convene a congressional hearing on the dysfunctional Congress.

The Congress holds televised congressional hearings on everything ranging from steroid-using baseball players to bailout-taking

Wall Street bankers and presidential Supreme Court nominees. One of the most critical issues confronting the nation today is that the majority of the American public sees the United States Congress as a part of the problem and not as part of the solution. We believe that perception is accurate.

Therefore, we recommend that the Congress convene a hearing on the dysfunctional Congress. The background material for that hearing should begin with the following statement, "Resolved the United States Congress is dysfunctional. It is in the best interest of the citizens of the United States and the country that the Congress be a functional body. This hearing is being held in order to identify the root causes of Congress's dysfunction and to develop recommendations to make Congress functional."

Poll after poll has shown that the citizens are looking to Washington, D.C., for bipartisan problem solving. We believe that the current nature of the legislative system combined with the personalities of some elected officials prevent this from occurring.

Drawing upon the classic work of economist Mancur Olson and writings by Jonathan Rauch, James Fallows attributes this to a state of "demosclerosis—hardening of the arteries," in which special interest groups gain control of the process and make adaptation and change virtually impossible.[14] David Walker, the former comptroller general, blames a variety of factors including: "the incumbency disease" and the "failure of party politics" and calls for a citizens action movement and grassroots efforts to change the status quo.[15]

On his *Morning Joe* show on February 18, 2010, Joe Scarborough said part of the problem was due to the fact that there were fewer "grown-ups" in Washington, D.C., than when he was in Congress during the nineties. Joe went on to explain that one of the "grown-ups" in the Senate when he was there was Senator Alan Simpson who told him "to grow up" and to learn to reach across the aisle to get things done.[16]

There may be some reaching across the aisle today, but it is more often done with a clenched fist instead of an open hand. Congress has become a place of unintended comedy instead of comity. Therefore, we agree with Comptroller General Walker that citizens need to take the leadership in calling upon Congress to change.

We believe that the best way to make the public case for that change is by demanding that a congressional hearing be convened in order to conduct Congress's checkup in a fully transparent and accountable manner. Such a hearing would bring the doings of Congress out of the shadows and into the sunlight. That is the essence of democracy, and because of this and the critical importance of the topic, we predict that the hearing will be the most viewed in C-Span's history.

In conclusion, the United States is in crisis. There is an opportunity, and we are at a pivotal moment. As we noted in the title of this chapter, "Government Is Not the Problem." Nor can it be the only answer in this moment. Government at all levels has its own problems to deal with. As it corrects them, it will become an even better partner in moving the American enterprise forward.

11 | Business Is Not the Answer

"Greed, for lack of a better word, is good. Greed is right. Greed works."

Gordon Gekko in the movie Wall Street

BERNIE MADOFF WAS SENTENCED TO 150 YEARS IN PRISON. Dennis Kozlowski, former CEO of Tyco, got up to 25 years. Jeff Skilling, former CEO of Enron, got 24 years. Reading this, you might conclude that only businesspeople are venal and corrupt. Think again.

Three out of the last eight governors from the state of Illinois have done time as well. A fourth, former governor Rod Blagojevich (Blago), was impeached in January of 2009 and will stand trial in 2010. If Blago is convicted, that would make it four out of eight—.500 percent. Not bad for a baseball batting average, but not what you'd like to see for the CEOs of one of the biggest states in the union.

Our point is not that all businesspeople and politicians are corrupt—they aren't. People of all types and from all walks of life engage in criminal activities. Our point is that it's easy to stereotype an entire group based on the actions of a few.

For many, right now, that group resides on Wall Street. Some even want to extend that stereotype to include not only Wall Street, but all of capitalism and business.

BUSINESS IS NOT THE PROBLEM

Frankly, that's completely unfair and pretty stupid. Since it was established, the United States has existed at the intersection of democracy and capitalism. When the traffic lights are working and the gendarmes are ensuring that all folks are obeying the rules of the road, it's a great place to be. Significant benefits have accrued to our nation and its citizens because of this dynamic and the positive contributions of businesses and businesspeople throughout time.

Henry Ford led America into the industrial revolution with the automation of the assembly line. Just as importantly, he increased the wages of the workers on that line so they could afford to buy the cars they were manufacturing. That was enlightened self-interest at its best and a case of win-win.

Andrew Carnegie was notoriously tight fisted and controlling in all his business dealings. However, he believed in the importance of education. As a result, Carnegie basically funded the entire system of libraries across the United States. Go to the library in your hometown and look at the cornerstone. You'll likely find Carnegie's name on it.

Then, there's college dropout Bill Gates who helped fuel the expansion and growth of the information technology revolution. His company, Microsoft, has provided tens of thousands of good-paying jobs and supported tens of thousands of others. Gates didn't do badly himself and is now one of the richest persons in the world. He could have decided to take the money and run, but he didn't. Instead, with his wife Melinda, he established the Bill and Melinda Gates Foundation. The foundation's scope, mission, and mode of operation are worth studying as a model by any business that sees a link between corporate and individual success and social responsibility.

Gate's friend and fellow billionaire, Warren Buffett, is well known not only for his investing acumen, but also for the fact that he has pretty much promised his entire fortune—not to his children—but to the Bill and Melinda Gates Foundation. Actions truly do speak louder than words.

We're not just talking about the Fords, Carnegies, Gates, and Buffets—American businesses of all shapes and sizes have been collaborators in constructing the enormous economic playing field for achieving the American Dream. They have created jobs, paid decent wages, covered health insurance, provided retirement benefits, purchased goods, supplied goods, created economic value-added opportunities, promoted innovation, contributed to community economic development, supported charities, and paid taxes. And that's just for starters.

That doesn't mean that business is perfect. However, business is a work in process, and what we are learning today from the mistakes and problems of the past decade should only make businesses stronger.

BUSINESS SELF-INTEREST

It's a fact of life—business and public interest will not always align. For example, in May 2009, President Obama signed a bill called the Helping Families Save Their Homes Act. The act originally featured a section that would have allowed bankruptcy judges to lower the amount owed on a home. That section was removed after a confrontation between Senate Democrats and lobbyists representing the nation's biggest banks, including many that were getting big government bailouts.

The lobbyists worked tirelessly to garner support from Republicans and selected Democrats whom they had supported with generous financial contributions. As is usually the case on Capitol Hill, they prevailed. This caused Senator Sheldon Whitehouse (D-RI), to complain, "This is one of the most extreme examples I have seen of a special interest wielding its power for the special interest of a few against the general benefit of millions of homeowners and thousands of communities now being devastated by foreclosure."[1]

FINANCIAL FLOTSAM AND JETSAM

The Wall Street bailouts made under the Troubled Assets Relief Program (TARP) were allegedly done to stabilize the nation's financial system and to unfreeze the lending system. According to Leo Hindery, chairman of the Smart Globalization for the New America Foundation, the banks initially used the TARP funds as follows:

- 43 percent went to bolster capital
- 31 percent went to other investments
- 14 percent went to repaying debt
- 4 percent went to making acquisitions

Mr. Hindery noted, ". . . in the first half of 2009, the major banks, which received almost all of the TARP monies, actually used their bolstered capital cushions and the exceptionally high 25:1 leverage ratio permitted under the Geithner stress tests mostly for renewed proprietary trading, and, according to their very own statements, specifically NOT for much new lending."[2]

It appears to us that the life rafts were made available, but only to the luxury liners. It is interesting to note that the total bailout for AIG was $180 billion while the combined debt in mid-2009 for all of the states in the United States was approximately $166 billion.

Where does all of this end and when? There is very little question about where it began and why. The self-proclaimed smartest guys in the room who thought they were ingenious and infallible in collateralizing debt and securitizing risk, instead, proved to be financial idiot savants. What they were actually creating were WMDs—Weapons of Monetary Destruction.

These WMDs (e.g., collateralized debt obligations, structured investment vehicles, derivatives, and hedge funds) caused a global economic pandemic and financial meltdown. To quote Gillian Tett, author of *Fool's Gold: How the Bold Team of a Small Tribe at J. P. Morgan was Corrupted by Wall Street Greed and Unleashed a Catastrophe,* "the entire financial system went wrong as a result of flawed incentives within banks and investment funds, as well as the rating agencies; warped regulatory structures and a lack of oversight."[3] The creation of this international financial crisis was completely self-inflicted and a total team effort.

The collapse might have been okay if the culprits and the investors they represented had paid the price for their actions. It might have been okay if there had been some lessons learned or behaviors changed. But this does not appear to be the case. Wall Street is still obsessed with derivatives and hedge funds. Banking and trading of stocks is passé and for chumps.

The quant wonks are still in supremacy in New York City. They are the physicists and mathematicians engaged in quantitative finance. They apply their scientific methods and write software programs to manage derivatives and hedge funds even though some of them admit that this is a fool's errant. As one quant was quoted in *The New York Times*, "(the) market is a 'wild beast' that cannot be controlled . . . It's not like building a bridge. If you're right more than half the time you are winning the game."[4]

Those are the odds, and that is the game that Wall Street continues to play. Irresponsible financial institutions have done enormous damage in the recent past. They will most probably do much more damage in the future—the near future. Wall Street has built an accelerator machine that could crash the nation and the world almost instantaneously.

A QUESTION OF VALUE AND A QUESTION OF VALUES

There are two questions underlying all of this: When did money and making money become so important to the American economy, and what does it mean to the American Dream?

In *Bad Money*, Kevin Phillips foreshadowed the 2008 market melt-down. He talked about the accelerated growth of the financial services industry. Phillips attributed much of this growth and the focus on finance to "financial mercantilism"—a collaboration in which Washington and the financial sector sought to minimize unwanted market forces, meaning the failure of a major financial institution or the deflation-cum downward reevaluation of financial assets.[5]

Given Washington, D.C.'s hands off intervention during the Wall Street bailout as opposed to its heavy-handed intervention during the Detroit bailout, Phillips's assessment may be accurate. What is very clear is that there was a double standard. Those who make money were treated very differently from those who make things.

As we noted earlier, Washington, D.C. has been described as "40 square miles surrounded by reality." We feel that while Wall Street may not be 40 square miles, it is definitely surrounded by reality, too. It's also connected to Washington, D.C.—and not just by the Acela Express. Unreality meets unreality, and the rest of us live somewhere on the outskirts.

This brings us to the issue of value and values. Let's return to hedge funds and derivatives for a moment. One of the central concepts in business is provide something that is "value-added." This can be defined as an enhancement added to a product or service by a company before that product is offered to customers.

Where does the concept of "value-added" fit in when it comes to a financial instrument like a naked derivative, and who benefits from it? It could be argued that the value-add is risk mitigation or securitization of risk because of the nature of these products. Or, it could be argued that the value-add is the ability to make much more money than in normal business transactions with nominal exposure.

Given the meltdown in 2008, we feel those are hard arguments to make and defend. Paul Volcker would agree with us. In a Frank Rich op-ed column in *The New York Times* in January of 2010, he asserts that there is not "one shred of neutral evidence that any financial innovation of the past 20 years has lead to economic recovery."[6]

Could the true value-add be the tacit and symbiotic partnership between the financial sector and Washington, the result of which was an immediate Wall Street bailout? Given that the bailout had no negative consequences for most of those involved and an almost instantaneous return to business as usual, we think that seems like a more plausible argument. It is hard to defend how we let the big Wall Street players maximize their upside while taxpayers protect their downside.

There is an old saying, "You break it, you own it." In this case, Wall Street broke it, we paid for it, but they still own it. From what we saw through 2009, it looks like if left to its own devices, Wall Street may be getting ready to try to break it again. There are $600 trillion in derivatives in the world marketplace today—many of these are so-called naked derivatives because the holder is using the derivative to speculate (that is, gamble), not hedge.

What elevates the importance of the financial sector above every other sector of our economy? We think it says something about our values as a nation when such primacy is given to making money by repackaging and reselling financial instruments as opposed to making it by making things and providing services. What does it portend for our future when so much of our wealth is concentrated in a sector that benefits so few? These are not merely existential questions; they are central to the economic and social future of the nation and should be debated in the halls of Congress and in business and public policy schools across the country.

We are not opposed to hedge funds, derivatives, or the dicing up of risk into securities; all of these can be used for good. Remember, we're businesspeople and capitalists—we're all for making money. But like everything else, money needs to be put and kept in perspective. It should neither be idealized nor idolized, and those who are in the "money" business should not be protected or rescued when they engage in folly. We agree with Harvard University Professor Niall Ferguson, who sees finance developing and evolving through a process of evolution, including creation, selection, and destruction. This means if a flawed financial product or technique is applied, it should be allowed to die a natural death and not be resuscitated.[7]

MEANWHILE IN THE REAL WORLD

Just outside of the financial district which is centered in D.C. and New York City is the remainder of the United States. That's where the majority of businesses and businesspeople make their living. Businesses in all sectors and of all sizes have suffered significantly in this downturn. Many have filed for bankruptcy. Most have significantly reduced headcount and locations. Some of this is attributable to the meltdown of the economy. However, many were acting instinctively and impulsively, rather than engaging in a pragmatic and measured manner. They were falling prey to some of the same problems and demonstrating behaviors similar to those in the financial arena.

Jim Collins pinpoints some of the reasons and stages for this decline in his 2009 book *How The Mighty Fall: And Why Some Companies Never Give In*. Collins's third book talks about how the companies profiled in his two earlier books fell from grace.[8] Collins picked 11 of these "fallen companies" and compared them to "success contrasts." For example, he compared fallen company Circuit City to success contrast Best Buy and fallen company HP to success contrast IBM. Based upon this comparison, Collins identified the following five stages of decline and pinpointed markers that characterized each stage:

Table 11.1: Stages of Company Decline		
Stage	**Description**	**Sample Marker**
1	Hubris Born of Success	Success Entitlement, Arrogance
2	Undisciplined Pursuit of More	Unsustainable Quest for Growth
3	Denial of Risk and Peril	Amplify the Positive, Discount the Negative
4	Grasping for Salvation	A Series of Silver Bullets
5	Capitulation to Irrelevance or Death	None

What would happen if we applied Collins's stages to all publicly traded companies? What percent in total would be in one of the stages and what percent would be in each stage?

We're not betting people, but if we were, we would venture that the overall percent would be relatively high and primarily in stages 3 and 4 of decline. The reason for this high estimate is that the United States has been living in a bubble economy for far too long. We went from the dot-com bubble of the late 1990s to the housing bubble in the first half of the 2000s with no meaningful growth in between. We became a debtor nation, as did many of our major businesses.

Businesses and individuals alike thought that the good times would never end. Instead of engaging in rigorous and disciplined analysis, we threw caution to the wind and rode the bubbles. Now the bubbles have burst, and we are paying a very heavy price.

The problem is that businesses didn't take the right actions by changing their business models and strategic approaches to respond to the economic downturn experienced after the dot-com collapse and the potential economic catastrophe created by 9/11. Keep in mind that we were in the doldrums before 9/11 so the potential was pretty easy to see.

In 2002, there were a record number of corporate bankruptcies and many businesses looked to be at significant risk. The response to this crisis by most businesses was to employ what could be labeled an incremental approach:

- Eliminate services or benefits for customers
- Make customers pay for services once provided free
- Downsize the organization—in other words, fire or lay off employees
- Ask for concessions on wages and salaries
- Reduce pension benefits
- Cut administrative costs and overhead
- Make an across-the-board cut in operating costs/expenses
- Outsource selected functions or activities
- Increase costs/fees

Sound familiar? Fast-forward to 2009. It is déjà vu all over again—except that this tactical response will not work this time. Where organizational transformation has been required, many businesses have been engaged in the process of transference. They have been finding someone else to blame or pay for their problems. There is no new bubble on the horizon. The future belongs to those businesses that can build and float their own boat and not rely on bubbles for buoyancy.

BORN-AGAIN CAPITALISM

In 2008 American businesses got a wake-up call and a whack on the side of the head. While we do have our doubts about the Wall-Street crowd, we believe that businesses in general were reacting wisely to the crisis in 2009. Many used the experience as a flashpoint to conduct a complete strategic reexamination of their business models and industries.

They were not just cutting costs. They were taking a hard look in the mirror and at their businesses and all their moving parts. They were identifying and acknowledging their mistakes. They were preparing to get better. They were pinpointing where to stay the course, where to change the course, and where to chart a new one. Here are two examples.

Warren Buffett, chairman of Berkshire Hathaway, in his annual letter to shareholders, emphasized four goals going forward:

- Maintain Berkshire's Gibraltar-like financial position, with huge amounts of excess liquidity

- Widen "moats" around operating businesses that give them durable competitive advantages (through means such as patents, copyrights, and brand building)

- Acquire and develop new and varied streams of earnings

- Expand and nurture a cadre of outstanding operating managers

Buffett admitted that 2008 had been a tough year for Berkshire (the stock fell 32 percent). He took personal responsibility for the failures and confessed that he had made some dumb mistakes, such as purchasing Conoco Phillips's stock when oil and gas prices were near their highest and making large derivative investments that caused multibillion dollar markdowns.

In his typical down-home, folksy fashion on the Conoco deal, Buffett confessed to "sucking my thumb when new facts came in that should have caused me to re-examine my thinking and promptly take action." On the derivatives problem, he observed, "It is not just whom you sleep with but also whom they sleep with."[9]

Starbucks epitomized the bubble years and the resultant conspicuous consumption. Four dollar cups of coffee. Espressos. Mocha lattes. You name it. They had it and gave new names to it—even the size of the coffee cup that was ordered had a special name.

Starbucks, however, also symbolized the type of company Jim Collins wrote about in *How The Mighty Fall*. It grew far too fast. There was a Starbucks on every corner. It diversified too quickly and lost sight of its core business. The quality of its coffee suffered, and its baristas were not well trained.

When the bubble burst, away went much of Starbucks's fortunes. It bled cash and closed stores—approximately 1,000 in 2008 and another 900 in 2009. Dunkin' Donut and McDonalds got into the espresso coffee and latte business at a lower price point, taking away market share from the once-dominant player.

Howard Schultz, charismatic Starbucks founder, had seen the handwriting on the coffeehouse wall and stepped back in as CEO after a long hiatus from that position. Schultz immediately took the company back to its roots as a socially conscious, strong-culture business with a focus on quality products and customer service. One of his first actions was to close all of the Starbucks for a 3-hour period and retrain the baristas.

It looks like the back-to-basics move is working. Starbucks released very strong results for its fiscal year third quarter that ended in June 2009. Along with those results, Schultz proclaimed, "The entire Starbucks organization is committed to continually improving our customer experience as the roadmap to renewed growth and increasing profitability. At the same time, we will continue to innovate and differentiate two perennial hallmarks of the Starbucks brand."[10]

Speaking of innovation and differentiation—in June 2009, Starbucks also announced that it was opening 15th Avenue Coffee and Tea in Seattle. According to Starbucks's press release, "This coffeehouse design is reminiscent of a European mercantile and draws its inspirations from the original Starbucks location opened in Seattle's Pike Place Market 38 years ago."[11]

Starbucks stated that it plans to open two more 15th Avenue stores in Seattle but had no plans to take the concept elsewhere. We wouldn't bet on that. Sounds to us like it's back to the future.

CORPORATE SOCIAL RESPONSIBILITY

Howard Schultz of Starbucks has always placed a premium on corporate social responsibility (CSR) by sponsoring activities as diverse as mobilizing thousands of employees to go help rebuild New Orleans after Hurricane Katrina to giving away free coffee to everyone who voted in the presidential election in 2008. CSR, however, was not a hallmark for businesses in general in the bubble years.

In fact, trust busting was more the norm as many businesses ignored or minimized the importance of their customers and employees during the Go-Go, Grow-Grow era. As a result, public confidence in business ethics and practices ebbed to a new low.

In the aftermath of the 2008 financial collapse, businesses' attitudes and perspectives on social responsibility began to change. Businesses were not only concerned with doing things right. They were concerned with doing the right things.

The importance of CSR is captured by the fact that 63 of the world's largest 100 economic entities are corporations and not countries. The emphasis on CSR is not new. Michael Porter and Mark Kramer identify four traditional rationales for CSR:

- Moral Obligation. Emphasis on ethical values and respect for people and nature

- Sustainability. Emphasis on community and environmental stewardship

- License to Operate. Emphasis on the need for tacit or explicit permission from governments, communities, or stakeholders to do business in certain locations

- Reputation. Emphasis on the focus of the company's image, strength of the brand, and positioning potential.[12]

Porter and Kramer argued that by implementing this approach, organizations can create shared value because the results benefit the company and the community. McKinsey and Company takes Porter and Kramer's argument one step further by asserting that a company's environmental, social, and governance (ESG) programs create financial value through growth, return on capital, risk management, and quality of management.[13]

The bottom line for us as businessmen is that well-designed and implemented CSR programs that link to a business's purpose have a double bottom line: they can contribute to the business's financial performance and produce powerful social returns. Moreover, they can also build a shared commonality of interest and help bridge the divide that sometimes exists between the private and public sectors.

SOCIAL ENTREPRENEURS AND SOCIAL VENTURES

There is a distinct group of businesspeople and businesses that adapt a social purpose as part of their business model. They want to do well by doing good.

They are social entrepreneurs, or social ventures. They include companies such as Ben & Jerry's, Newman's Own, Patagonia, 7th Generation, and The Body Shop.

There is no accurate count of how many businesses fall into this category. However, given the rise of social investors and social capital, it appears that those interested in combining their instinct for social responsibility with a financial motivation are definitely on the increase.

This is evidenced by the fact that in 2008, 630 people attended a new conference, Social Capital Markets. As *The New York Times* reported,

> *"According to Kevin Jones, the creator of the conference and a principal in Good Capital, an investment firm focusing on social business, two-thirds of the participants signed up after the collapse of Lehman Brothers which he called a sign that people are flocking to what he calls a 'new asset class.'"*[14]

Given the current economic conditions, the strains on the social safety net, and the decreased funding of government programs and capacity for those most in need, it would seem this "asset class" could become a growth stock.

An argument for the social entrepreneurship or for-profit model is that it may be implemented more quickly than a nonprofit or governmental model. On the other hand, experts note that some social problems such as early childhood may not respond well or be appropriate for the for-profit model because a business might have to cut quality in order to ensure its profit.

We believe this tension will be worked out in the marketplace. And, it already is in some cases. For example, look at the battle that has played out over the past 25 years between those in the free software and open source code camps and the proprietary software providers. Or, consider the change in the educational playing field that is occurring today with the new emphasis for funding for charter schools as opposed to maintenance of the existing educational delivery system.

The business landscape has been irretrievably altered by the events of 2008. We believe that one of the key dimensions of that alteration will be many more opportunities for social entrepreneurs and small businesses to initiate social ventures that provide equal returns in terms of financial and psychic benefits to the founder/owner of a social venture.

GOVERNMENT CAPITALISM

American taxpayers now own General Motors. They also own AIG. If there were ever an accurate analysis of their assets and balance sheets, taxpayers would probably own most of the big banks in this country.

General Motors (GM) was restructured by a team of Wall Street financial deal maker types, none of whom had any significant industry experience or operational expertise. In July 2009, the U.S. Treasury named four directors to represent the taxpayer-owners on the General Motors board: Daniel F. Akerson (Carlyle Group), David Bonderman (TPG Capital), Robert D. Krebs (Burlington Northern Santa Fe Railroad), and Patricia F. Russo (Alcatel–Lucent).

Sounds like an illustrious group. Time will tell whether they have any strategic insights and whether they bring the right skill set to the General Motors boardroom is another question. They did replace two of the executives who helped drive this car into the ditch. Rick Wagoner resigned in June 2009 shortly after the bailout, and 8 months later, Frederick "Fritz" Henderson, who was elevated to the CEO position, was summarily dismissed. GM is now firmly in the hands of board Chair Ed Whitacre, Jr. who has assumed the reins of CEO.

We're not just concerned about GM, however. The overriding issue that must be resolved is—what should the government's appropriate role and responsibility be after the bailout. Should it bail out? Should it stay and play? Should it be somewhere in between? It is commonly argued that the government doesn't do a good job at running anything. Therefore, it shouldn't take over anything.

It is rarely argued that business doesn't do a good job of running anything despite the fact there are countless bankruptcies, mergers, and reorganizations that take place every year. Logic would dictate that it should be argued that businesses should not take over anything either. Logic need not apply in this instance. If it did, we'd have no options left.

Fortunately, there are options. They entail not blindly affixing blame but doing a reasoned analysis and then carving out a solution that is appropriate for these turbulent and tumultuous times.

RENEWING BUSINESS RECOMMENDATIONS

The market collapse and economic meltdown of 2008 will inevitably lead to new regulations, more aggressive enforcement, and tougher sanctions for businesses. That's an appropriate pendulum swing given the deregulatory shift that began with Reagan and culminated in the laissez-faire approach of the Bush years. However, this must not just be about command and control. Equal concern should be paid to enlistment, enablement, and empowerment. We need to protect that which has been fundamental to the nation's economic success. We need to correct that which erodes it.

America's strengths as a place to do business are unrivalled. In a special report in *The Economist* in 2009, a World Bank report cited America as the third easiest place to do business in the world. American businesses (both home-grown and adopted) have been the driving engine for the economic development of this country and the American Dream.[15] Recognizing this, the recommendations that follow are presented to make American businesses better and to make the United States an even better place to do business in the future.

Business Primary Recommendations

1. Establish an independent oversight board to monitor the work of the Federal Reserve Bank.

2. Establish tax and financial incentives for firms to create or bring jobs to the U.S.

3. Create a social entrepreneur venture and tax credits fund.

Business Subsidiary Recommendations

4. Develop an industrial and innovation policy that spurs investment and creativity in targeted sectors.

5. Engage in transformational thinking and planning to create the business of the future.

6. Revamp the curricula of business schools and schools of public policy.

7. Enhance corporate social responsibility programs.

8. Create business and industry advisory panels for businesses in which the government has significant ownership positions.

The primary recommendations are discussed here. The subsidiary recommendations are addressed in the Appendix.

1. Establish an independent oversight board to monitor the work of the Federal Reserve Bank.

A small permanent board should be established to review and oversee the performance of the Federal Reserve Bank. The board should have a full-time set of directors appointed by the president and a professional staff with skill sets similar to those at the bank, plus individuals with human resources, business, public policy, and financial markets experience.

The board should function as a combination of the Government Accounting Office and the National Transportation Safety Board. It should be a watchdog on an on-going basis with special investigative capabilities if problems or abuses occur. The first thing that board should do is conduct a complete program and performance audit of the Fed. In January 2010, Chairman Ben Bernanke was calling for the GAO to do an audit of the Fed's actions during the financial crisis. If this is done, the study should be a starting point for a fuller audit of the entire agency.

There are three reasons for making this recommendation: First, the Federal Reserve Bank today is independent. In effect, it answers to no one but itself. Since its establishment, it has operated as a fiefdom. It has also conducted much of its business in a secretive manner. In an era where "transparency and accountability" have become the buzz words, the Federal Reserve still operates in the netherworlds of high finance and monetary policy.

Second, the Federal Reserve's relationship to those it would regulate appears to have become far too cozy and cordial. The Wall Street bailout may have saved the "financial system," but at what cost and to whose benefit?

Third, there is the issue of performance. The Federal Reserve is responsible for establishing and maintaining a regulatory system that ensures financial stability. If we were to assign a letter grade to its efforts, it would receive an "F."

2. Establish tax and financial incentives for firms to create or bring jobs to the U.S.

The Homeland Investment Act of 2004 allowed companies to take a large one-time tax break on overseas profits, but only if the money was used in the United States for specified investments. The problem with the act wasn't its intent, but rather its execution. The failure to put the proper language in the bill to ensure that the money was spent as intended enabled businesses to bring the money back to the U.S., take it, and run. When Congress said, "Show me the money," it was long gone. (Can anyone say, "Wall Street bailout"?)

Congress should develop an updated version of the Homeland Investment Act focused on creating or bringing jobs back to the United States. The act should give businesses the ability to redeem overseas profits with a tax break and also add tax incentives to the mix to facilitate investment in specific types of job creation. The Act should include strict monitoring and enforcement provisions.

The new economic realities globally and the availability of a large pool of unemployed and underemployed skilled workforce in the United States makes this an ideal time to pass and implement legislation of this type. A Homeland Job Creation Act would accelerate this trend. It would help to build a public and private partnership for job creation and begin a trend of insourcing lost American jobs back to the United States.

3. Create a Social Entrepreneur Venture and Tax Credits Fund.

Over the past several years, a number of groups such as the Acumen Fund, Calvert Group, and Good Capital have developed social venture capital funds to provide financial support to businesses and organizations that are implementing responsible market-based solutions to social and environmental issues. In addition, there are other groups that provide financial support focused on the nonprofit social entrepreneur.

The federal government should consider expanding and leveraging the resources of these investor groups in two ways: First, by creating a social entrepreneurship venture capital pool that would be financed with a mix of funds from the private and public sectors. The pool should be administered by a third-party NGO that could establish a competitive process for awarding funds in response to business plans and proposals from social ventures. Second, creating a tax credit vehicle similar to New Market Tax Credits—this would allow businesses to reduce their tax burden by allocating a percentage of their profits to support social ventures.

The United Kingdom has a Social Enterprise Unit as part of its government. *BusinessWeek* has reported that President Obama has suggested starting a new government agency to help socially conscious start-ups gain more access to venture capital.[16] On June 30, 2009, President Obama held a press conference to recognize innovative nonprofit programs such as *Teach for America* and the *Harlem Children's Zone* that were making differences in communities across the country. At that conference, he called on foundations, philanthropists, and the private sector to fund and invest in these solutions.

We'd recommend that the federal government add its substantial brawn and brains to that mix of investors. It will sweeten the pot significantly and bring additional rewards to those who want to blend passion with compassion as social entrepreneurs.

America cannot be renewed without business leadership. When American businesses grow stronger and assume the appropriate level of corporate social responsibility and invest in the homeland, they advance the cause of the American Dream and the interests of the American citizen. To do this, businesses need not put country first. But, they must not put country last.

12 | Citizens All

"Politics ought to be the part-time profession of every citizen who would protect the rights and privileges of free people and who would preserve what is good and fruitful in our national heritage."

Dwight Eisenhower

Barack Obama started his meteoric rise to success at the Democratic Convention of 2004 when he gave the keynote address in which he declared that the United States was purple. What now-President Obama actually said was "There's not a liberal America and a conservative America, there's the United States of America . . . We worship an awesome God in the blue states, and we don't like agents poking around our libraries in the red states. We coach Little League in the blue states, and, yes, we've got some gay friends in the red states."

The then-Senator Obama used his keynote to strike a unifying and positive theme to try to counteract the negativity and divisiveness that had grown increasingly intense in the country after the bitterly disputed 2000 election. One United States. Red and blue—together they make the color purple.

Unfortunately, there are some people who don't like the color purple—whether it's a book, a movie, or a cow. They're purple people eaters. They much prefer red or blue. More precisely, they prefer red states or blue states. That's how these folks make their living or stay in power—by stoking the coals of their respective constituencies. To them, you are either right or you are left—there's no middle ground.

THE GREAT DIVIDES

In spite of what President Obama said in 2004, there are divides in America that take many forms, including political, personal, and historical. In his book *Don't Think of an Elephant*, George Lakoff provides a useful framework for looking at political divides by classifying these differences as follows:

Table 12.1: Political Divides[1]	
Progressives	**Conservatives**
Stronger America	Strong Defense
Broad Prosperity	Free Markets
Better Future	Lower Taxes
Effective Government	Smaller Government
Mutual Responsibility	Family Values

The "progressive" values are on the left, and the conservative values are on the right—as they should be. Lakoff uses words to frame issues. Note that he uses the word *progressives* instead of *liberals*. That's because the "L" word has become a no-no unless you are referring to the HBO series.

In our opinion, most progressives and conservatives support all 10 of the values listed in the table. It's just a matter of primary orientation or focus. For example, we believe that conservatives support a "stronger America" and progressives support a "strong defense." The difference between the two groups is that the progressives emphasize domestic priorities and the conservatives emphasize defensive priorities.

We also think that conservatives are as interested in a "better future" as progressives, but where a conservative would favor lower taxes, a progressive would favor reasonable or fair taxes. Finally, we think both groups have family values, but progressives lean toward shared and democratic values while conservatives lean toward more rigid or enforced values.

You can see that things may not be all that black and white (or red and blue). The divide between us is more gray or purple. Seeing it this way provides the potential for bridging the gap.

Robert Burgess provides a framework for capturing personal divides by issue area:

- Politics
- Education
- Religion
- Immigration
- Race Relations[2]

In political parlance, these are areas in which wedge issues exist or are born: abortion; same-sex marriage; don't ask, don't tell; the right to bear arms; illegal immigration—to name a few. These are topics on which hardened beliefs prevail and dictate the nature and tone of our dialogue. Hardened beliefs are your core values, attitudes, and opinions. They are usually developed early in life and relate to areas such as those listed above.

Social psychologist Milton Rokeach from Michigan State University was one of the foremost experts on belief systems. His research disclosed the fact that Americans basically share the same values, but that we each have a value hierarchy and the ranking and weighting of the values in that hierarchy varies considerably from individual to individual.

Rokeach also developed a psychology of dogmatism. He found that dogmatism was a measurable personality trait created by the convergence of a closed cognitive system, authoritarianism, and intolerance.[3]

What this means simply is that if you are dealing with a person with a closed mind—forget it. There are some immutable values and opinions that simply can't be changed no matter what. Nevertheless, that doesn't mean that there can't be an acknowledgment but not acceptance of the other person's position—in other words, agree to disagree and agree to an honest debate without being disagreeable.

As the Civil War so dramatically and tragically illustrates, that which divides us is not of recent origin. In fact, we have always had disagreements, dating as far back as the founding of our nation. In his book *The Thirteen American Arguments: Enduring Debates*

That Define and Inspire Our Country, Howard Fineman identifies those arguments as:

1. Who Is a Person?

2. Who Is an American?

3. The Role of Faith

4. What Can We Know and Say?

5. The Limits of Individualism

6. Who Judges the Law?

7. Debt and the Dollar

8. Local Versus National Authority

9. Presidential Power

10. The Terms of Trade

11. War and Diplomacy

12. The Environment

13. A Fair, "More Perfect" Union

Fineman uses the word *argument* to describe these debates deliberately. He reminds us that James Madison "proposed that the multiplicity of 'factions' was essential to a just and equitable society." Fineman asserts "arguing is good—in fact, indispensable." He emphasizes, however, that there should be some rules of engagement for the arguing: "Each side needs to accept the others' humanity, and understandable emotional intensity, so the debate can really begin. For argument is inert without a measure of goodwill."[4]

We agree, but unfortunately, the problem today is that there are more and more destructive debates or angry arguments, with less and less constructive conflict. We've got more name calling, hollering, body slamming, and no-holds-barred cage wrestling events than we do gentlemanly disagreements. Where is Bill Buckley when we really need him?

We agree that argument is necessary. But, we need to ensure that those who are arguing are educated and have knowledge of the facts. We need to learn how to communicate authentically and constructively and respect our opponent's position. Ed Crego often heard his mother say what was firmly believed by her generation of Americans, "I may disagree with your opinion, but I will defend to the death your right to hold and express it." While we're at it, a little anger management training probably wouldn't hurt either.

POLITICIANS AND THE DIVIDES

Most of the time, the vast majority of Americans don't think about politics or civic engagement. In fact, most of us have an inherent distrust of politics. E. J. Dionne, Jr., columnist for *The Washington Post*, put it a little more strongly in a book titled *Why Americans Hate Politics.*[5] Why do we distrust or hate politics? One reason is that politicians rarely seem to get anything done when it comes to big issues.

For a variety of reasons, the domestic and economic issues both parties agreed to address through the end of the 1990s and under the Bush administration were all minor. Many big issues—healthcare, labor, environment, and energy—were either ignored or addressed peripherally. As a consequence, during that time period, most of us continued to hate politics. This was not because we saw "false choices," but because we saw "no choices."

In 2009, when the Obama administration came into office, things seemed to change suddenly and dramatically. Everything was on the table and all topics were up for full discussion and debate. We thought that was a good thing.

Based on the interaction of both parties throughout 2009 on items such as the stimulus bill, the energy and climate change bill, and most notably, the healthcare legislation, it became painfully obvious that problem solving and dispute resolution would be greatly restricted in both scope and nature. *Bipartisanship* was a word that went out of vogue by the end of the first quarter of 2009.

To understand why this was the case, look at the current composition of the Congress. The Republican-elected officials are a distinct minority in the House and the Senate. Overall, they represent a narrow segment and section of the country. They tend to be to the right or far right. Thus, they braced themselves to resist compromise and voted almost unanimously and consistently against the major bills presented by the president and the Democratic majority.

In contrast, about one-fifth to one-quarter of the elected Democratic officials are moderate or conservative—more center and center right than center left. This bloc constituted the swing vote. These representatives swayed the content and design of legislation. They were the focus of compromise because they were willing to compromise.

Politics is the art of comprise, and getting legislation passed has been compared to making sausage. These Democrats became the compromisers in charge and the chief sausage makers. They didn't define the issue, but they shaped the choices. From false choices to no choices to limited ones. Still, limited choices are better than none.

Politics is not about perfection, but it is about perfecting. Perfecting means there is some progress. When so little has been made for so long, progress becomes our most important product. It moves the ball out of the end zone and up the field. This is a good thing for democracy. It also helps reduce our disdain for politics, or what we prefer to call the alienation or anomie of the average voter and your typical American citizen.

There's another factor that we believe tends to promote alienation and anomie among the less partisan among us—negative ads and personal attacks that are sometimes employed in an attempt to win political contests, as well as the inappropriate and inexplicable behavior of politicians.

Politics in the United States has always been a full contact sport—more pugilism than persuasion. Cases in point from the twentieth century include the "nuclear destruction" ad run against Barry Goldwater in the 1964 presidential contest and the Willie Horton "racial hatred" ad run against Michael Dukakis in the 1988 contest.

Fast-forward. The twenty-first century gave birth to the Swift Boat ads that were run against John Kerry by a small group called Swift Boat Veterans for Truth (think political/social capitalists) to discredit Kerry's heroic service in Vietnam. These misleading ads were so effective in creating doubt about Kerry among "low-information voters" that they gave rise to a new term for attack politics called "swift-boating."

Swift-boating is now in the American political vernacular. In the 2008 presidential election, former Alaska governor and Republican vice-presidential candidate Sarah Palin was accused of swift-boating and of being swiftboated. She herself said, "The heels are on, the gloves are off . . . From now on until Election Day, you know, it may get kinda rough here. Campaigns have to take the gloves off and start telling the truth." On the other hand, Palin felt that the media was constantly swift-boating her on a range of issues from the $150,000 wardrobe that had been purchased for her by the Republican National Committee to her choice of newspapers. It will be interesting to see how Ms. Palin feels now that she is a media commentator herself.

Tough attacks go on during primaries as well. The Hillary Clinton campaign employed what was called the "kitchen-sink strategy" against Barack Obama in the 2008 Democratic presidential primary. Mitt Romney was continuously bombarded by many of his opponents in the Republican primary for his liberal leanings when he was governor of Massachusetts.

Finally, as we've seen recently, the behavior of politicians can be less than exemplary and edifying. Sometimes it's private behavior in personal life (such as the indiscretions of ex-governor Eliot Spitzer (Democrat) of New York and Governor Mark Sanford (Republican) of South Carolina. At other times, it's the reckless and flamboyant behavior of someone like ex-governor Rod Blagojevich of Illinois. The public disapproves of conduct of this type, but the black eye goes to the individual involved and not as much to the political process. Put it all together: negative ads; personal attacks; spin; intraparty power struggles. The American public is watching, and too often, they are seeing a very ugly picture.

When the political process becomes a demeaning one, we all suffer—our desire to participate in the process is diminished. The United States is at a critical juncture where we need all hands on deck. Those politicians who set bad examples and put personal interest and petty politics above the need to change are being unpatriotic. They are stealing the political spirit and will from those of us who need to be politically engaged in order to ensure our country's future.

THE STATE OF POLITICAL ENGAGEMENT

Harvard Professor Robert Putnam found that there was a decline in political engagement and participation in elections at the national level from the early 1970s through 1998.[6] (Part of this decline in electoral participation can probably be explained by the fact that 18-year-olds were given the right to vote in 1972. The turnout of 18-to-21-year-olds has been low since that right was given.) What's happened since 1998? There's been some bad news, some good news, and some news.

The bad news is that participation in the presidential election of 2000 stayed at a low level (51.3 percent) compared to participation in the elections 1952 to 1972 (60 percent). The good news is that participation in the 2004 election went up to 55.5 percent, and that in the 2008 contest between McCain and Obama, the participation was estimated at 61.7 percent—the first time turnout has been above 60 percent since 1968. You might conclude that we have begun a renaissance in political engagement, or at least in election participation.

An alternative interpretation could be that there were drivers in both 2004 and 2008 that drove participation up. The 2004 driver on the Democratic side was anger and a firm conviction that the 2000 election had been stolen by George W. Bush and the United States Supreme Court. The 2004 driver on the Republican side was evangelicals and social conservatives seeing an opportunity to consolidate the gains made after the Bush election in 2000. In 2008, the drivers were youthful idealism and economic anxiety.

In spite of the participation spike in 2008, we are inclined to believe the latter interpretation. The real story will be told in 2012, so we will withhold our judgment on whether there is a reengagement in presidential election years until the results of that election are in.

The inside story about political engagement, though, is told by participation in the mid-term elections in the off years. The comparative stair-step table that follows presents participation in elections in both general presidential election years and off-year elections from 1980 to 2008.

An analysis of the data shows a very wide range in participation in general election years—from a low of 49.8 percent to a high of 61.7 percent (the 11.9 point difference represents a 23.9 percent range). In contrast, the data show a very narrow range in the off years—from a low of 38.1 percent to a high of 42.1 percent (the 4 point difference represents a 10.5 percent range). If the outlier high years were excluded from both the general and off years, the general election range difference would only be 6.9 percent and the off-year range would be below 1 percent at .8 percent. That's still a substantial difference between the election cycles.

Table 12.2: Election Participation in Presidential and Off-Year Elections		
Year	**General Election Participation**	**Off-Year Participation**
2008	61.7 percent	
2006		40.3 percent
2004	56.7 percent	
2002		39.5 percent
2000	51.3 percent	
1998		38.1 percent
1996	49.8 percent	
1994		41.1 percent
1992	55.1 percent	
1990		38.4 percent
1988	50.1 percent	
1986		38.1 percent
1984	53.1 percent	
1982		42.1 percent
1980	52.7 percent	

We might see an uptick in 2010 elections as we did in the off-year elections of 1982 and 1994 because of a chance to vote against a sitting president and his party. The tea partiers were making concerted efforts in states such as Florida to run Republican candidates and to mobilize support to accomplish this. They also appeared to be trying to take control of the Republican party itself. Indications in early 2010 were that the Republicans would pick up a good number of seats in both the House and Senate—whether that will be because or in spite of the tea partiers will be determined at the polls.

The turnout in mid-term elections has been, and always will be, lower than in general election years. Therefore, the true test of whether we have begun to move the needle on political engagement is whether participation rates can be increased in both general and off-year elections. If this occurs and we see "average citizens" getting more engaged in activities such as canvassing, poll watching, and voter registration, then we will be persuaded that civic engagement is on the rise for good. We know, however, that we are fighting an uphill battle.

Alan Gitelson, a professor of political science at Loyola University, has been studying citizen cynicism and skepticism toward politics and government for more than 20 years. Over that period, he found that cynicism and skepticism toward both have increased significantly.

As Professor Gitelson explains, the cynicism rating is more important than the skepticism rating because cynical citizens do not participate in politics. Skeptical citizens might, if they can be persuaded and given an opportunity and reason to set their skepticism aside for a time—to engage in what the sociologists call "the willing suspension of disbelief."[7]

As citizens, if we want to make a difference in the conduct of public affairs and public policy, we need to be able to move from skepticism and cynicism to a sense of realism and pragmatism about politics. We can accomplish this through more civic education and political engagement. This demands, though, that we be given more reasons and opportunities to participate actively and meaningfully in that process.

BRIDGING THE DIVIDES

Numerous proposals have been made on the appropriate role for citizens in our Democratic society and to increase citizen engagement. They come from conservatives such as Newt Gingrich and Charles Krauthammer to liberals such as William Greider, best-selling author and national affairs correspondent for *The Nation*, and Professor Putnam of Harvard, who, in his book, advocated a 2010 agenda for civic engagement. We present ours later in this chapter.

Before we do so, we thought it would be helpful to posit a set of core principles for what it means to be a citizen in the United States. What are the essential requirements for civic and political engagement?

The list below was drawn from "Our American Voice," a civic engagement program designed for middle-school students. We believe that they provide a useful frame of reference for Americans of all ages to think about and reflect on what it means to be a citizen:

- Citizenship is a way of life and not a singular event.
- With our rights and freedoms come responsibilities.
- The success of the individual and the community are inter-dependent.
- The informed participation of the people shapes and sustains our democracy.[8]

In other words, citizenship begins with the right mind-set. That mind-set leads to involvement. Involvement enables the bridging of divides and progress for America in the twenty-first century.

RENEWING CIVIC ENGAGEMENT RECOMMENDATIONS

In our opinion, the great divides and dissent are natural. They cannot, and should not, be eliminated. They should, however, not be allowed to be amplified or exaggerated by those who would manipulate them and others for personal ends. These divides help to create the dynamic tension that moves us forward—sometimes lurching, sometimes stumbling, but always moving in the right direction.

We offer the following primary and subsidiary recommendations to contribute to that forward momentum and to bridging the divides:

Civic Engagement Primary Recommendations

1. Prepare future generations of citizens by teaching civics and civic engagement from middle school.
2. Permit in-person voting for an extended period of time and allow mail-in voting for everyone (with proper safeguards).
3. Implement a national fair districting initiative.
4. Convene town halls and community discussions about issues of concern to citizens and the role of government in America's future.

Civic Engagement Subsidiary Recommendations

5. Develop and enforce a code of conduct for candidates for political office.

6. Demand more transparency and accountability from all groups involved in campaign financing.

7. Involve our higher educational institutions in addressing failures and breakdowns in government and the political process.

We present our primary recommendations in this chapter. The subsidiary recommendations are in the Appendix.

1. Prepare future generations of citizens by teaching civics and civic engagement in middle school.

Former Supreme Court Justice Sandra Day O'Connor identified the lack of sufficient and appropriate civic education as one of the most significant problems in America today. She put addressing that problem at the top of her personal agenda now that she is a private citizen again. Justice O'Connor worked with the Georgetown University Law Center and Arizona State University to develop a Web site and an interactive civics curriculum for seventh- through ninth-grade students called Our Courts.

According to Justice O'Connor, "At least half of our states no longer make the teaching of civics and government a requirement for high school graduation. This leaves a huge gap, and we can't forget that the primary purpose of public schools in America has always been to help produce citizens who have both the knowledge and skills and the values to sustain our republic as a nation, our democratic form of government."[9]

The federal government should make civics a requirement and provide adequate funding to support implementation of scalable and replicable civic education and civic engagement programs on a national basis. State legislatures should provide support for and make civics a requirement as well. Foundation support should be solicited to magnify the efforts.

These civic education and engagement programs should be designed to build knowledge, attitudes, and skills. They should be targeted to middle school, in-school, and after-school classes because educational research indicates that formation of a positive orientation toward an area earlier in a student's career increases the potential for sustained interest and participation.

We know of three models, each with a different primary focus, which could be employed nationally:

- *Project Citizen.* This is a national curricular program for middle, secondary, and postsecondary students, youth organizations, and adult groups that promotes competent and responsible participation in local and state government (www.civiced.com).

- *Our American Voice.* This after-school program involves middle-school students directly in the democratic process by employing the action learning model to help them develop the core knowledge, attitudes, and abilities for citizenship. It enables students to understand the critical role they play as citizens in a democratic society. The program is currently run in the state of Illinois by the Barat Education Foundation (www.ouramericanvoice.org).

- *Kids Voting.* Kids Voting USA® gets student involved and ready to be educated and engaged citizens. Students learn about democracy through a combination of classroom activities and authentic voting experience and family dialogue (www.kidsvoting.org).

We read recently that middle schools in Scarsdale, New York, have begun to teach empathy to privileged teenagers so they can understand the needs of those less well off than they. The focus on empathy is not restricted to Scarsdale. The Character Education Partnership reports that 18 states require programs to foster core values such as empathy, respect, and integrity.[10] If we don't place a renewed emphasis on civics in middle school, we will unwittingly be teaching apathy toward citizenship instead of empathy and active participation.

2. Permit in-person voting for an extended period of time and allow mail-in voting for everyone (with proper safeguards).

Although we pride ourselves on the manner in which elections are conducted in the United States, we are still far from perfect. Over the years, we have had, and continue to have, our fair share of problems with issues such as voters' rights, voting equipment, and the voting process. Our concern here is a limited one. It is that the process itself is one that, whether intentionally or unintentionally, can make it difficult for a citizen to participate in the electoral process.

As we noted earlier in this chapter, the average voter turnout in presidential election years is in the 50 percent range and 40 percent range in nonpresidential years. This is an appallingly low figure. Various studies have ranked the United States anywhere from 28 to 40 among nations that vote democratically. A few countries like Australia and Belgium make voting mandatory. However, the majority of countries that do better than the United States don't make voting mandatory.[11]

There are a variety of factors that influence voting turnout. These include: voter registration—who is registered; salience—will my vote really matter; and voter fatigue—how frequently elections are held. In this case, we are concerned simply with the "ease of voting."

In the United States, we have more restrictive voter registration processes than many other nations. In addition, access to the voting process itself as determined by factors such as the hours for voting, availability of locations, and the time period for absentee balloting varies substantially from state to state and, indeed, by districts within a state. To counteract this, we should implement a minimum national standard that promotes maximum feasible participation in the voting process. This standard should extend the length of the time period for voting and include mail-in balloting. All voting in Oregon is done by mail ballot.

We should also give consideration to changing the voting dates to weekends as opposed to weekdays or making Election Day a national holiday. Both of these options would likely boost participation significantly. Finally, voting electronically as an option to increase electoral participation should be tested and evaluated.

3. Implement a national fair districting initiative.

It is commonly accepted that politics today is more polarized than it has ever been. One of the reasons for this is that gerrymandering and redistricting has made electoral districts at both the national and state levels more partisan than they have been historically. It makes bipartisanship virtually impossible.

At the national level, only around 10 percent of the 450 congressional races in general elections are considered to be competitive districts.[12] The real contest occurs in the primary. Whoever wins there takes the whole enchilada. The same principle applies at the state level. That's why in 2006, only seven out of the 153 legislative and congressional races in California were considered competitive.[13]

Gerrymandering is nothing new. It dates back almost to the establishment of the democracy. Patrick Henry and the Anti-federalists drew the boundaries of a district in Virginia to keep future President James Madison from winning a congressional seat there. They were unsuccessful.

That wouldn't be true today because what was once an art has become a science. With sophisticated software and the click of a mouse, the "gerrymanderers" can restructure a district in their own images and likenesses in an instant. And they do.

The persons who redraw the district lines in most instances in the United States are elected officials, and the redistricting is controlled by the power in party. There is no way that those in power can do redistricting in an impartial manner.

The self-interest maxim dominates, and the mantra, although spoken sotto voce, is "to the victor belongs the spoils." This is accomplished by "packing" voters of the other party into a single district or "cracking" the center of the opposition's strength by dispersion of opponents to districts where they will be a minority.

We think this approach to developing districts is totally unacceptable. It causes many voters to vote in districts where their votes are "wasted"—either in the majority or minority. It contaminates democracy by elevating the concerns of the elected officials above those of the citizenry and letting the politicians select their own constituents. In a sense, the politician becomes judge, jury, and executioner.

2010 is a census year. All states will be required to redistrict in this decade as they are, after all, censuses. This redistricting must be done in as fair and neutral a manner as possible. In June 2009, a bicameral, bipartisan group in Congress introduced the Fairness and Independence in Redistricting Act (FAIR). FAIR calls for congressional districts to be drawn to "adhere to the Voting Rights Act, equal population, geography, and local boundaries." It also suggests using an independent commission to draw lines. While FAIR does not apply to district lines for state and local elections, we recommend that a similar process be used for those races as well.

In an op-ed piece, John Tanner (D-TN) and Mike Castle (R-DE), two of the cosponsors of FAIR, wrote, "It will not be easy to convince our colleagues to reform a process that often helps ensure their re-election."[14] This is a sorry commentary on the quality and values of our legislators. Because of it, we have one final recommendation here: Identify all the elected officials at both the national and state levels who oppose reforming the redistricting process. Then, vote the rascals out!

4. Convene town halls and community discussions about issues of concern to citizens and the role of government in America's future.

Neutral entities such as institutions of higher education and local civic organizations need to be encouraged to take the lead in convening forums in local communities on civic and political topics of interest, such as healthcare, energy, and immigration. These discussions should be on-going and not tied to an election cycle, an advocacy group's position, or a politician's agenda.

Town halls and community listening tours have become the stock-in-trade for politicians during campaign seasons and now even between campaigns. These meetings are valuable for both candidate and community because they create the opportunity for an exchange of information. They do not, however, provide much in terms of new knowledge creation because they tend to reinforce preexisting biases due to their political and partisan nature.

Independently convened town halls or community discussions featuring speakers with a diversity of opinions on a topic or a panel with a range of information provide interested citizens with the chance to get unfiltered ideas and information. They can then make their minds up themselves—not just about who to vote for at election time but on the issues that matter year-round. Numerous organizations, such as the Foreign Relations Council, the New America Foundation, and the Chicago Council on Global Affairs, provide citizens with this type of access and opportunity.

The Chicago Council of Global Affairs takes it one step further. It picks a class of emerging leaders and has them work on a project for 2 years. In the first year, they examine timely issues, such as the global economy and climate change. In the second year, the class prepares and presents a report on the most pressing global challenge confronting Chicago and the Midwest.

SCOPE (Sarasota County Actively Plans for Excellence) takes it one step further as well. SCOPE's mission is to connect and inspire citizens to create a better community. It was established in 2001 as a community-wide project to bring people together to discuss issues related to Sarasota County's future and what it will take to make it a good place to work, live, and raise a family. Since its establishment, SCOPE has issued five Community Report Cards and also produced a variety of reports on topics such as affordable housing and school dropout that have prompted community initiatives to respond to them.

To repeat, there are numerous examples of community-sponsored initiatives. In a society where we are becoming more and more isolated from one another and more and more dependent on the electronic media for our news on civic and community issues, there needs to be many more community-sponsored initiatives. We need to expand their scope substantially—not just to build knowledge but also to rebuild an appreciation of what it means to be a concerned and involved citizen.

13 | Bowling Together

"Jesus was a community organizer."
Popular T-shirt during the 2008
presidential election campaign

Norman Rockwell was an artist who had a unique gift for capturing and reflecting the American experience. He depicted perfectly those small and large social events that mattered to all Americans—Thanksgiving dinner, a visit to the doctor, a baseball game.

During his life, Rockwell painted more than 570 magazine covers for *The Saturday Evening Post* and *Look*, both of which are long gone. Rockwell's most famous paintings were the four freedoms that he did for the *Post* during World War II:

- Freedom of speech and expression
- Freedom to worship
- Freedom from want
- Freedom from fear

In the new millennium, there are four freedoms that can be added to that list:

- The freedom to tweet
- The freedom to text
- The freedom to Facebook
- The freedom to TiVo

Americans today live in electric currents not brushstrokes. Ironically, while we enjoy greater connectivity, we have greater disconnectedness. Chat rooms and chatter appear to have replaced meaningful social interaction and communications.

NO LEAGUE OF OUR OWN

It seems that in addition to political divides, there's something else that divides us from one another—who we are as Americans and what we are becoming as a society. That's not just our opinion. Robert Putnam, professor of public policy at Harvard, did the seminal research on this and reported it in his book with the evocative title, *Bowling Alone* published in 2000.[1]

In a much-discussed *Journal of Democracy* article with the same title as his book, Putnam observed that ". . . more Americans are bowling today than ever before but bowling in organized leagues has plummeted. Between 1980 and 1993, the total number of bowlers increased by 10 percent, while league bowling decreased by 40 percent. The rise of solo bowling threatens the livelihood of bowling proprietors . . . The broader social significance, however, lies in the social interaction and the occasional civic conversations over beer and pizza that solo bowlers forego . . . bowling teams illustrate yet another vanishing form of social capital."[2]

Social capital binds us together and helps us to engage collaboratively and constructively in activities and areas that matter to us. Based upon his research, Putnam concluded that America has experienced a precipitous decline in its social capital over the past 25 years: "For the first two-thirds of the twentieth century a powerful tide bore Americans into ever deeper engagement in the life of their communities, but a few decades ago—silently, without warning—that tide reversed and we were overtaken by a dangerous rip current."

Where has that rip current caused us to lose social capital? Everywhere! Putnam looked at seven measures of social capital: (1) political participation, (2) civic participation, (3) religious participation, (4) workplace networks, (5) informal networks, (6) mutual trust and honesty, and (7) altruism and volunteering. His conclusion was that we have lost capital in them all.

No matter whether it's in turnout rates for elections (see Chapter 12), attendance at church, membership in groups like the Chamber of Commerce, volunteerism, or charitable giving, our social capital has been going down the gurgler. Putnam found four exceptions to this significant drop over the past 3 decades: (1) increased volunteerism among youth, (2) the growth in telecommunications, (3) evangelical conservative grassroots involvement, and (4) self-help support.

Does social capital matter? Putnam makes a persuasive case that it does because social capital

- Makes collective problems easier to resolve because of less opposition, resulting in improved social environments such as safer neighborhoods.

- Makes business transactions easier because of trust resulting in less time and money enforcing contracts.

- Widens the awareness of our mutual connectivity improving the quality of civic and democratic institutions.

- Increases the flow of information improving our education and economic production.

- Increases our health and happiness through both psychological and biological processes which require human contact.

Social capital does have its downside, however. Think of groups like the KKK, the John Birch society, skinheads, and the Taliban. Information from groups such as these can influence individual deviants who bowl alone to commit targeted acts of violence. Both the killing of the innocent guard at the Washington, D.C., holocaust museum and the killing of Dr. George Tiller, the doctor who ran an abortion clinic in Kansas, were committed by solo bowlers.

Putnam argues that in spite of what we would label the "splinter groups/elites" of social capitalists, his empirical evidence suggests that social capital, freedom, and equality are mutually reinforcing. We accept that argument on its face because it coincides with our worldview. Each of us has our hardened beliefs and the prisms through which we see things—we just need to be aware of them.

STRIKES OR GUTTER BALLS IN THE TWENTY-FIRST CENTURY?

The overriding question is where do we stand today in terms of social capital. How have we been bowling in the first decade of this new century?

We have not seen any studies that update Putnam's research. But, we believe we know the answer and don't need a study to confirm it. Consider the following:

- The 2000 presidential election. The Florida "butterfly ballot" fiasco and the Supreme Court's intervention. Capital builder or capital destroyer?

- Millions of jobs lost and a decline in real wages for the blue-collar and middle-class worker. Capital builder or capital destroyer?

- Hundreds of thousands of jobs and businesses off-shored. Capital builder or capital destroyer?

- The market meltdown of 2008. Capital builder or capital destroyer?

- The home foreclosure crisis. Capital builder or capital destroyer?

- 47 million people without health insurance. Capital builder or capital destroyer?

- Bailing out General Motors and Chrysler, including the closing of thousands of dealerships in small towns and communities across the country. Capital builder or capital destroyer?

The list goes on. As Bob Dylan would put it, you don't need a weatherman to know which way the wind is blowing. Or, as we would put it, an ill wind blows no good and builds no social capital.

The inevitable conclusion must be that America's social capital account is in much worse shape than it was when Putnam completed his research. There have been far too many withdrawals and not enough deposits. America's social capital account is not bankrupt, but it is seriously overdrawn. As a result, it is in need of a major bailout.

We don't have the social scientist's scalpel or the time to pinpoint with precision the factors that have negatively impacted our social capital in recent years. However, based upon selected information and informed intuition, we nominate the following as major candidates for consideration: rampant individualism, random socialization, Internet interference, organizational obsolescence/irrelevance, evangelical political involvement, and heightened fear/anxiety.

Rampant Individualism

The end of the 1970s was a period of rampant inflation, high interest rates, and great uncertainty. It still, however, resembled the old social order. Then, in 1980, Ronald Reagan was elected and ushered in a new era of individualism that continues to this day. The priority was placed on individual opportunity and achievement as opposed to collective effort. The me generation was upon us.

Reagan broke up the air traffic controllers union, proclaimed big government the problem, and called for cuts or elimination of domestic social programs. Bill Clinton, in conjunction with the Republicans, instituted welfare reform.

The jury is still very much out on whether welfare reform was good or bad, and it may change its verdict based upon the new and altered state of the American economy. The one conclusion that can be reached is that the reform radically changed the nature of the social safety net and placed responsibility on the individual as opposed to society.

George W. Bush began his administration with some "compassionate conservative" concepts such as faith-based initiatives and "No Child Left Behind." But after 9/11, his attention and that of his administration focused almost entirely on security and national defense. Faith-based initiatives floundered. "No Child" became an underfunded mandate and a point of contentious debate within the educational community. Community action agencies, the social safety net organizations in 1,000 communities and all 50 states across the country, were routinely zeroed out of the budget that President Bush presented to Congress each year.

After 9/11, President Bush could have called upon the nation to come together in unity and establish some common social purpose. Instead, he encouraged the nation's citizens to go out and buy something and placed the emphasis on the creation of an ownership society. An ownership society certainly sounded good. However, due to the lack and nonenforcement of regulations and exploitative lending practices, people got loans they shouldn't have at terms that never should have been offered. The ownership society became the onerous society—a society in which capital of all forms (social, financial, and human) has been reduced or destroyed. In the end, unconstrained capitalism and rampant and unrestrained individualism collided at a very high cost.

Random Socialization

In his best seller, *The Medium Is the Massage*, Marshall McLuhan predicted that the emerging media (at the time, television) would become a primary socializing agent.[3] Putnam's findings confirm that McLuhan's crystal ball was a good one.

Prior to the emergence of the electronic media, the primary socializing agents were family, school, church, and community. Working in combination and in an admittedly simpler time, these agents built social capital in consistently aligned and mutually reinforcing ways.

In contrast today, television is controlled by the individual with the remote—unstructured and unsupervised. Cable. Digital. High definition. 500 channels. Push the button. Find what appeals you. Turn on. Tune out. Become what you watch. Spend more time alone.

Internet Interference

Television was thought to be an inhibitor of social capital development. Well, you ain't seen nothing yet. Enter the Internet and the opportunities become boundless. The Internet was emerging as a social factor in larger society when Putnam did his study. It had gained prominence and significant utilization in the business and academic worlds but had made lesser inroads with the lay users. In spite of this, Putman forecast that it would be a significant future influencer of social capital.

One can only wonder what Putnam would find if he were to replicate his study today. It seems to us that the Internet has 10 times, 100 times the potential to be a social capital destroyer as television. The Internet is television on steroids.

The younger generation gets its news, watches TV shows, surfs, downloads games, and communicates—all using the Internet. These are essentially singular activities—even the exchange of e-mails, text messages, or tweets. They emanate from one person and can be done in isolated solitude—one singular sensation. As with television, the time that could be spent in this splendid isolation is only restricted by the need to sleep.

It's not that the Internet can't be used to build social capital—it can. Probably the most innovative—and certainly the best-known—application was in the Obama for President Campaign. The Obama team used the Internet, in conjunction with community organizing tactics, to expand its support base exponentially by implementing a citizen- and community-centered campaign approach. The result was 7 million members conversing online and half a billion in contributions over Obama's 21-month campaign for the presidency. That's a lot of capital—social, political, and financial.

It could be argued that the Internet is the ultimate social capital tool. The Internet has spawned a number of applications for "social networking." Facebook, MySpace, Plaxo, LinkedIn, Twitter. Each of these applications allows people to connect electronically. The connection can be made easily, frequently, and at a low cost in terms of time and dollars spent. The question is whether these apps make us more connected in human terms and build social capital. We believe the answer is "not yet."

In fact, they create the potential for social entropy. We could mistake constant contact with authentic communication. We could perceive the state of virtual connectedness as the existence of a meaningful connection. We could substitute superficial and shallow exchanges for legitimate involvement. Compare a handshake or a hug to a text message or tweet. We could be sacrificing part of our humanity on technology's cross.

Do the social networking sites have the potential to be used for the development of social capital? Absolutely. We have more to say on that later in this chapter.

Organizational Obsolescence/Irrelevance

Beginning in the early 1980s, American companies began an endless cycle of downsizing. Each round of downsizing was supposed to be the last, but it wasn't. So, by the time we got to the 1990s, something had to give. That something wasn't downsizing. The reduction of the employee workforce was given a new name—*reengineering*. Downsizing accelerated under a euphemistic label that sounded more scientific and humane than "laying off," "firing," or "terminating."

At the same time this was going on, America continued to become a place that made money by doing transactions and not by making things. All the things that American companies used to make here were made elsewhere at lower labor costs—then shipped back here so that we could buy them. They cost a little less. But of course, American workers were out of jobs or earning less. That was the trade-off. Doesn't sound like much of a trade-off to us.

The virtual company became the new buzz word and a reality. You didn't have to employ anyone full-time. You just got out your cell phone and your Rolodex, placed the calls, assembled the folks to put up the big top, held the circus, took the tent down, and then moved on to the next town. Consultants told people to thrive on being "free agents." Diversify and build up your "skill sets." Be your own boss. Create your own opportunities. Relish your independence. *Freedom* is just another word for nothing left to lose.

There's only one problem. Companies were one of the primary places in which people built communities and created social capital. They gave workers some of the sense of self-respect we all need. It's where workers satisfied some of their affiliation needs. People used to bleed IBM blue, International Harvester red, or John Deere green—no longer.

In America today, because of the financial crisis of 2008, the concept of organization as it was traditionally known is becoming increasingly more obsolescent or irrelevant. Many of the companies that had survived up to this point went out of business or took bankruptcy. Many of those that didn't were downsizing (again), cutting salaries, and gaining concessions from employees so they could keep their doors open. In response, workers who were still hanging on were tightening their belts and their resolves. They were just happy to have a job and a paycheck—to be able to say in the words of another Bob Dylan song, "It's all right, Ma, I'm only bleeding."

Evangelical Political Involvement

Putnam cites evangelical political involvement as one of the four areas in which new social capital was being built when he did his study. Beginning in the mid-1990s and then proceeding into the general elections of 2000 and 2004, the evangelicals bonded together to demonstrate that the concept of separation of church and state was not as American as motherhood and apple pie.

They proved, instead, that the integration of social capital and political capital could be a winning combination. Joined by the Catholic Church which added its social capital congregation to the mix in the 2004 general election (and again in 2008 but to a lesser extent), the evangelicals were one of the primary reasons for George W. Bush's victory over John Kerry that year. Religious dogma (or at least a part of it) became political dogma.

Is evangelical political involvement a force for good or evil in the battle to restore community? It all depends on who is looking at it and what is meant by *community*. The one thing that is certain is that there is, and will be, a divided opinion on this issue—and, as Miles Maxim goes, "where you stand depends on where you sit."

If that seat is in the evangelical pew, the answer would be most assuredly "yes." If you worship in another congregation, are nondenominational or agnostic, the answer would most likely be "no." Or, as the rational pragmatist might say, it all depends, and time will tell. Our opinion is that the evangelical's political involvement up to now has been more harmful than beneficial to the broad concept of a shared community in the United States and worldwide and also to the Republican Party as it exists today.

Heightened Fear and Anxiety

After 9/11, everyone felt some degree of fear and anxiety. But the bulk of it was on the coasts and in the major cities. After the meltdowns of

2008 and the continued economic decline in 2009, fear and anxiety were almost everywhere and in almost everyone at dangerous levels entering 2010.

If there were a fear and anxiety threat warning level as there is for national security, it would be "red," meaning a large number of Americans are concerned about their own ability to survive. Being in this condition makes it hard to think about building social capital.

THE NEED AND OPPORTUNITY FOR POSITIVE POPULISM

Combined, these factors have strained and not strengthened our social fabric. They have moved the nation and its citizens further apart, rather than bringing us closer together.

The one exception was the reaction we had to the bailout that included the payment of huge and exorbitant bonuses to the same Wall Street crowd who had caused the collapse of the financial system. We rose up in a national outcry and expressed our populist outrage at something that was too egregious.

Up until that time, we suffered in silence. We Americans tend to be stoic. But too much was too much. This was the straw that broke the camel's back. It was almost as if Peter Finch had been channeled from the 1976 movie *Network* to admonish the American public to "Go to the window and shout as loud as you can: 'I'm mad as hell, and I'm *not* going to take it anymore.'"

We had had and heard enough and were moving from fear and anxiety toward fear and loathing. We shouted our objections, and Washington responded. *Power to the people* might be taking on some meaning again.

Indeed, the nation may be poised for an era of new populism. We've had populist movements throughout our history. Most of the time, they've been reflected in third-party movements such as the Progressive Party of 1912 headed by Theodore Roosevelt, Robert La Follette's Progressive Party of 1924, and Huey Long's Share Our Wealth movement launched near the beginning of the Great Depression. The most recent significant populist third-party candidacy was that of Ross

Perot in the economic tough times of 1992 and 1996. In 2010, the tea partiers appear to be a third-party movement that is coalescing to try to gain control of the Republican party. If that occurs, there is a real question about what it will mean for the American two-party system as we have come to know it.

These are the circumstances. Economic times are tough and getting tougher. People are on edge. Populism presents both an opportunity and a threat. The threat is that populism can be used for purely political purposes and to turn groups against each other. The opportunity is for *positive populism*.

Positive populism is based on the understanding that the answer to America's future lies in its citizens and not in Washington, D.C., or the Fortune 500. Positive populism begins with the recognition that we are all in this together—whether you are at the top or the bottom of the heap, you're still part of it.

Given this recognition and understanding, positive populism can be used to channel and harness the energy and talents we all have by getting more involved and working together on issues that are most relevant and important to the American community at all levels. Positive populism compels engagement in the search for solutions instead of the placing of blame. Positive populism enables the replenishment of our social capital accounts.

RENEWING SOCIAL CAPITAL RECOMMENDATIONS

Barack Obama is the nation's new bowler in chief. He's not that good a bowler, as he proved during the Pennsylvania primary when he bowled a 37 and threw many gutter balls. He is committed to getting better, however, as he demonstrated when he rolled a 129 once he could practice in the White House bowling lanes.

We believe that President Obama wants to get better, not because it's that important to him as an individual (although having seen him on the basketball court, we're certain he has a competitive streak), but because he realizes it is important to us as a country. President Obama wants to unify the nation. He understands that one of the ways to do this is to get Americans bowling together again—to get us talking in meaningful ways and involved in working cooperatively on issues that matter.

Obama demonstrated that this is not a partisan effort on his part when he went down to Texas A&M in October 2009 and spoke with President George Bush, the elder, at the Points of Light meeting there. President Bush and President Obama were both eloquent in making the case for civic engagement and social capital development. Together, these two leaders proved that this is not a Democratic issue or a Republican issue. It is an American issue. This issue must be addressed through a shared venture or enterprise between the institutions of our society and all of us working together collaboratively on concerns and matters that are of relevance for building community.

We have provided recommendations for public sector and private sector involvement and citizen political engagement in Chapters 10, 11, and 12 of this book. In this chapter, we round out our recommendations by making the following primary and subsidiary social engagement recommendations that can be employed to build America's "social capital":

Social Capital Primary Recommendations

1. Articulate a social compact for the twenty first century.
2. Establish "Interdependence Day" as a national holiday for celebrating our connectedness as citizens.
3. Require mandatory national service for all youth 18–21.

Social Capital Subsidiary Recommendations

4. Invest in activities that blend community economic development (CED) and community building.
5. Increase support for those organizations that are focused on community service and volunteerism.
6. Exploit the power and potential of the Internet for development of social capital and community building.
7. Stimulate the private sector's participation in community-building activities.
8. Encourage interdenominational, faith-based initiatives directed at enhanced communications and community problem solving.

Our primary recommendations follow. The subsidiary recommendations are in the Appendix.

1. Articulate a social compact for the twenty-first century.

The social compact has always been at the heart of American democracy. The compact is framed by the Declaration of Independence and the Constitution but is also bracketed by the involvement and relationship of government in citizens' lives.

The American social compact has evolved over time in response to attitudinal, economic, and societal conditions and values. In the twentieth century, the compact evolved as follows:

- 1900–1930: Emphasis on rugged individualism
- 1930–1945: Emphasis on creating a social safety net
- 1945–1965: Emphasis on creating social stability and normalcy
- 1965–1980: Emphasis on equality and extension of the social safety net
- 1980–2010: Emphasis on individual and organizational achievement

We are a decade into the twenty-first century and given the events of the past 2 years, the compact definitely warrants revisiting.

The social compact for the twenty-first century should be developed by a citizens' committee. That committee should be drawn from a broad cross-section of society. The composition should be similar to that of the National Global Competitiveness Commission. However, it should also be structured to reflect the diversity that makes up America in terms of demographic factors, such as age, ethnicity, and religion, as well as geographic factors, such as rural and urban locations and regions of the country.

The committee should be charged with reviewing the evolution and current status of America's social compact and developing a recommended social compact that responds to contemporary times and factors. At a minimum, that compact should address the roles of government, business, free enterprise, and that of the individual. It should also address the interface of democracy, capitalism, and social justice. The compact should identify key requirements for creating the social capital that is necessary to move America and its citizens forward.

The compact should be apolitical. It should be developed based upon hearings held across the country. It should be prepared as a reference document of nonpartisan "best thinking" provided to inform future discussions and actions related to social capital development. It should serve as a companion to the competitive advantage strategic plan drafted by the National Global Competitiveness Commission.

2. Establish "Interdependence Day" as a national holiday for celebrating our connectedness as citizens.

American holidays are held primarily to recognize past accomplishments and contributions as opposed to celebrating the present and future. We're suggesting the addition of *Interdependence Day* as a federal holiday to be held on either July 5 or on the day after Thanksgiving. This holiday should focus on who we are as a nation and recognize what we are becoming. The Statue of Liberty should be made central to this holiday. E pluribus unum should be its theme.

America is a nation of immigrants and continues to be so. The United States remains a unique vessel of being and becoming. This day should be dedicated to celebrating the nation's diversity, progress that has been made, and the opportunities and challenges ahead. In 2009, the Statue of Liberty reopened certain viewing areas, and Ellis Island opened a new visitors' center. Interdependence Day could take these symbols in combination with others from around the country that demonstrate our common humanity and elevate the importance of what brings us together.

Our interdependence is reflected in many ways from business to the arts. It has probably never been more vividly portrayed than in the mass and spontaneous outburst at the rally in Chicago's Grant Park on November 4, 2008, when Barack Obama won the presidency. How ironic that this scene could take place 40 years later on the same site as the confrontation between the Chicago police and protesters. The Days of Rage became the Days of Engage.

Interdependence Day is one way of beginning to deal with the red and blue divide by building bridges and a shared community of choice. That which we celebrate can bind us together. That which we ignore can keep us apart.

3. *Require mandatory national service for all youth 18–21.*

In 1960, President John F. Kennedy famously said, "Ask not what your country can do for you; ask what you can do for your country." In 1964, President Lyndon Baines Johnson called upon us to build a "Great Society." Note that President Johnson used the word "society" and not "country." In the mid-1970s, President Jimmy Carter asked that we sacrifice by reducing our gas consumption.

Since the early 1980s and until recently, requests for shared commitments or sacrifices have not been too visible on the country's radar screen. Until recently, the national refrain appears to have been "Ask what you can do for yourself." Service to country seemed to belong to those in the armed forces, the well off, or the do-gooders.

We are not advocating that the draft be reinstated. But some type of national service should be made mandatory. The service could take one of many forms, for example, military, civic, or education.

John McCain and Barack Obama both expressed a desire for more Americans to be engaged in national service when they shared the stage at Columbia University at a forum commemorating the seventh anniversary of the 9/11 attacks. Jim Lehrer spoke most eloquently on this topic.

As the commencement speaker at Harvard University in 2006, Mr. Lehrer stated, "I have come with only one major commencement-like point to make . . . I believe we should consider adapting some form of national service. No, not a return to the military draft, something entirely different, and completely new for us. National service in its fullest meaning." Jim proceeded to recall the lessons he learned about life and himself in the diverse company of his fellow marines during his 3 years of service. He then observed why he felt national service was so necessary:

". . . I have never seen us more disconnected from each other than we are right now . . . Our racial, cultural and religious differences, always our great strength, have become an instrument in our great disconnection. Our growing economic differences . . . are feeding this.

Our politics at the moment actually seem to be encouraging it; and our otherwise terrific explosion in new media outlets for information and debate . . . I believe what we need is a new, hard real-world dose of shared experience." [4]

We couldn't say it any better. The Serve America Act as well as service learning projects for students are starting to move us in the right direction. But overall service still remains somebody else's business. We need to make it the nation's business—service to country and our fellow citizens. That is the measure of true patriotism. It is not about waving the flag or pledging allegiance. It is about standing up and doing what is required to make America the very best it can be.

14 | The Renewal Model

"Genius is 1 percent inspiration and 99 percent perspiration."
Thomas Edison

THE AMERICAN DREAM WAS BORN OUT OF GREAT IDEAS. BUT IT WAS realized through blood, sweat, and tears shed over a sustained period of time. Renewing it demands no less. And, as we've written in the earlier chapters of this book, requires:

- Informed and involved citizens
- A twenty-first-century competitive advantage strategy for the nation
- Policies and programs that create jobs, rejuvenate the middle class, reignite the manufacturing sector, unleash the potential of small businesses and entrepreneurs, and ensure a vital news media
- Government redirection
- Business redirection
- Working together in a shared venture to revitalize all aspects of America and the American Dream

These are big ideas. They provide a blueprint.

THE RENEWAL COMPONENTS

Implementing that blueprint requires three essential components: leadership, organizational, and individual renewal. This renewal engaged in across the board and around the country will rebuild all the forms of American Dream capital: individual capital, social capital, economic capital, intellectual capital, organizational capital, community capital, spiritual capital, and institutional capital.

As depicted in the illustration that follows, these three components work individually and in combination to create the Renewal Model.

Figure 14.1: The Renewal Model

As the model implies, American renewal will require a self-initiated effort, rather than a dictated one. It will require an integrated effort, rather than an isolated one. It will require a shared enterprise, rather than an independent one. In combination, these efforts will renew the American Dream. It all starts with leadership.

LEADERSHIP RENEWAL

Leadership can take two primary forms: (1) institutional (working within an existing organization to drive change) or (2) entrepreneurial (starting a new organization to create change). There are different requirements depending on whether an organization is just starting up or well established. The principles of leadership, however, are essentially the same for both.

One of our favorite leadership models is Harvard Business School Professor John Kotter's 8-Step Change Model.[1] The model has been implemented successfully by countless organizations since he introduced it back in 1995. The eight steps that make up the model (paraphrased somewhat below) are especially relevant for leaders today who need—and want—to facilitate major change:

1. Create a sense of urgency

2. Form a powerful coalition to direct the change process

3. Create an appropriate vision for the change

4. Communicate the vision broadly

5. Empower individuals and remove obstacles

6. Create short-term wins

7. Build on the change

8. Anchor the changes in the corporate culture

Jack Welch's accomplishments as the leader of General Electric (GE) are legendary. During his tenure, he kept the organization in a continuous state of reinvention and renewal. His motto could have been "If it ain't broke, break it."

Whether you love or hate Jack, GE was extremely profitable early in his tenure. He could have sat on his laurels. Instead, he drove the business into new areas. His philosophy was to be in the top three in an industry or not be in it at all. GE divested itself of units that didn't meet that criterion. Welch also established tiger teams comprised of specially trained company managers and employees who would swoop into a business unit that was not performing effectively and develop a plan to turn it around almost overnight.

With the assistance of Noel Tichy, who left the University of Michigan for 2 years to facilitate the process, Welch completely revamped GE's Leadership Development Center to make it the envy and model for the business world. Together, Welch and Tichy transformed GE's corporate university into an action-learning platform for change. Through the center, they trained the top 10,000 GE leaders to teach and lead change and implemented and launched *Work-Out,* a program in which line managers ran their own workshops on change.

Welch put GE into the change and renewal business. He understood that the status quo was the enemy and that standing still in business was moving backward.

Alan Mulally is CEO of Ford Motor Company—the only one of the Detroit Big Three automakers that didn't declare bankruptcy or take bailout money. For that alone, President Obama should award Mulally the Citizens and Taxpayers Medal of Honor. Mulally was able to maintain Ford's independence because he had the strong support of the Ford family and because of the actions that he took to renew and reinvent Ford from the time that he arrived on the scene at Ford from Boeing Corporation.

Mulally has done significant restructuring and streamlining of Ford since he joined the company in 2006. He sold off brands like Land Rover, Jaguar, and Aston. He cut vehicle models from 93 to fewer than 20. Since 2005, Ford has eliminated 50,000 jobs and shut 17 plants.

In late 2006, Mulally raised $23 billion by mortgaging much of what the company owned, including vehicle stocks and factories. This capital allowed the firm to survive the severe downturn and not to have to go to Washington with hat in hand. Mulally doesn't apologize for the cost-cutting measures. He says, "You have to look at the world the way it really is and then deal with it. I've done that a number of times, both at Boeing and here." [2]

George Muñoz is not nearly as well known as Mulally or Welch. The feat he accomplished, however, after being appointed the CEO and president of the Overseas Private Investment Corporation (OPIC) by Bill Clinton in 1997, is also quite impressive as an example of renewal leadership.

When Muñoz took the helm of OPIC, the agency's usefulness was being questioned in Congress. In fact, the House of Representatives had voted to abolish the agency. But Muñoz saw OPIC differently and went out to prove it.

He began by showing how OPIC could be a useful economic tool to create jobs in this country by helping U.S. companies grow beyond our borders. OPIC became the largest producer of political risk insurance for U.S. private sector investments in the emerging market countries at no cost to the taxpayer. Muñoz also worked to renew OPIC by making it a "high-performance organization," with such high levels of efficiency and productivity that OPIC was able to operate with user fees at no cost to the taxpayer. Some of the same leadership planning and execution techniques we are recommending in this book were put to work at OPIC. *The New York Times* paid a tribute to Muñoz and the employees at OPIC in a news report titled, "Development Agency's Survival Tale":

> *"How OPIC went from being the symbol for a Republican crusade against government subsidies to being the champion of American entrepreneurs in the global economy is also a story of how the agency's new, politically astute leadership used a grass-roots campaign to translate its business projects and policy goals into something that all lawmakers understand: jobs."* [3]

Frank Islam also had to renew the QSS Group, Inc. The Group started as a one-employee business eligible for government SBA assistance and grew to become a 2,000-person firm with no government safety net. When the QSS Group graduated from the SBA program in 2001, it was required to enter full and open competition for future business. Over 90 percent of the companies that graduate from this program don't make this transition successfully. The QSS Group did.

In large measure, that was because of Frank's leadership style that came from his humble background. When the Group graduated, he reinforced that being attentive to customers and employees alike, with a desire to serve, were to remain the driving forces for his firm. Frank insisted that all employees deserved to be treated with dignity and respect. As Frank repositioned and renewed the business, he did not leave his employees behind. Quite the contrary, he gave everyone the authority (and corresponding responsibility) to make decisions as if it were their company. His only instruction was to put the customer first.

That "ownership" feeling was made real for many of the employees. As a result, the QSS Group continued to grow and to flourish until the company was sold to Perot Systems in 2007.

We define *leadership renewal* as follows:

> *Establishing the vision, values, and strong strategic and operational focus that enables the organization to create a sustainable competitive advantage and to succeed in the future.*

Are there special things that a leader should do to accomplish this in difficult and chaotic times such as these? Unfortunately, there's no textbook answer on this because we are in uncharted water. However, based upon our own experience as executives and leaders and a review of much of the advice that has been written for, and by, leaders since the economic collapse of 2008, we offer the following guidelines:

1. *Ask, What Would Peter Say?* The Peter is Peter Drucker, probably the most influential management thinker of all time.[4] Based on what we've read, we're pretty sure he would say three things: (1) management should be a profession, and its responsibility is to look after the long-term health of the organization—both social and financial, (2) workers need to be motivated, not controlled—they need intrinsic as well as extrinsic rewards, and (3) nonprofits are an essential part of a healthy society in which businesses can thrive. They should be cultivated and supported financially.

2. *Calibrate Your Approach.* Each organization's circumstance is unique. Leaders need to assess their own situation thoroughly in order to determine the correct course for their organization: (1) transition—modest change and incremental adjustments, (2) turnaround—major change, or (3) transformation—total reconstruction of the business model.

3. *Play to Your Strengths.* Leaders have their own personal styles and strengths. Leaders need to know theirs and use it to their advantage. For example, flamboyant Gordon Bethune turned around Continental Airlines in the mid-1990s and made it an industry award winner. In 2004, Bethune was succeeded by Larry Kellner. Kellner had a much different and more subdued

style than Bethune. But he still managed to maintain Continental's position as an industry leader. In the 1980s, flamboyant Lee Iacocca turned Chrysler around while the more taciturn Donald Peterson did the same at Ford. They each knew how to play to their strengths.

4. *Pay Attention to the Basics.* Even though many organizations lost sight of it during the years of easy credit and easy money, there is a discipline to management. The organization should always be managed efficiently, effectively, and profitably. Cash and capital reserves should be king. In trying times, leaders need to pay greater attention than ever before to the discipline of management.

5. *Pay Attention to Your Core Group.* The core group is that small team (usually four–eight individuals) of executives who make implementing the vision and agenda possible. They work with upper and middle managers in the organization to keep them motivated and enable them to cope with the stress related to crisis.

6. *Keep Your Eye on the Ball.* The ball for all organizations—public, private, and nonprofit—should be their customers. Most organizations that get into trouble have failed to realize this and as a result, either deliver lousy products and/or services or implement policies and programs that do not relate to their customers' needs. Leaders need to ensure that everything the organization does is customer-centered, regardless of who the customer is.

7. *Think Inside the Circle.* One of the most hackneyed organizational admonitions is "think outside the box." We certainly support non-traditional thinking, but we feel it's even more important for leaders to get their organizations to "think inside the circle." This involves identifying the critical few priorities or goal areas for the organization and then getting everyone to focus on them obsessively. If an "outside the box" idea makes it to the finals, it gets converted to reality by "thinking inside the circle."

8. *Convey Confidence.* Consumer confidence in 2009 was down as was employee confidence. Employees and citizens look to their

leaders for reassurance, a sense of security, and anxiety reduction. Leaders need to project cautious and realistic optimism in order to avoid fear pandemics. An old saying goes, "If you can keep your head while those around you are losing theirs, then you'll be the boss."

9. *Be a Risk Taker but Manage Risk.* One of the natural tendencies in uncertain times is to hunker down. Leaders need to realize that uncertain times can create new opportunities. They need to position the organization to take advantage of those opportunities. At the same time, the appropriate level of due diligence needs to be done before action is taken and mechanisms need to be put into place to manage the potential downside. There are too many recent examples of too much risk-taking and not enough risk management (e.g., Bank of America's acquisition of Merrill Lynch).

10. *Communicate Values and a Future Vision.* There has been enormous erosion in public trust and employee loyalty. To counteract this, leaders need to communicate a positive set of values and vision that people can believe in—*really* believe in. This will enable them to take positive actions. Fear can lead to pessimism and paralysis. Anger can lead to hostility and negative reactions that impede progress and productivity. Leaders need to demonstrate through both words and actions that there is a future for the organization and its employees—a future that will help give meaning and worth to employees' lives.

Those aren't the only things that leaders can do to renew an organization. They're just the ones at the top of our list. What is not on our list—and does not belong there—is simple cost-cutting and lay-offs with no defined future strategy. Those are survival, not renewal techniques. We're not saying there is never a time when these unfortunate steps aren't necessary. What we're saying is the steps taken after those steps are the ones that matter in the renewal process. We believe that if a leader follows the guidelines suggested here, it will facilitate positive organizational change and lay the foundation for organizational renewal.

ORGANIZATIONAL RENEWAL

There are many excellent models for organizational renewal. Before we present our favorite, let's ask the question, "What is the purpose of a business?"

This is a question we ask of others frequently. About 90 percent of the time, the answer we get is "to make profits." After people volunteer that answer, we respond, "No, the purpose of a business is to acquire and retain customers." If an organization does that and has the right business model, profits follow.

Without customers, nothing else is possible. Peter Drucker made this point decades ago. He also made the point that although organizations don't do this nearly enough, finding out what customers value may be the most important thing you do. That's why our preferred organizational renewal model is the Customer-Centered Renewal Triangle we present below:

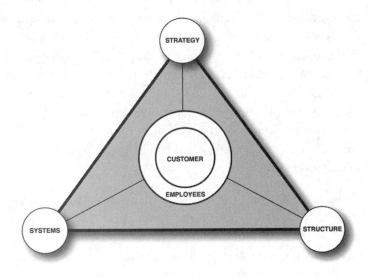

Figure 14.2: Customer-Centered Renewal Triangle

Ed Crego and Peter Schiffrin developed this model in the mid-1990s as a holistic approach for reengineering an organization.[5] Because of its comprehensive nature, it is perfect for implementing *customer-centered organizational renewal*, which we define as:

> *Reinventing the organization from the outside in by realigning the organization's strategy, systems, and employees around employees so they can create total customer value.*

There are seven principles to customer-centered organizational renewal:

1. An organization is a complex organic system comprised of four major interdependent components—strategy, structure, systems (processes), employees—that function together to create value for customers. The components comprise the organization's current *customer value map*.

2. The process of renewal involves realigning those components around the customer.

3. To accomplish this realignment, it is essential to have a clear and precise understanding of customer expectations.

4. The purpose for renewal is to create a state of *total customer value*.

5. For renewal to create maximum benefit for the organization, it must be directly connected to the organization's strategic business purpose.

6. For renewal to have the maximum long-term impact, it must be strategically integrated into all aspects of the organization's way of doing business—policies, procedures, practices, processes, and core value streams such as leadership, human capital, and information technology.

7. Renewal is not a one-time event. It is a continuous process of innovating to surpass customer expectations and empowering employees to manage relationships in a manner that maximizes customer satisfaction and creates customer loyalty.

The customer-centered organizational renewal model is implemented in seven phases:

1. Executive Awareness and Commitment Building
2. Organizational Assessment

3. Renewal Strategy Development

4. Renewal Plan Development

5. Renewal Plan Implementation

6. Organizational Performance

7. Monitoring and Continuous Improvement

The customer-centered model works for business, government, non-profits, you name it—because every organization has a customer. This model has been used successfully with organizations such as Bausch & Lomb, Volkswagen, Jewel Food Stores, and the American Medical Association. The Australian Department of Administrative Services (DAS) proved how well the model can work for a government agency.

At the time DAS implemented the model, it was the largest non-military agency of the Australian federal government comprised of 20 business units and a budget of approximately A$1 billion. The Australian Parliament had decided to commercialize DAS in a move to achieve greater efficiency and effectiveness in government operations. DAS was required to compete with other private and public sector providers for 90 percent of its business.

DAS used the customer-centered model to transform itself. They implemented the model comprehensively across the organization and in each business unit. The implementation included surveying customers, realigning strategies, redesigning systems, and changing processes. The program reawakened DAS's employees.

Five years after the change process was initiated, DAS went from a loss of A$100 million to a profit of A$50 million. Other accomplishments in that time frame included: 6 percent productivity increases annually—more than twice that of other government agencies; and cost savings of more than A$300 million. When Noel Tanzer, secretary and CEO of DAS, commissioned the customer-centered transformational journey, he wasn't certain how it would end up. It ended up extremely well, as evidenced by the fact that Tanzer was knighted by the Queen for his achievements and those of his DAS teammates.

The challenge confronting most businesses and organizations today is greater than cost containment and growth. The need and opportunity is to refine the business model and template for the twenty-first century. This demands thinking about all of the organization's moving parts and relationships and how they work together.

Many organizations won't recognize this and instead will implement incremental responses such as eliminating product lines, downsizing their workforces, asking for concessions from employees, reducing benefits, outsourcing functions, and increasing prices. The sad fact is that this will probably be the predominant response. It is incorrect, insufficient, and inappropriate to ensure the future needs and existence of the organization—whether that organization is public, private, for-profit, or nonprofit.

When it comes to true organizational renewal, many will be called but few will be chosen. Those leaders and organizations that renew themselves by defining their primary customer(s) correctly and reinventing themselves around those customers will be in that select group of the chosen ones.

INDIVIDUAL RENEWAL

As Americans, we engage in individual acts of renewal all the time ranging from religious activities to working out at the gym. There are big acts of renewal like that of David Duval. Only a golf fan would be familiar with David Duval's story, but it's a great example of individual renewal.

In 1999, David Duval was the number-one golfer in the world. He and Tiger Woods held specially scheduled and televised one-on-one shootouts. After that, Duval's game fell apart and he sank to as low as 882 in the rankings of professional golfers. By 2009, it appeared Duval's career as a top competitor was over. Then came the U.S. Open at Bethpage Black in June of 2009. Duval tied for second two shots behind the winner and was back. But it wasn't an easy journey.

Part of the journey for Duval was rediscovery. After consulting with many of the top golf teaching professionals and getting nowhere, Duval sought out Puggy Blackmon, his college coach from Georgia Tech. Blackmon examined Duval's swing and worked with him to re-create his old swing. Duval did exactly that, but it took 4 years to get to the near win at Bethpage Black. What sustained Duval over that time period was his confidence and determination. As he said, "I knew it would come." Something else that sustained him was his new wife Susie. Coach Blackmon said of her, "If David searched the whole world over, he couldn't find a better soul mate."[6]

David Duval redeemed himself. Dan McAdams, professor at Northwestern University, tells us that the redemptive life is characteristically American. A redemptive life is one in which a person begins life relatively blessed, suffers or stumbles, and then reestablishes one's self and does good things to make life better for the next generation and those in need.[7] If you look at the life of Senator Ted Kennedy, one of the most respected politicians in history, you'll see a great example of someone who went through this process. Senator Kennedy went from the scandal of Chappaquiddick and drinking to becoming one of the most revered and respected public servants in recent history.[8]

For the American Dream to flourish—and the nation to regain its competitive advantage and spirit—the majority of us will have to engage in some level of individual renewal. Individual renewal is what will enable us to perform those acts—both personal and at work—that promote the renewal of America. We define *individual renewal* as:

> *Developing the mental discipline, personal competence, and empathy to be a peak performer and to collaborate with others to ensure that organizational goals are accomplished successfully.*

What is required for that form of individual renewal and to make that kind of contribution? A large part of it is proper preparation. This requires discovering your "inner citizen" and getting into "citizen shape."

As with leadership, there is no single textbook or reference manual on how to do this. But, based on our own experiences and advice from others, here are the favorite techniques that we try to practice:

1. *Take Your Own Stress Test.* There are many new books on the market designed to help individuals assess their own stress level and develop strategies to deal with it. Here's a simple approach that psychologists have been using for years. Imagine there is a circle

comprised of four equally sized quadrants with the following labels: Love Given. Love Received. Play. Work. If you are relatively content and the quadrants are approximately the same size, you will probably have minimal stress in your life. If, on the other hand, the quadrants get out of balance, you experience stress. To deal with this, you should develop a personal action plan for the quadrants that are out of balance. For example, if work is taking up too much of your time, set aside a specific time dedicated to play.

2. *Know Yourself.* Each of us has our own personal styles. They influence how we deal with stress and interact with others. One of the most common ways of looking at style is in four major areas: (1) introvert/extrovert, (2) feeler/thinker, (3) big-picture person/ detail person, and (4) present oriented/future oriented. There is no right or wrong style. You probably fit somewhere between each of these areas. In other words, you may feel you are somewhere between being an introvert and extrovert. What does that mean about your approach to communication and problem solving? Remember, we all have blind spots—things we don't know about ourselves and our styles that others do but haven't told us. What do you think your friends would say yours are? If you really want to know, ask them. With that courage comes the insight and potential for greater individual change and renewal.

3. *Understand Others.* It's human nature—we are attracted to people with styles similar to our own. Likewise, research has shown that the larger the gap between a person's preferred style in an area and another person's, the more likely they will have difficulty in interacting. Steps that you can take to flex your style and improve interactions with those with styles different from yours include: understand their style, speak in their terms, look for nonverbal clues (body language), and solicit feedback ("Have I been clear?").

4. *Assess the Facts.* A recent study led by researchers from the Universities of Illinois and Florida found that many people do not even attempt to secure data if it does not agree with their viewpoints.[9] If you want to avoid falling into this category, think of Joe Friday from Dragnet: "All we want are the facts, ma'am." Gather the facts

objectively. Get the facts and nothing but the facts. Then, define and implement your own systematic approach for using those facts in a "rational" manner. One of the most common of such approaches is the six-step problem-solving model: 1. Define the problem. 2. Analyze the facts. 3. Generate alternatives. 4. Make the decision. 5. Test the solution. 6. Evaluate the results.

5. *Be a Fox, Not a Hedgehog.* Even if you employ a systematic process for decision making, getting around your own ideological biases is not easy. Political scientist Philip Tetlock demonstrated this when he evaluated predictions from "experts" in different fields regarding specific events and compared them to the predictions of well-informed lay people. The lay people did just as well as the experts in most instances and outperformed them in many. Tetlock labeled these people as "foxes" because they had an open mind and no preconceived positions. In contrast, the experts were labeled "hedgehogs" because they had strong filters through which they interpreted things.[10] Think about Alan Greenspan or Dennis Kucinich. The message in the bottle here is to think for yourself.

6. *Avoid Thinking Traps.* There are a number of traps that can impede the rational decision-making process in addition to the "hedgehog" trap. Some of the most common include: "the assumption that everyone thinks like you do"; "too much has already been invested to pull the plug"; "we don't need any data to support our decisions." We're that you can add to this list. Do that and then identify the traps which you fall into with the greatest frequency and develop "thinking trap detectors" that you can apply as a screen before making decisions on critical issues.[11]

7. *Embrace Your Irrational Side.* Lately, behavioral economists such as George Akerlof, Robert Shiller, and Cass Sunstein and Richard Thaler have done an excellent job of disabusing us of the "rational man theory" of economics.[12] Akerlof and Shiller based their analysis on the activities leading up to the economic collapse of 2008. We thought the stock and housing markets would go up forever, even when there were strong indicators to the contrary.

We substantially overestimated upside potential and significantly underestimated risk and the consequences on the downside.

8. *Trust Your Gut.* In *Gut Feelings: The Intelligence of the Unconscious*, Gerd Gigerenzer describes how simple "rules of thumb" and the "advanced capacity of the brain" allow individuals to employ intuition to enhance the human interaction and decision-making process.[13] To discover the power of your own intuition, try the following advice: If you're having a problem that you have been working on and can't seem to resolve it, think about it again just before bed. Go to sleep. If you are like many who have tried this, the "eureka" answer will be there as soon as you wake up or as you towel off coming out of the shower. The subconscious mind can rule the conscious.[14]

9. *Simplify.* If you're like most Americans, you have too much clutter in your life. That clutter can range from physical possessions stuck in closets to negative emotions and harmful relations.[15] In economically difficult and stressful times, clutter can become immobilizing and increase stress. That's why this is a time that you should de-clutter and let go of what you don't need or want. Eliminating excess stuff from your life can provide the springboard to address the clutter in other areas.

10. *Maxi-Task.* Over the past decade, Americans have become obsessed with multitasking. Until recently, it seemed that everyone was competing for the multitasker's badge of honor. The award would go the person who could do the most things simultaneously. You shouldn't enter that competition, or if you're already in it, you should withdraw. You should concentrate instead on doing one task at a time, doing it as well as you can until it's completed. A Stanford University study released in August of 2009 showed that the most frequent multitaskers performed extremely poorly in a number of areas including: not focusing as well as nonmultitaskers; being more distractible; being weaker at shifting from one task to another and at organizing information. Most surprisingly, the multitaskers were worse at multitasking than the people who didn't ordinarily multitask.[16]

11. *Be a Brainiac.* A recent Oxford study showed that eating food with high fat content such as hamburgers made an individual sluggish and slowed down decision-making capability.[17] Realizing this, one of the things that you can do to renew yourself mentally is to eat brain food—food that enhances the brain's decision-making power such as those that are high in omega-3 oils. Get enough sleep: Research has shown that sleep deprivation significantly impairs the quality of an individual's reasoning and response time while sleep boosts it. Finally, take control of your information intake. This will enhance your ability to concentrate and focus. Even though we can consume an avalanche of varied data almost instantaneously now, we can only pay careful attention to one thing at a time.

12. *Exercise Caution.* The caution here is that you should exercise. The ancient Romans had a saying, "Mens sana in corpore sano—a sound mind in a sound body." The Romans knew what they were talking about. There is overwhelming evidence that physical exercise reduces stress, increases health, and improves mental acuity and the quality of decision making.

13. *Be Kind to Yourself.* In order to be kind to others you need to be kind to yourself first. In times of crisis, personal time and personal space become even more important to ensure the level of renewal that allows you to provide support and assistance to others. Research shows that those involved in doing emotional labor such as nurses and social workers can suffer from burnout and emotional fatigue. Today, almost everyone is involved in some type of emotional labor. Implementing an exercise regimen, simplifying, maxi-tasking, and nourishing your brain are all things you can do to be kind to yourself.

Individual renewal must also be spiritual. Spirit is the individual force that moves each of us and the organizations of which we are a part. As we work together to renew America, we need that shared spirit and a spirit of sharing.

15 | Implementing the Renewal Process

"The plan is nothing. Planning is everything."
Dwight Eisenhower

ON JANUARY 15, 2009, CAPTAIN CHESLEY "SULLY" SULLENBERGER lifted the nose of U.S. Air Flight 1549 off the tarmac at New York City's La Guardia Airport. Minutes later, Sully notified the control tower that he was going to land the plane in the Hudson River. Seventy-two seconds later, he did just that.

Miraculously, all 155 passengers and crew were successfully evacuated from the plane. There were no fatalities and no serious injuries. The entire event elapsed in less than 30 minutes. However, **preparing** for it took a lifetime.

Captain Sullenberger, a former fighter pilot, had been flying for U.S. Air for 29 years. Sully had considerable expertise in addition to his basic flying ability. He specialized in studying crash and emergency landings and what made them successful—he was a nationally known expert.

Sully was the right person in the right place at the right time to put that Airbus 320 down in the Hudson. He was a pro. But he was also a lifelong learner who knew that no matter how good he was, he could always get better. As Captain Sullenberger said to Jeffrey Brown on the Jim Lehrer show in the week of October 23, 2009, "I've learned not only from my own experiences but from the experiences of others."

Sully didn't accomplish this feat all on his own. He did it by **involving** others. He orchestrated the actions of his crew, who enlisted the passengers in the effort. The passengers didn't panic. They remained calm, and many of them assisted others in the deplaning process.

Together, they were all responsible for **executing** this miracle. But even though they did it together, they didn't do it by themselves either. They had the volunteer help of the tugboat operators who were the first responders on the scene to help evacuate the passengers. They also had the substantial assistance of New York's first responders.

The process of execution was not completed until Captain Sullen-berger took one last walk through the entire plane to ensure that all passengers had gotten off safely. Satisfied that was the case, Sully himself left the plane—appropriately, as the officer in charge, he was the last person off this plane, which was soon to become a submarine.

THE P-I-E CYCLE AND RENEWAL

The "Miracle on the Hudson" provides an excellent compressed time example of the P-I-E Cycle as depicted below:

Figure 15.1: The P-I-E Cycle

We introduced this cycle earlier in the book. To repeat, we define the elements of the cycle as follows

- *Preparation*. Planning, organizing, and ensuring the level of competence to perform professionally and properly.

- *Involvement*. Securing the engagement of the appropriate stakeholder groups and individual citizens to ensure participation and ownership.

- *Execution.* Putting the proper procedures and processes in place to do the work, manage performance, and to take corrective actions as necessary.

P-I-E plays out quickly in daily events. When we apply it to implementing public policy and programs as well as in organizational life (of all types), it takes much longer and becomes a more complicated process. Senator Mark Warner (D-VA) understands this. That's why his first speech on the Senate Floor in March of 2009 was about management. He opened that speech by stating:

> *"I rise today to state a principle that is known well by those of us who have spent any time in the private sector—and it is this: 'What is measured gets done. . . .' Now, the American people are not expecting miracles. But at the very least they can—and they should— expect competence. So we must put in place the people with the right skills and insist on the appropriate measurements, and then demand transparency and accountability."* [1]

Warner thinks like this because he was a very successful businessperson—one of the cofounders of Nextel. He knows how to run things and get things done. He proved that not only while he was at Nextel but also in his term as governor of Virginia. Warner left office with an approval rating of 80 percent because he managed the state and its budget in a fiscally responsible manner.

Unfortunately, the majority of our legislators don't have Warner's background. A large number of them at the federal level are lawyers. There are businesspeople. But they are outnumbered. Is it any wonder that so many of these representatives on Capitol Hill think that the work is done when the final version of the legislation is drafted and the bill is passed? In fact, just the opposite is true.

The real work begins after legislation is passed. The result of that work determines whether the legislation achieves its intended results. We agree with Senator Warner about the importance of measurement. That's why we are pleased that in October 2009, Senator Kent Conrad (D-ND), chairman of the Senate Budget Committee, named Senator Warner to lead a bipartisan Task Force on Governmental Performance.

The Task Force will look at how government measures the cost-effectiveness of federal agencies and programs with the goal of boosting efficiency and finding cost savings.[2]

We agree with the need to wring all of the unnecessary costs out of government. As businesspeople, we also know that is only part of the equation for success. The other is realizing each organizational unit's vision and achieving its performance targets. This is accomplished not just through prudent financial management but by implementing a structured approach to renewing organizations.

For America to be renewed, its organizations in all sectors—public, private, nonprofit—must be renewed. Renewal requires focused and sustained effort over time. The P-I-E Cycle addresses this requirement because it provides a systematic and disciplined process for organizational renewal.

The P-I-E Cycle blends and integrates the essential elements of leadership renewal, organizational renewal, and individual renewal. It addresses the complexities of organizations and organizational life. It also addresses the fact that people and organizational cultures are change-resistant and that the appropriate mechanisms must be put in place in order to effect change. The cycle has been developed based upon our experiences combined with what we consider to be best practices in organizational turnarounds and transformations. It begins with proper preparation.

PROPER PREPARATION

Vince Lombardi, the extremely competitive head coach of the Green Bay Packers, is alleged to have said, "Winning is everything." What Coach Lombardi *actually* said was *"Preparing to win is everything."* He knew what he was talking about.

Robert Rubin, secretary of the U.S. Treasury during the Clinton administration, also emphasized preparation. In his book, *In an Uncertain World: Tough Choices from Wall Street to Washington*, Rubin explains how his decisions were not as important as the "decision-making process."[3] George Muñoz observed this firsthand when he served as assistant secretary of the Treasury under Rubin. "At our senior staff meetings, Rubin asked more about how we arrived at the decision than justification for it. What mattered was: getting as many facts as possible, getting the views and input of all stakeholders, and weighing that information against established objectives."

It is virtually impossible to achieve desired organizational outcomes without proper preparation. There may be occasional "happy accidents" for organizations and sporting teams. Renewal and sustained success over time, however, usually come from being prepared. The two major ingredients for that are: (1) the strategic planning process, and (2) competency development and enhancement.

The Strategic Planning Process

As noted in Chapter 14, a leader's primary responsibility in beginning organizational renewal is to "establish a vision, values, and a strong strategic and operational focus that enables the organization to create a sustainable competitive advantage and to succeed in the future." Putting the right strategic planning process in place enables a leader to discharge that responsibility.

Notice the emphasis here is on the strategic planning process and not on the strategic plan. In many instances, strategic planning and strategic plans have gotten bad names—and deservedly so. That's because too often planning is a meaningless exercise that is totally disconnected from the organization's day-to-day operational realities. The top management team gets together for a couple of days in an off-site retreat. The team writes a plan. It then puts that plan on a shelf to gather dust until the team gets together again in another off-site retreat to update the plan which hasn't been looked at since the last retreat.

There is a much better way for thinking about and doing strategic planning. Henry Mintzberg advised that strategy is "crafted," rather than planned.[4] What he meant is that strategy is implemented in a dynamic and changing environment. Therefore, plans need to be reviewed and renewed regularly. That is why the focus needs to be on ensuring the right planning process to promote crafting strategy. This enables making the most important strategic decisions for the organization on an on-going and timely basis.

Based on their work with large organizations, Michael Mankins and Richard Steele concluded that organizations could improve the quantity and quality of decisions by doing "continuous issues-focused strategic planning." They recommend doing planning throughout the year by debating one issue at a time until it is resolved and then implementing the strategic decision for that issue.[5]

We absolutely agree with the need for continuous planning. When renewal is what is in order—as it is with most organizations today—we recommend an integrated process that blends elements of traditional strategic planning with continuous planning. It is a process that Ed Crego has been employing quite successfully with consulting clients for more than a quarter of a century.

The five critical requirements for implementing that integrated strategic planning process are:

1. Attain participation and commitment from the relevant stakeholders throughout the planning process.

2. Undertake a thorough, realistic analysis of the organization's situation relative to the current and expected environment.

3. Articulate or rearticulate the organization's vision, mission, and values.

4. Set the goals and define the strategies and action programs to enable accomplishment of the goals and achievement of the vision, mission, and values.

5. Develop a monitoring and feedback system to evaluate progress against the plan and to make adjustments as necessary.

The following approaches and methodologies are useful for addressing those requirements.

Stakeholder Input. Conduct individual interviews with a cross section of key individuals in all stakeholder groups. Use focus groups and survey instruments to give as many as practical the chance to voice their opinions and provide feedback. This builds consensus and commitment along the way and buy-in for the planning process and the plan.

Situational Analysis.   Combine an external Environmental Scan of the organization's operating environment, looking at factors, such as the competition, regulations, and customers with an internal assessment of the organization's strengths, weaknesses, opportunities, and threats (SWOT analysis). Synthesize these two analyses to identify the critical considerations and Key Result Areas to be addressed in the strategic plan.

Vision, Mission, and Values Statement.   Develop a clear and cogent statement. Evaluate the statement to ensure that it addresses the following: What the organization wants to be (long term); who the organization is/what business is it in (short term); and what the organization believes in. Determine whether the statement passes the 3-M test (i.e., is it meaningful, memorable, and motivational for those associated with the organization). Research has shown that people will go the extra mile for an organization they believe is making a real difference and contribution to society.

Goals, Strategies, and Action Programs.   Set no more than three to seven goals (the fewer the better) that are measurable and challenging but realistic. Review the goals to ensure that they are attainable by taking into account the market, financial, and business realities of the organization. Define actionable strategies. Develop an action program for each strategy that spells out steps, responsibilities, resource requirements, and time frames. Ensure that there is an appropriate alignment of all goals, strategies, and action programs. Remember that eventually everything degenerates into work and it is the actions of those to be involved in strategic plan implementation that will determine whether it succeeds. Unless these individual actions are carefully aligned, the plan will fail.

Monitoring and Feedback System.   Put a monitoring and feedback system into place that permits tracking progress against plan milestones, reevaluate strategies as necessary, and make changes to keep the plan on track. No planning process is perfect. Therefore, use that process to address strategic issues that emerge during the course of the year. Markets, competitors, and internal resources are never static.

Consequently, the key to successful implementation is to make the plan a living document and to continue to craft strategy on a regularly scheduled and on-going basis.

Competency Development and Enhancement

The second element of preparation is putting the right process in place to ensure that employees can "perform properly and professionally." In this regard, there is an old adage that "practice makes perfect." That is absolutely incorrect. What is correct is that "*perfect* practice makes perfect."

Perfect practice is what separates master craftspeople from novices and apprentices. Perfect practice is what separates professionals from amateurs. Perfect practice is what will separate a successful strategic renewal effort from an unsuccessful one. Perfect practice enables competency development and enhancement. Perfect practice takes place in the work environment as opposed to the classroom. In the classroom, students gain knowledge. It's what we learn in the work setting that develops the skills, abilities, and habits that form a competency.

Think about it. On-the-job training and mentoring are critical for developing the skill sets to make individuals peak performers and to make organizations successful. It's why accounting firms take the graduates right out of school and spend a couple of years or so to make them real "accountants." It's why medical school graduates do internships. It's why folks with IT degrees who are sophisticated at programming are trained in project management skills by the firms that hire them. Hotel and restaurant workers are put through some type of orientation and work with a lead employee to learn the ropes. Manufacturing employees do apprenticeships. Those who want to become teachers student teach.

Historically, despite the preponderance of training directed at developing competencies, much of it has not been well done. The consequences can be negative for the individual, the organization, and society as a whole. As an example, in October 2009, Education Secretary Arne Duncan gave a speech at Columbia University's Teachers College where he decried the poor state of teacher training in the United States.

In that speech, Duncan called for a "revolutionary change" in teacher training. Secretary Duncan related that he had spoken with hundreds of teachers while he was serving as Chicago's school chief and universally heard two complaints from them: (1) they did not get the practical training they needed to manage their classroom, and (2) they weren't taught how to use data to improve student learning.[6]

As another example, during the 1970s, 1980s, and 1990s, employees were receiving on-the-job training in apprenticeship programs being run in metalworking companies across the country. While this sounds like a good idea, it wasn't. The majority of the programs weren't competency-based. The skills being developed were nontransferable.

For example, a worker would learn how to run a machine in plant A. However, if plant A were closed and plant B was looking for new employees, unless plant B had exactly the same machine as plant A, the worker wouldn't be qualified for a position there. As the metalworking industry in the United States changed in the 1990s, a serious supply and demand problem arose. There were thousands of workers losing jobs as the industry shrank. But those workers weren't competent to fill the job openings that still existed in other metalworking companies.

The major trade associations in the metalworking industry took steps to correct the problem by establishing the National Institute for Metalworking Skills (NIMS). NIMS develops manufacturing skill standards and competency assessments for occupations in the metalworking industry. In 2006, with support from the Department of Labor and industry stakeholders, NIMS developed the first competency-based apprenticeship program for the metalworking industry. NIMS built on this in 2007 by developing a competency-based Structured O-J-T System to enable metalworking companies to do a high-quality job in training their own trainers.[7]

We think the NIMS model is an excellent one for organizations to look at as they develop their own competency-based programs. There are other organizations such as the Federal Aviation Administration, Marriott International, the United States Coast Guard, Walt Disney World, McDonald's, and Toyota that do an excellent job in developing the core competencies of their own workers as well as the managers, supervisors, and lead employees who do the training and mentoring that is required for workforce competency development. Finally, there is a wealth of material available through organizations, such as the American Society of Training and Development, the International Society for

Performance Improvement, and consulting firms that can be employed in the development of competency-based programs.

The important point we want to emphasize here is that organizational renewal depends on competent people and management. Competent people and managers are created through competency-based programs. No matter what the nature of the job or position, the development of competency-based programs follows a closed-loop process similar to this:

1. Identify the core competency areas and needs of the trainees
2. Identify the underlying knowledge, skills, and ability requirements
3. Identify the critical tasks to be performed in the core competency area
4. Develop the customized training material for those tasks and competencies
5. Deliver the training
6. Evaluate the training and results

Competency-based training provides a bridge between the organization's past and future. It equips individuals with the skills needed to participate effectively in a renewal effort. Competency-based training does not guarantee the success of an organizational renewal effort. Failing to do training or doing the wrong type of training as part of a renewal effort, however, significantly limits the likelihood of its success.

TEAM USA

Organizational renewal is a team effort—it is more important to have a championship team than a team of champions. A team of champions is a team with a lot of individual talent, but one that may not be able to put the pieces together to optimize performance and win the big game. A championship team is a disciplined one that works together to maximize group potential and achieve results through collective efforts and synergy that would have been impossible otherwise. Think of the amateur and collegiate U.S. hockey players that took home the Olympic gold medal in 1980, a great example of a championship team.

There won't be any gold medals awarded to the championship teams in organizational renewal. The contributions they will make to renewing America and the American Dream, however, will be as important to America's psyche and its spirit as winning the gold medal was for the U.S. hockey team.

A championship team is a disciplined one. Jon R. Katzenbach and Douglas K. Smith have identified five characteristics of high-performing teams:

1. A meaningful common purpose that the team has helped shape
2. Specific performance goals that flow from that purpose
3. A mix of complementary skills
4. A strong commitment to how the work gets done
5. Mutual accountability[8]

These characteristics are important for any organizational team. They become especially important when an organization is engaged in a renewal initiative. When Ed McManus was president of Jewel Food Stores in the Chicago area, he initiated a program that demonstrated the power of teams. With consulting assistance, he launched a service quality improvement initiative.

The initiative was rolled out to the more than 200 stores in the Chicago metropolitan area over a 3-year period. Each store manager and his or her five-person team were brought into a combined training and planning session. In that session they received customer and employee survey results for their store, along with the survey results for other stores in their region and the entire Chicago metropolitan area. They analyzed the data and then put together a store service quality improvement plan including goals and action programs.

The teams went back to their stores and implemented their plans. They received updated survey data on a quarterly basis and adjusted their plans accordingly. The results were extremely positive. The majority of the stores significantly improved their customer and employee satisfaction, share of customer spending, traffic, and profitability.

Teams, whether existing or newly formed, are the basic building blocks of organizations. They take many forms, such as stores in the Jewel case, business units, divisions, departments, offices, self-directed teams, quality circles, and matrix management teams.

Matrix management teams can be especially useful as part of a renewal process. Ron Gunn is one of the foremost experts on matrix teams. He says, "For a couple of decades, the mantra in organizations has been we need to break down the silos, but these initiatives rarely get past the chanting stage. Matrix teams are cross-functional teams that pursue shared objectives with shared resources. They break down the silos by placing staff drawn from different disciplines shoulder-to-shoulder, either physically and/or virtually, with one another to pursue a common objective." Organizations like Boeing, ExxonMobil, the Navy Bureau of Medicine, and the Defense Finance and Accounting Service have used these teams to great advantage.[9]

An organization's strategic success will be determined in great part by how well its teams of all types perform. Therefore, it is essential that they have a chance to review the organization's plans and goals and determine what contribution they can make to its success.

As importantly, these teams need to be able to do an assessment of their own situation and identify what changes will be required of them in order to achieve their goals. Regardless of the type of team, the following questions need to be answered:

- Are we truly committed to the renewal?
- Do we agree with the goals?
- Are we structured correctly to implement the renewal?
- Do we have the right team composition for the renewal: skill sets, experience, and personal styles?
- Do we work well as a team? Or, do we need to do some team building?
- Are we results-oriented with a strong commitment to getting the work done?
- Are we willing to hold ourselves and the team accountable for results, or are we conflict adverse?

This all might seem like common sense. However, based upon our experience, many organizations neglect the process of team development when they are attempting a major organizational transformation or turnaround. They simply send the change message from on high and assume that it will be implemented seamlessly throughout the organization. This is a fatal error for two reasons.

First, many teams are teams in name only. Team members may share common office space or a building. They may be in units that are part of a common supply chain such as supplier–manufacturer–distributor–customer in the private sector, or federal-state-local government units in the public sector. Apart from that, they may have little or nothing in common.

Second, existing teams have evolved their own norms and culture. They have defined roles and expected behaviors for team members. Any change to their way of doing things and the nature or responsibilities of the team threatens the balance of power and influence within the unit's social network. Teams and team members do not take kindly to those threats.

This is a lesson Ed Crego learned many years ago in a major customer-centered change project with Volkswagen in the United States. Volkswagen's top management team had come up with a plan to do significant reengineering of the company. When the plan was introduced to the next level of management for input and buy-in, it became apparent to the president of Volkswagen U.S. that some of the executives responsible for implementation were not supportive.

The president asked Ed what to do. He said let it play out for a while to see what happened and recommended that if they didn't embrace the plan, or tried to block it, they should be confronted and told, "You are either on the bus or off the bus" (the Volkswagen bus, of course). The president followed Ed's advice. He gave the recalcitrant executives enough rope, and they hung themselves. Within 1 year, none of the obstructionist executives were still with the company.

Our point here is that if you are going to renew an organization—public, private, nonprofit, for-profit—you must be sure that everyone agrees on what needs to happen. If someone doesn't agree, you need to either find out if their reasons have merit (and then adjust your plans accordingly) or find someone else who will support your renewal efforts. In this case, one bad apple can ruin the whole bunch.

MASTERING EXECUTION

No matter how well you prepare, the game is won on the playing field. To do that, organizations, teams, and individuals need to excel in execution. Marriott and Warren Buffett's Berkshire Hathaway investment company are masters of execution.

J. W. "Bill" Marriott, Jr., the CEO of Marriott, is famous for saying "Success is never final." He and his team have been constantly upping their game since Bill became CEO in 1972. Marriott continued renewing itself in 2009 by restructuring its divisions worldwide and integrating Ritz Carlton more closely into the company. Part of this was done in response to the economic downturn that had affected the entire hospitality industry. Of greater importance, however, was the opportunity to use these changes to make Marriott a truly global international brand and not just an American business.

Marriott has performed so well that *Fortune* recognized it as the most-admired company in the hotel and resort industry for 9 consecutive years (1999–2008). The company achieved the most-admired status for a variety of reasons, but the primary one was its ability to "execute with discipline." Two key principles were central to this: (1) rigorous adherence to standard operating procedures will result in flawless execution and (2) making employees (and, in turn, guests) central to Marriott's execution formula. In other words, if the organization takes care of its associates, those associates will take care of Marriott's customers (guests).

That's been more than a belief or principle for Marriott as evidenced by the fact that in surveys, Marriott's employees rate their satisfaction with how the company treats them much higher than employees at industry competitors. That's because Marriott has a good compensation and benefits package and builds emotional ties with its employees. Turnover is low, and nearly half of the promotions come from within. As a result of its human resource practices, Marriott is consistently rated in the Top 100 companies to work for by *Fortune* and among the best companies by *Working Mother*.[10]

Like Marriott, billionaire investor Warren Buffett also used 2009 for renewal. He did it by executing an investment philosophy and strategy that he has employed since he started investing. The philosophy was expressed in an op-ed column for *The New York Times* in September 2008 titled, "Buy American. I am." In that column, Buffett wrote, "A simple rule dictates my buying: Be fearful when others are greedy, and be greedy when others are fearful."

In November 2009, Buffett put his money where his mouth was by acquiring the Burlington Northern Santa Fe railroad for $34 billion. Buffett is a value investor. The purchase of Burlington Northern was perfectly consistent with his approach. As a value investor, Buffett took into account the following criteria: sound management; demonstrated earning capacity with a likelihood it will continue; consistently high returns and a prudent approach to debt; and a business that is easily understood.

Burlington Northern met all of these criteria, and more. The railroad business is older than the trucking business and will undoubtedly become more important as the United States looks for more cost-effective and cleaner alternatives for transporting goods. Buffett knew a lot about Burlington Northern because Berkshire Hathaway owned 22 percent when the acquisition offer was tendered.

Where else has Buffett invested recently? In September 2008, he helped bail out Goldman Sachs to the tune of $5 billion. In the fall of 2008, Buffett also bought 10 percent of BYD, a relatively new Chinese company that make batteries, cell phones, and a plug-in electric car for $230 million.

At first, that investment may not seem to fit with Buffett's investment criteria.[11] But, when you put it into a broader context along with the investment in Goldman Sachs and the Burlington Northern acquisition, the investment strategy that Buffett is executing becomes startlingly simple and straightforward. It is, indeed, a Buy American strategy. Buy or invest in those businesses that the American government will support directly or indirectly and/or will be critical to America's future. In some cases, that means back to the future (the railroad and Goldman Sachs). In others, it means fast-forward (BYD and the plug-in car).

Marriot and Warren Buffett's Berkshire Hathaway Investment Company are each exemplars of execution and each has lessons to offer. So do Larry Bossidy and consultant Ram Charan in their 2002 best-selling book, *Execution: The Discipline of Getting Things Done.*

Bossidy and Charan spell out three core processes for execution: (1) people, (2) strategy, and (3) operations—and how all three should interface. They stress that the people process is the most important because it is an organization's leaders who must develop executable strategies and convert them into operating plans with accountabilities. They also highlight the need to develop strategy that can easily be put into operation and position the business strategically in the marketplace, the economy, and against its competitors.

Bossidy and Charan make the point that the operating plans must be specific, detailed, and actionable in order to achieve the desired results. They emphasize that successful execution requires: establishing the leader's personal priorities, doing a good job of selecting and appraising people, and addressing the company's cultural issues.[12] While this may seem like Management 101, it is amazing how many American businesses and organizations of all types have flunked this course in the past few decades and not attended to the basics.

As an example, look at General Motors. At one time, GM was considered the best-run company in America and the world. That was definitely not the case by 2009. In fact, almost the exact opposite was true. But sometimes there are cases that make even General Motors look good. Consider the Tampa Bay Buccaneers during their start-up years.

John McKay was the first coach of the Buccaneers. When McKay coached the Bucs, they were a hapless bunch and almost never won a game. After an especially embarrassing defeat, a member of the press corps asked Coach McKay about his team's execution. He thought for a minute or so and then said with dead-panned seriousness, "I'm in favor of it."

We've been talking about a different form of execution here, but it still helps to have a sense of humor. That's because execution is hard work and even with the best people, strategy, and operations, things don't always go as expected. That's when those who excel in execution pick themselves up, dust themselves off, and start all over again.

CHANGES IN LATITUDES, CHANGES IN ATTITUDES

Implementing the P-I-E Cycle and engaging in organizational renewal require change. The extent of the change required will depend on the scope and nature of the renewal effort. Regardless of the extent of the change, there will be some resistance to it. It's human nature to be resistant to change—we don't like to be told we have to do things differently.

As individuals, our natural tendency is to try to achieve *homeostasis*—a relatively steady state of equilibrium in our personal and professional lives. Most people strongly resist any change that seems likely to upset that equilibrium. While many of us say we want change we can believe in, most of us want it to happen somewhere else—not in our own backyard or on the job.

Organizational change or renewal can threaten us on a number of levels and in a number of ways including:

- *Loss of Status.* What will this change mean to someone in terms of position power and personal influence?
- *Loss of Job.* The past 2 years have caused even the most seaworthy of employees to question whether or not they will have a job.
- *Loss of Security.* Security is both psychological and financial. Significant cuts in hours and wages have caused heightened levels of anxiety in individuals.
- *Loss of Structure.* Most people prefer some structure and order in their lives. Organizations and work help provide that structure through routines, rituals, and standard operating procedures.
- *Social Disruption.* For many people, the most meaningful relations outside of family are with associates and colleagues. A change can dramatically alter the social order and affiliation patterns.

Anyone who is leading a renewal initiative must understand that while the change effort may seem logical or rational to them, it is also an emotional experience that can affect personal perceptions, feelings, and attitudes of those involved. Recognizing this, we recommend that the organizational renewal process should include a transition management plan.

That plan should allow for individual buy-in and set out the path and expectations regarding the transition. Individuals within the organization working alone and in teams are in the position to create success or failure—their concerns have to be dealt with as part of that plan.

Based on the research of Gene Hall, a professor from the University of Texas, these concerns exist at six levels:

1. Information: What is the change?
2. Impact: What does this change mean to the individual?
3. Implementation: How will this change be conducted?
4. Intent: Why is this change important?
5. Involvement: What can the individual do to affect the change process?
6. Investment: What can the individual do to extend the change into other areas?[13]

The transition management plan should be structured and designed to address these concerns in a stepwise manner. This will maximize individual buy-in and facilitate full integration of the changes within the organization.

At the end of the day, the success of any renewal effort will be determined by whether the players involved have the will along with the mental and emotional toughness to stay the course. That's why during World War II, Winston Churchill admonished the boys at Harrow School, "Never give in—never, never, never. . . ." It's also why Calvin Coolidge proclaimed forcefully, "Nothing in this world can take the place of persistence. Talent will not; nothing is more common than unsuccessful people with talent. Genius will not; unrewarded genius is almost a proverb. Education will not; the world is full of educated derelicts. Persistence and determination alone are omnipotent. The slogan 'Press On' has solved and always will solve the problems of the human race."

Renewing America and the American Dream will be accomplished because of millions of acts of will. It starts with a call to arms and a commitment to participate in this war of necessity. To become, as Thomas Friedman calls it, part of "The Regeneration"—the generation that renews, refreshes, reenergizes, and rebuilds America for the twenty-first century.[14]

There is no management system or method that will guarantee results. We hope, however, that the framework provided in this book will give you a sound basis to do what Americans have always done in times of crisis—come together to think, reason, and act in order to make America and the world a better place for ourselves and future generations.

Epilogue:
The Dream Renewed

"Ask not what your country can do for you. Ask what you can do for your country."

John F. Kennedy

THE COVER OF THE NOVEMBER 4, 2020, ISSUE OF *TIME* WAS AN aerial photo taken from space of millions of American citizens holding hands and forming a human chain that stretched across the breadth of the United States from California to New York. The cover story was titled, "Citizen Nation," and it began as follows:

> When the United States entered this decisive decade, there was considerable doubt about the future of this country and the American Dream. Today, there is little doubt. America and the American Dream is stronger than ever. A Pew Research Center report released this week revealed that Americans feel better about their opportunity to realize the American Dream than at any time since the early 1970s.
>
> This accomplishment was fueled by a number of factors, including small businesses and entrepreneurs creating jobs at record levels in the last half of the decade, manufacturing as a percent of GDP increasing from below 10 percent to almost 20 percent, and real wages going up by more than 10 percent over the course of the decade. Most importantly, however, it was driven by an unprecedented

level of civic and social engagement by millions of American citizens across the country.

This massive involvement helped to transform America. The story of American renewal is one unique to the United States. When things seemed the darkest at the beginning of the decade—when politicians and talk-show hosts were polarized and polarizing—citizens took matters in their own hands.

They pulled America up by its bootstraps through independent thinking and collective action. As they have in the past and will in the future, American citizens provided the brains and brawn, and the will and the spirit for America to come together to restore the country's competitive advantage—and with it the American Dream.

We know that it's impossible to predict the *Time* magazine cover story for November 4, 2020. Just as we know that it's impossible to predict what things will look like in 2020. We also believe, however, that it is much better to have 2020 foresight than 2020 hindsight. Hindsight won't renew America or the American Dream.

Foresight establishes a vision and a perspective about what's happening now and what needs to be done to move ahead. We have presented our view in this book. We have attempted to be nonpartisan and independent in our assessment and recommendations in doing so. You will be the judge of that.

We know full well that citizens can look at the same set of facts and reach different conclusions. That's okay. Our primary goal in writing this book was to make "a call to arms" and provide a foundation for a serious dialogue with you and other citizens about our role and responsibilities in reviving the American Dream. That's because we believe implicitly in the power of the citizen's voice.

We also believe that America's best idea was, and is, America. It was a brilliant idea in 1776. It remains a brilliant one today and will be even more brilliant tomorrow when we come together to ensure that our citizens' voices are heard.

Appendix: Renewal Recommendations

We present recommendations for renewing the American Dream throughout this book. This Appendix lists all of the recommendations from the following chapters:

- Chapter 1:   Competitive Advantage for the Twenty-First Century
- Chapter 6:   Manufacturing Matters
- Chapter 7:   Small Businesses and Entrepreneurs Matter
- Chapter 10: Government Is Not the Problem
- Chapter 11: Business Is Not the Answer
- Chapter 12: Citizens All
- Chapter 13: Bowling Together

We discuss the subsidiary recommendations from these chapters here. We address the primary recommendations in the chapters in which they are provided.

CHAPTER 1: RENEWING AMERICA'S COMPETITIVE ADVANTAGE RECOMMENDATIONS

Competitive Advantage Primary Recommendation

1. Establish a national global competitiveness commission to develop a twenty-first century competitive advantage plan for the United States

Competitive Advantage Subsidiary Recommendations

2. Form regional competitiveness councils to piggyback on the national plan and to develop regional solutions
3. Encourage enhanced local economic development and competitiveness planning

2. Form regional competitiveness councils to piggyback on the national plan and to develop regional solutions.

A national plan can not address regional differences. The United States is a large nation comprised of diverse regions. The diversity of those regions is acknowledged by the fact that the Federal Reserve Bank has 12 districts and the federal government has six regional offices.

The Fed's beige book for June 2009 showed that almost all of the regional economies were struggling or weakening. However, there were differences in the reports by region, with five of the 12 districts reporting that the pace of decline was tapering off and districts such as Dallas and Richmond were reporting slight up ticks in demand. Things started to improve gradually later in the year. In December the Fed reported that eight districts indicated some pick up in activity, while the remaining four—Philadelphia, Cleveland, Richmond, and Atlanta were little changed or mixed.

Regional competitiveness councils should be established to develop plans to deal with this diversity and the differing economic needs and drivers of the regions. The regional councils should use the national global competitiveness strategic plan as a reference and starting point and then create regional plans that respond to their particular situations.

The regional councils should have charters similar to and be patterned after the National Commission in terms of scope, structure, and composition. Unlike the National Commission, however, we believe the regional councils should be standing bodies. We also believe the primary funding for these councils should come from private and charitable sectors. Government grants could be used to support the establishment of the councils or to conduct special economic analyses. However, on-going operations should be sustained through voluntary contributions. This will ensure the appropriate independence of the councils from governmental control and intervention.

No one provides better insights or writes more eloquently about the need for regional planning than Dick Longworth in his book, *Caught in the Middle: America's Heartland in the Age of Globalism.* Dick is a fellow at the Chicago Council on Global Affairs and was twice nominated for the Pulitzer Prize for his reporting.

Dick sets out his prescription for a regional approach in his book's final chapter titled, "Global Midwest."[1] It includes establishing a Midwest think tank and new collaborations among the players—cities, universities, and industries—to develop and implement the requisite plans to move the Midwest forward and to make it a player in the global world.

What's most interesting is that what Dick was advocating in his book (published in 2008) has already started to happen. In May of 2009, the Task Force on National Energy Policy and Midwestern Regional Competitiveness released a report that presented four key findings and a series of recommendations to put the Midwest in the middle of the action on energy.

The Task Force Report was sponsored by the Chicago Council on Global Affairs and supported financially by some of its members. It had 32 experts from various stakeholder groups from around the region.

Dick Longworth doesn't include government in his recommended regional planning approach. We believe they must be at the table. Governments are either part of the problem or part of the solution. To try to divorce them from the process altogether we believe is unrealistic and impractical. On the other hand, to think that they have capacity to solve problems single-handedly or to even take the lead in doing so is foolhardy.

3. Encourage enhanced local economic development and competitiveness planning.

Having argued for regional councils, we need to add a couple of caveats. The regional councils will be advisory bodies. As such, they will have no decision-making or implementation authority. They will need buy-in and ownership from governments, businesses, and communities from areas across the region in order to translate their ideas into action. This will require that regional plans be matched by local plans.

In addition, there is a saying that all politics is local. The same is true for economic development. It is possible to have a struggling city in a thriving region or state. For example, Brownsville, Texas, and Hartford, Connecticut, house the two poorest school districts in the United States despite the fact that these two states are doing relatively well economically.

It will also be the case that a regional approach will of necessity ignore sections of a region. The route for a bullet train, the location of a manufacturing site, the placement of a research center will benefit some but not help others. Larger and more urbanized areas may profit more than mid-sized or rural ones. Therefore, it will be imperative for those communities that want to succeed to do economic development and competitiveness planning of their own.

Currently, most, if not all, state and local governments engage in some form of economic development planning. The other locus for this sort of planning has historically been institutions of higher education that have departments or institutes that specialize in this type of activity.

Some of the work that is done by these groups is very good, while some is not. Much of it is issue-focused, narrow in scope, tactical in nature, and frequently disconnected from the input and participation of the broader community.

Just as we need more strategic and collaborative thinking at the national and regional levels, we need it at the local level as well. We also need to have that planning being done collaboratively by concerned stakeholders outside the governmental/academic context.

Recognizing this, the national and regional approaches should be replicated at the local level. The funding for this should come from the community (foundations, charities, businesses) and the local governments in more affluent areas. The federal government should establish local competitiveness planning grants for impoverished communities that need assistance and support for their planning. Those grants should be awarded on a competitive basis.

Communities of all sizes and shapes have begun to change the process and approach to economic development. Here are four examples that can serve as models for enhancing nongovernmental cooperative planning at the local level:

- **Chicago Council on Global Affairs:** The council was established in 1922 as the Council on Foreign Relations. It has now morphed to be a "leading independent, nonpartisan organization committed to influencing the discourse on global issues through contributions to opinion and policy formation, leadership dialogue, and public learning." The Report of the Task Force on National Energy Policy and Midwest Regional Competitiveness discussed earlier provides an example of the work being done by the council. The council has also released other reports of significance and in early 2010, sponsored a briefing to promote the release of a Brookings Institution report on Great Lakes Venture Capital Building.

- **Sarasota Economic Development Commission (EDC):** The EDC of Sarasota is a private, not-for-profit corporation leading the community's economic development strategy to add high-wage jobs and diversification to the local community. The EDC's most recent plan focuses on leveraging the strengths and characteristics of Sarasota, which include a thriving arts and cultural community, an affluent and aging population, and a diverse set of higher educational institutions.

- **Human Development Commission, Caro, Michigan:** This community action agency in upstate, rural Michigan has implemented a model for conducting a complete community needs assessment and developing a comprehensive strategic plan to guide the revitalization of rural communities. These plans are holistic in nature and typically address concerns such as affordable housing and Main-Street projects. The process includes involving and managing volunteers as part of the planning and implementation of revitalization efforts and activities.

- **Garrett County Community Action Committee (GCAC), Western Maryland:** In collaboration with the Garrett Chamber of Commerce, the GCAC has created a model for rural economic development. It has used that model to turn a historically distressed county in Central Appalachia into a vibrant economy. The strategies employed to drive that change included small-town revitalization, community-based economic development, workforce housing, childcare and workforce development.

CHAPTER 6: RENEWING MANUFACTURING RECOMMENDATIONS

Manufacturing Primary Recommendations

1. Develop and fund an industrial and innovation policy focused on driving research and development and the rapid growth and restoration of manufacturing in targeted sectors.

2. Reform corporate tax policies and create strong incentives for American manufacturers to establish plants and manufacture products domestically.

3. Create vehicles for public-private financial support for targeted R&D and manufacturing/industrial initiatives.

4. Continue to expand funding and heighten public awareness of the importance of STEM and how basic workforce competencies and cutting edge expertise in these areas can make American manufacturing second to none in the world.

Manufacturing Subsidiary Recommendations

5. Implement a major jobs program focused on creating manufacturing and construction jobs related to rebuilding America's crumbling and critically important infrastructure.

6. Develop an integrated education and training plan that rationalizes the nation's approach for developing a skilled manufacturing workforce.

7. Ensure the manufacturing technical training and support capabilities of America's community college network.

8. Ensure the level of financial and technical assistance required to make small businesses leaders in manufacturing.

9. Provide assistance to small manufacturing companies to help them reduce their healthcare costs.

10. Establish a trade agreement with China that is based on the principle of reciprocity.

11. Heighten public awareness of the importance of manufacturing and manufacturing careers.

5. Implement a major jobs program focused on creating manufacturing and construction jobs related to rebuilding America's crumbling and critically important infrastructure.

Wherever you look—whether it's roads and bridges, electrical grids, water mains, or waterways—things are deteriorating and crumbling. We recommend that the president and Congress pass legislation to fund a major long-term program (5–10 years) focused on revitalizing all components of the infrastructure. This program should be front-loaded and time-phased. It should treat the nation's infrastructure as a "public good" and minimize or eliminate local or state obstacles that prevent properly repairing or maintaining the infrastructure.

There are two compelling reasons for launching a massive infrastructure program:

1. A sound and "state-of-the-art" infrastructure is a source of a competitive advantage. America's infrastructure in the twentieth century—most especially after the initiatives launched during the Great Depression and during and after World War II—gave American manufacturing and industry an engine for economic development domestically and the basis for international trade advantages. For the most part, that infrastructure "edge" is now gone.

2. The infrastructure is "job- and shovel-ready" right now. There is some R&D and high-tech manufacturing that needs to be done to generate new "green" solutions, but much of what needs to be addressed can be done with existing technology and resources. This means that a large number of projects can be initiated, and

good-paying jobs can be created quickly. This is of utmost importance for America to implement a sustainable approach to begin to work its way out of this "jobless" recovery.

6. Develop an integrated education and training plan that rationalizes the nation's approach for developing a skilled manufacturing workforce.

We recommend developing a Skilled Manufacturing Workforce Education and Training Plan. The plan would be standards- and competency-based and take a systems approach. It would identify all of the key players responsible for educating and training a skilled manufacturing workforce and define and assign roles, responsibilities, and performance expectations of each participant. It should establish a specific agenda and timetable for implementation.

The plan should assess the current performance of each participant and establish performance improvement goals based upon the desired performance expectations. The plan should precisely and thoroughly depict the linkage and articulation among and between the participants. It should spell out how the various players will communicate and cooperate to implement the plan and address how apprenticeships and on-the-job training would be structured (and how it would contribute to the development of a fully skilled manufacturing workforce).

Manufacturing and technical training have received the short end of the training and education stick for far too long. The emphasis has been placed on higher education and 4-year degrees and preparing youth for white-collar careers. There have been few blue-collar initiatives. This stands in stark contrast to countries such as Germany, Northern Ireland, and China, which place a policy and investment priority on creating a skilled manufacturing workforce.

7. Ensure the manufacturing technical training and support capabilities of America's community college network.

America's community colleges are uniquely positioned to assist in implementing a national skilled workforce education and training agenda because they sit at the juncture between secondary education and higher education and vocational education and technical training. Many community colleges have dual missions of job/career preparation and educational advancement.[2]

The Obama administration has put an emphasis on community colleges as a vehicle for retraining the workforce and has directed $12 billion for that purpose. It is important to ensure that all of the participating community colleges have the capability to deliver the type and quality of technical training to prepare workers for new careers. This is especially critical when it comes to equipping individuals to participate in the skilled manufacturing workforce.

Of 1,013 colleges, 55.1 percent offer specialized training in manufacturing skills. These colleges should be the "first responders" in helping create the new skilled workforce and act as allies with manufacturing in providing the workforce training that is required to make them competitive. Qualified community colleges should apply and/or compete for funding by demonstrating that they have the capacity to deliver manufacturing skills training that will ensure a high-performing workforce and good jobs for the workers that they train.

8. Ensure the level of financial and technical assistance required to make small businesses leaders in manufacturing.

More than 99 percent of the manufacturing companies in the United States are small- and medium-sized businesses. Because of their size, these businesses are likely to have difficulty in securing loans or lines of credit. They will also have difficulty in getting high-quality assistance on how to operate most effectively and efficiently, as well as access to the latest advice on innovation.

Therefore, a special provision should be made to ensure that low-cost direct loans and lines of credit are available for small- to medium-sized manufacturers. The limits on these loans and credit should not be capped arbitrarily but customized and scaled to the need of the individual applicant.

For more than 20 years, the government has operated the Manufacturing Extension Partnership (MEP) out of the National Institute of Standards and Technology in the Department of Commerce as a public–private partnership to increase the competitiveness of America's industrial base. The MEP is a national network comprised of 59 centers in 392 locations in every state of the Union and Puerto Rico. It has 2,500 affiliated partners representing private and non-profit organizations with specialized expertise in areas, such as manufacturing and business processes, as well as technological applications and economic development.

The MEP is funded through a combination of federal and state dollars. Since its establishment, the MEP has worked with thousands of manufacturers and helped to produce tens of billions of dollars in cost savings and increased or retained sales for its manufacturing clients.

At the end of 2008, the MEP issued a "Next Generation" Plan that put a strong focus on innovation and expanded assistance to manufacturers in five key areas: (1) continuous improvement, (2) technology acceleration, (3) sustainability, (4) supplier development, and (5) workforce.[3] The stimulus bill provided additional funding for MEP, and in June 2009, Commerce Secretary Gary Locke asked MEP Director Roger Kilmer to lead an effort to make it easier for "Main-Street businesses" to access service from the bureaus of the Commerce Department by establishing one-stop operations in the field.

We think this streamlining is especially important for manufacturing companies because of the complexity of their operations and the nature of their needs. Because of the excellence of its reputation and track record, the MEP should be given the level of funding necessary to ensure that it can implement its Next Generation Plan on an expanded and accelerated basis. This will help level the playing field for American manufacturers by enabling them to get the type of technical assistance they need to compete with global competitors—many of which receive substantial governmental support in their homelands.

9. Provide assistance to small manufacturing companies to help them reduce their healthcare costs.

Most manufacturing companies are small businesses. They will be impacted by the healthcare reform legislation that was passed in March 2010. The legislation requires these businesses to provide coverage but includes state-based insurance exchanges and provides tax credits of up to 35 percent of insurance costs for those manufacturing companies that employ less than 25 employees.

Thus, it appears that will be some relief and assistance for businesses. However, many groups that represent small businesses feel that the bill does not address the question of underlying healthcare costs—we agree—and that the imposition of new taxes and government mandates will make healthcare more expensive—we're not certain about that.

We are certain that the healthcare reform bill must be seen as a work in progress. The actual impact of implementation must be assessed and the bill should be revised accordingly. As we note at other points in this book, costs must be driven down and quality must be improved. State-based exchanges will probably have a minor effect on cost—the potential for exchanges across state lines needs to be revisited.

Consideration should also be given to providing appropriate assistance to small businesses and manufacturing companies to help them reduce the cost of their coverage. This could be accomplished by creating and providing some financial support to small business association health plans. This recommendation was made by the U.S. Department of Commerce in 2004 and endorsed by President Bush.

10. Establish a trade agreement with China that is based on the principle of reciprocity.

There is nothing that has hurt the state of manufacturing in America more than the one-sided trade relationship that currently exists between the United States and China. The current relationship is not reciprocal and can be characterized as when someone hits you, turn the other cheek.

The United States has lost millions of jobs, and China accounts for more than one-half of the entire U.S. trade deficit once expenditures for oil are excluded. The deficit in 2009 was projected to be approximately $350 billion, with China accounting for more than $220 billion of it. Peter Navarro attributes this condition to China's protectionist and mercantilist trade policies.

Protectionist policies are those that exclude access to a country's domestic market and include policies such as quotas and tariffs, port-of-entry restrictions, local content rules, import licensing restrictions, and discriminatory tax policies. Mercantilist policies are those that abridge free trade principles, and include export subsidies, currency manipulation, counterfeiting and piracy, forced technology transfer, lax environmental and health and safety regulations, and unfair labor standards and practices.

According to Peter Navarro and almost all knowledgeable observers, China not only practices all of these policies and more—it has written the book on them![4] Still, the United States has been reticent to confront China on its violations.

Some of this reticence may be attributable to an ideological belief in free trade. Some may be due to the fact that the current arrangement benefits corporations doing business in China. Whatever the reason, a reciprocal trade agreement is needed—now. The longer there is no such agreement, the more likely it is that the American economy will continue to recover at a snail's pace, and the recovery will become even more jobless and hopeless.

The Obama administration put its first iron in the fire for fighting fire with fire by imposing tariffs on consumer tires coming into the U.S. from China for the next 3 years. These tariffs were levied based upon the recommendation made by the International Trade Commission (ITC), an independent body that advises the government on trade.

The ITC found that China violated an agreement it made upon entering the World Trade Organization by creating a "market disruption" for domestic American producers. The ITC found a similar violation four times during the Bush administration, but no action was taken.

In manufacturing terms, the die has been cast. It will most likely lead to some form of retaliation from China. That retaliation will probably lead to retaliation from the United States. The retaliation to the retaliation will probably lead to real negotiations and eventually reciprocity. That's how things normally work out in the real world where actions have consequences.

Alan Tonelson makes a persuasive case that for manufacturing to be restored to a position of strength, the United States will have to reform its trade policies, not only with China but with other nations in which the agreements have historically been too one-sided and favored others' interests more than ours.[5] We agree with Tonelson's perspective overall but signify on China here because it is the most egregious offender in the international trade arena.

11. Heighten public awareness of the importance of manufacturing and manufacturing careers.

Manufacturing has driven economic growth in the United States for a long time. That growth has been responsible for a better quality of life for millions of her citizens. We firmly believe that much of the public does not grasp what manufacturing has meant in creating America's past and what it means for our future.

For manufacturing to play a leading role in recovery and growth, it needs to be valued. Industry and government need to come together to create a full-scale and multifaceted educational campaign to accomplish this. The campaign should outline the "Reindustrialization Imperative" and strike a bold and compelling manufacturing vision for the future. It should be led by high-profile spokespersons who can appeal to all age groups. In addition, school curricula should include not only a study of the industrial revolution but how manufacturing is the backbone of the nation.

We all need to understand that no matter whether we are talking about smokestacks or laptops, we built this country on manufacturing. As manufacturing goes, so goes the nation.

CHAPTER 7: RENEWING SMALL BUSINESS/ ENTREPRENEURSHIP RECOMMENDATIONS

Small Business/Entrepreneurship Primary Recommendations

1. Increase funding and expand the current direct and guaranteed loan program for start-ups
2. Implement small business-friendly tax policies and incentives
3. Merge the SBA into the Department of Commerce

Small Business/Entrepreneurship Subsidiary Recommendations

4. Implement a targeted jobs program for entrepreneurs and small businesses

5. Enforce and increase the federal government's goals for small business contracts

6. Increase the funding for SBIR and STTR initiatives

7. Ensure the effective implementation of target group initiatives

8. Listen to and make the voices of small businesses and entrepreneurs count in policy making

9. Implement small business-friendly healthcare programs

4. Implement a targeted jobs program for entrepreneurs and small businesses.

In Chapter 4, we recommend implementing a massive four-component jobs bill with one of the components being focused on small business. That recommendation is critically important, and that's why we reiterate it here. Small businesses and entrepreneurs should get the direct and guaranteed loans described and targeted jobs tax credits for creating jobs that meet established criteria.

In addition, federal money should be concentrated to support entrepreneurship and business development in states and regions within states that have been the hardest hit by the recession in terms of job losses. The federal government should encourage and promote participation from state, local, and regional governments in those areas by implementing sliding scale matching fund investment requirements.

Consideration should also be given to establishing special dedicated funding streams for gazelle businesses and entrepreneurial businesses that appear to have high-job development potential. Research should be done to assess the characteristics of the Inc. 500 companies over time, as well as growth clusters and corridors to determine whether investments to support entrepreneurs in those locations make sense. Governments at all levels need to use available research and develop policies that create programs, which promote entrepreneurship, new business development, and job creation.

5. Enforce and increase the federal government goal for small business contracts.

The federal government's goal for contracts with small businesses in 2009 was 23 percent. This goal should be raised to a minimum of 25 percent in future years. No large business contracts should be counted toward goal accomplishment.

The SBA should be required to review its own reports and eliminate all companies from the list that do not satisfy the standards for being a small business. It should establish a system for true and honest reporting and be held accountable if it does not. The overstatement of small business contract awards by characterizing contracts with large businesses as small business has been going on for nearly a decade. There have been a variety of reasons given for this, but the fact is—no reason is acceptable.

6. Increase the funding for SBIR and STTR initiatives.

The Small Business Innovation Research (SBIR) program was established by Congress in 1982 and the Small Business Technology Transfer (STTR) program in 1992 to help meet the federal government's research and development needs though small businesses. The SBIR/STTR Reauthorization Act of 2009 was in a conference committee at the end of 2009. New features of the bill from the House and Senate include: 8-year reauthorization, increased funding for both SBIR and STTR, a stronger emphasis on outreach, and commercialization of products and venture capital participation in the programs.

The funding for SBIR and STTR should be increased two- to fourfold in 2010 and 2011. As part of this increased funding, the amount for commercialization of research products in the pipeline should be quintupled.

Small businesses generate 14 times more patents than big businesses and are technological pioneers. These patents lead to job growth. Increasing this funding for the short term will ensure that significantly more new products are developed faster, resulting in more jobs more quickly. The United States has always been an innovation nation. Both entrepreneurs and small businesses have been the primary innovators and job creators. This increase unleashes their potential to help solve the nation's current jobless recovery.

7. Ensure the effective implementation of target group initiatives.

The SBA currently operates a number of programs for targeted groups including women-owned businesses, minority-owned businesses, and veteran-owned businesses. Under its new leadership, the SBA has reaffirmed its commitment and placed renewed emphasis on these programs.

Kauffman Foundation research showed that in 2008, the two groups that significantly increased their business start-up activities were immigrants (.46 percent) and seniors (.36). While these numbers may appear small, the U.S. as a whole was .32 percent. They also note that immigrants start more high-income potential types of businesses when compared to native-born Americans.[6]

We recommend that the SBA consider implementing targeted programs for three other specific groups: immigrant entrepreneurs, senior entrepreneurs, and youth entrepreneurs. These programs should include set-asides for government contracts and also grants or loans to support business start-ups. Additional support might be provided to those entrepreneurs who launch "social enterprises" focused on addressing the needs of their target group or providing employment for members of the group.

8. Listen to and make the voices of small businesses and entrepreneurs count in policy making.

In September 2009, the Department of Commerce announced the establishment of a new Office on Innovation and Entrepreneurship (OIE) and of a National Advisory Council on Innovation and Entrepreneurship (NACIE). This could be either a game changer or, as frequently occurs in Washington, D.C.—the "symbolic use of politics." When you want to ensure that nothing happens, create a new assistant secretary position or a special study commission. Then, go on with business as usual.

To ensure that the OIE has a true impact, it should be given a substantial budget, appropriate staffing, and a leader with a title and job description that assigns the stature to make the OIE important within the Department of Commerce. When the SBA is merged into Commerce as we recommend, much of the excellent work and "cutting-edge" research that is being done through the SBA's Office of Advocacy can be rolled into the OIE. We also recommend establishing a formal working relationship with the Kauffman Foundation to piggyback and support their significant entrepreneurial research.

We agree with the establishment of NACIE. However, a National Council gives disproportionate weighting to a few voices. The council should be matched by regional advisory councils with a broad base of membership selected from highly qualified and representative small business owners and entrepreneurs.

Most importantly, systematic research should be done to gain quantitative confirmation of the qualitative input that will be expressed by both the regional and national councils. This will ensure that the "voice of small business and the entrepreneur" is heard in an unbiased and unfiltered fashion.

There are 27 million small businesses in the United States—no one trade group, association, appointed, or elected official can accurately reflect their opinions. Small businesses need to have their voice magnified. This can best be accomplished through private–public sector cooperation in implementing a continuous nonpartisan listening program that is objective in nature and rigorous in its design while being responsive to the messages received.

9. Implement small business-friendly healthcare programs.

An overwhelming message from the small business community is that the escalating costs of healthcare impose a tremendous burden on them—a burden that has become increasingly unbearable.

The Kaiser Family Foundation found that the average annual cost of employer-sponsored healthcare increased 119 percent between 1999 and 2008. It typically costs a small business 18 percent more than a large business to provide coverage for its employees.

Because of these factors, small businesses have been forced into cost-sharing, cafeteria-type plans, and even providing no coverage. In 2008, 16 million employees—almost 25 percent of the wage-and-salary workers—in small businesses with fewer than 500 employees had no coverage.

Studies released by the NIFB and the Kauffman Foundation in 2009 confirm that healthcare remains a paramount issue for small business owners and entrepreneurs. The NIFB study showed that 9 percent of the respondents rated healthcare as the "single-most-important problem."[7] In the Kauffman study, 27 percent ranked "reforming healthcare" as "the most important thing that the federal government should be doing to boost the economy."[8]

Given the foregoing, it is imperative that the needs of small businesses be adequately addressed as part of this healthcare reform. As we noted in our healthcare recommendation for small manufacturing companies, careful attention must be paid to the actual impact of this legislation on small businesses. If that impact is negative rather than positive, the bill should be revised as soon as possible.

There is a sort of trial period for the legislation from now until 2014 when various provisions go into full effect. This same window should be used to study the needs of small businesses more rigorously and to tailor the bill to address them directly.

CHAPTER 10: RENEWING GOVERNMENT RECOMMENDATIONS

Government Primary Recommendations

1. Have each federal government agency conduct a zero-based strategic organizational assessment and develop a strategic blueprint to become a high-performing organization.

2. Implement a government-wide operational excellence initiative with maximum feasible employee involvement.

3. Ensure on-the-job training and mentoring to transfer essential knowledge and skills to new government employees.

Government Subsidiary Recommendations

4. Establish stronger performance management capabilities in the executive and legislative branches and government agencies.

5. Ensure appropriate performance management training for all government employees.

6. Enhance the government hiring process.

7. Identify innovative and successful governmental models that can be used to stimulate integrated economic development and problem solving.

8. Build Congress's capacity and capabilities for performance management.

9. Eliminate television coverage of Supreme Court nominee hearings.

10. Provide capacity-building assistance to state and local governments.

4. Establish stronger performance management capabilities in the executive and legislative branches and government agencies.

On April 18, 2009, President Barack Obama named Jeffrey Zients to be the United States chief performance officer (CPO) and deputy OMB director for Management. He was confirmed on June 19. Zients receives assistance in his CPO role from Vivek Kundra, the government's chief information officer, and Aneesh P. Chopra, the chief technology officer.

On November 13, 2007, President George W. Bush signed Executive Order 13450: Improving Government Program Performance, which made it official policy to spend taxpayer dollars effectively, and more effectively each year. The order called for the establishment of a Performance Improvement Council (PIC) comprised of performance improvement officers (PIO) to be appointed by each agency head. The responsibilities of the PIO include:

- Development and improvement of each agency's strategic and performance plans, annual performance reports, and budget justifications

- Ensuring program goals are aggressive, realistic, and accurately measured

- Convening agency program management personnel to assess and improve program performance

- Assisting the head of the agency in the development and use of performance measures in performance appraisals

As noted earlier, GAO's mission is "to help improve the performance . . . of the federal government." One of the key functions GAO performs to accomplish this is "reporting on how well programs and policies are meeting their objectives."

What this all means is that there is now a stronger three-legged stool in place for performance management: CPO (executive); GAO (legislative); and PIO (federal agencies). This represents an improvement, but there are still some wobbly legs on that stool.

One is that there is a single person or small group of individuals with a scope of responsibilities that would normally require a large team to execute. Another issue is that the current approach is more reactive than proactive. It relies primarily on completing activities (e.g., strategic plan, annual plan, program or performance assessments, performance appraisals), rather than focusing on contributing directly to the achievement of improved performance results or outcomes.

In addition, there may a problem in terms of the actual level of authority for those in performance management positions. There was a classic *Harvard Business Review* article written about the senior human resources officer in private-sector organizations with the wonderful title, "Big Hat. No Cattle." That may be the case here. Why performance improvement officer instead of chief performance improvement officer? What's in a title? In this case, maybe everything—maybe nothing.

Given the foregoing, the performance management capabilities in all three areas should be strengthened significantly. Dedicated performance teams should be established, and those teams should have the capabilities to work directly on resolving performance issues and enhancing performance. These teams should be sized according to the nature and scope of their responsibilities. Team members should be recruited from inside and outside government and should have proven track records in areas such as organizational analysis and development, quality improvement, and performance management.

The Performance Improvement Council should consider forming "tiger teams" drawn from across agencies to deal with issues that are boundary crossing or interagency in nature. We suggest looking at the tiger teams used by GE as examples.

The case for strengthened performance management capacity and capabilities is clear and compelling. It should be at the top of the government's agenda going forward.

5. Ensure appropriate performance management training for all government employees.

The federal government has a highly professional workforce, including accountants, lawyers, engineers, economists, and computer programmers. While our government's workforce is proficient in the area of their technical expertise, many may be lacking when it comes to performance management.

The training that is required for most federal employees is primarily to ensure compliance with policy and program changes. Many organizations in the private sector provide wall-to-wall and on-going training in critical areas, such as quality management, lean manufacturing, and process improvement.

In contrast, the federal government's training on these topics tends to be episodic, related to a reform initiative and more voluntary in nature. If the government wants its employees to be competent at performance management, they need to receive adequate and appropriate training to develop the requisite knowledge, skills, and abilities. They also need to be trained on how to work effectively in problem-solving teams.

The federal government should make performance management training a requirement for all employees. The training should include how to use the performance measurement data that are currently collected, as well as how to gather new data. It should also include a component on contractor management given the large amount of work that the government is outsourcing. If possible, that training should be done in teams using an actual workplace issue. That would allow a team to identify performance improvement needs together and develop a plan to address them as part of the training and then implement that plan upon return to the workplace.

The Office of Personnel Management (OPM) should conduct a review of available courses and resources and develop a list of approved courses and vendors that agencies can choose from to implement training. As part of that review, OPM should identify courses and materials that have been developed by government agencies in the past, such as those created by the Federal Quality Institute in the late 1980s and early 1990s, Malcolm Baldrige Award materials, and material developed as part of the Clinton-era reinvention initiative. Each agency should be required to submit its performance management training plan to OMB as part of the annual budget and performance planning process. OMB should require that the training be "fast-tracked" so that the agencies can begin to implement their performance improvement initiatives as soon as possible.

No matter whether government is rowing or steering—both are hands-on activities. So is performance management. Providing mandatory performance management training for all federal employees will ensure that they can do the hands-on work that is necessary for performance improvement.

6. Enhance the government hiring process.

Now is the time for fixing what is broken instead of engaging in what President Obama refers to as "the default position is inertia" in Washington. Based upon Peter Orszag's June 11, 2009, budget and performance planning memo, it looks like OMB is trying to break the inertia in the federal personnel arena—at least as it relates to streamlining the hiring process.

In his memo, Orszag directs agencies to use a new tool called the End-to-End Hiring Roadmap. The Roadmap was created in 2008 to help agencies break out of hiring gridlock, but it has not been widely used so far. Orszag sets out four clear benchmarks for improving the hiring process: (1) mapping the current hiring process to improve timeliness, (2) plain language and streamlined announcements, (3) communicating with applicants, and (4) involving hiring managers.[9]

How important was Orszag's focus and how serious is the need to improve federal hiring? *The Washington Post* ran an article on the memo titled, "The Memo That Roared." It cited one particularly egregious case where a mapping effort at the Federal Student Aid agency disclosed a 110-step hiring process that required the input of 45 people. The article concluded by noting that Orszag's memo also made the point that it was not good enough just to accelerate hiring; it was also necessary to retain employees once they were hired.[10]

We agree with Orszag and the *Post*. However, we'd also like to add *recruitment* to the list of factors to be considered for enhancing the hiring process. Specifically, we recommend that the government develop an outreach program to targeted segments to replenish the federal workforce. These segments should include baby boomers from the private sector workforce who have lost their jobs, recent college graduates from institutions and programs who, in the past, might not have considered federal employment as an attractive career option, and state and local government employees who have been part of reductions in force at that level.

In January 2008, the Partnership for Public Service issued a report that noted many of these "older Americans" had somewhat negative opinions about government and federal service. Given the collapse of the economy later that same year and the increased joblessness among the baby boomer generation throughout 2009, it seems to us the government has the opportunity to bring these experienced and skilled workers into the workforce.[11] Just as the government was looking for "shovel-ready" projects for the stimulus bill, the government should be making the recruitment of these "job-ready" individuals into the workforce a priority.

Replace a baby boomer with a baby boomer. Seems like a good trade. Good for the worker, the economy, and the federal service.

7. Identify innovative and successful governmental models that can be used to stimulate integrated economic development and problem solving.

The words "innovation" and "government" are not frequently used in the same sentence. Government is often characterized as sluggish, lethargic, and slow moving at best, and wasteful and inefficient at worst. It doesn't have to be that way.

Government should promote innovation within the economy, in its policy applications, and in the programs it operates. The government should identify best practices and successful governmental models for accomplishing this, document them, and provide them to agency heads for possible replication. Given the challenges facing the United States on all fronts, innovation cannot be ignored.

In describing a meeting hosted by Harvard Business School Professor John Kao in *The New York Times*, Steve Lohr wrote, "Governments are increasingly into the innovation game, declaring innovation agendas and appointing senior innovation." Lohr noted that the most advanced nations in terms of their focus on innovation include Britain, India, and Finland. All three nations have dedicated resources and programs that promote innovation.[12]

On the other hand, the United States lags behind when it comes to governmental innovation. However, the Obama administration has stuck its toe into the innovation pond in its new budget that directs the Bureau of Economic Analysis to develop statistics that "uniquely measure the role of innovation" in the economy. Aneesh Chopra, the government's new chief technology officer, has boldly declared that one of his job responsibilities is to build "innovation platforms" to spur growth.

The call for policy innovation also came from a meeting convened in June 2008 by the Accenture Institute for Public Service, the Georgetown Public Policy Institute, and OMB Watch. The meeting report included the following observation: "Where there continues to be a need to hold government programs to account, the president needs to encourage and support innovation and reasonable risk-taking within federal agencies to develop more creative solutions to larger and more complex problems."[13] Sometimes those crosscutting solutions already exist, but they are not being duplicated or replicated to deal with multi-faceted problems like the current economic crisis or implementing the stimulus bill rollout.

As an example, the Defense Department has an Office of Economic Adjustment (OEA). Patrick O'Brien is the office's executive officer. OEA was created in 1961 to assist state and local government efforts to aid communities, workers, and businesses as they respond to base closures as well as mission growth activity. From its start, OEA has operated very successfully.

The OEA has prepared a short white paper that provides a description of the manner in which the OEA works and how its approach can be used for other economic discontinuities.[14] The heart of OEA's approach is the project manager who acts as the "pivot person" for the intervention. The departure of a major employer like Maytag from Newtown, Iowa, or the closing of recreational vehicle plants in Elkhart, Indiana, are just as potentially devastating to a community as the closing of any military installation. Therefore, the federal government should explore expanding and implementing the OEA model and other integrated ones like it nationwide and in nondefense-related situations.

8. Build Congress's capacity and capabilities for performance management.

Earlier, we recommended that the performance management capabilities of the executive, legislative, and agency branches of government be strengthened significantly. Specifically, we recommend that GAO establish a dedicated performance management unit and have that unit be available to work directly with congressional staffers to resolve performance issues as well as enhance performance and the policy-making process.

In addition, each member of Congress should be allowed to hire one additional seasoned performance management analyst at a salary commensurate with experience and expertise. The analyst should assist in the review of performance management data and contribute to the development of policy proposals and appropriate interventions. The key committees should also add two performance management analyst positions.

Finally, a review should be done of congressional budgets to determine if they are adequate to recruit and retain the quantity and quality of staff necessary to manage a high-performing government. While many might argue that this is a time to cut costs, we argue that cost-cutting does not necessarily improve performance, nor does it automatically enhance either efficiency or effectiveness.[15]

We are entering an era when the nation needs results. We need to do the appropriate level of investment to ensure those results can be realized. False economies in D.C. can destroy the national economy. If we need an additional 30,000 troops in Afghanistan and Iraq, we send them with few questions asked. If we want to add 300 or 3,000 positions to the government, we hold a grand inquisition.

Homeland security and economic security are equally important. Let's size the force in both instances to the nature of the need and problem.

9. Eliminate TV coverage of Supreme Court nominee hearings.

Even though the judicial branch was not in our direct line of sight for the chapter on government, the Supreme Court confirmation hearing for Justice Sonia Sotomayor necessitated a recommendation.

The hearing was held but little hearing was going on, and certainly not a lot of listening. The members of the judicial committee went on at length espousing their positions and philosophies while Justice Sotomayor said as little as possible in a completely scripted manner. There were lots of talking points but few thoughtful ones. We agree with former Supreme Court Justice Sandra Day O'Connor. The only thing these hearings were good for was to allow the cable channels to fill up their broadcast agenda at a low cost, and for the judicial committee members to get a little camera time.

In the future, these hearings should be closed. Or, because no nominee is going to make the mistake that Robert Bork did and speak the truth, maybe they shouldn't even be held. In any case, the Supreme Court does not allow cameras in the courtroom partially to ensure the right atmosphere and decorum. We should apply the same rule to the nomination hearings. Perhaps it would result in a little more comity and a lot less comedy.

10. Provide capacity-building assistance to state and local governments.

State and local governments are in dire straights. Early in 2010, it was reported that all states, with the exception of Montana and North Dakota, had tight budgets and would run fiscal deficits with a potential shortfall of $350 billion nationally. Federal government handouts under the ARRA may have stemmed the tide just a little, but they most assuredly did not prime the pump or stop the bleeding.

The federal government is going to have to look very seriously at its unfunded mandates and their impact on state and local economies.

When times were good, it was possible to pass the bill and the buck, but not the dollars, down the line. Times are no longer good, and the federal government needs to do its part.

In 2009, state and local governments cut budgets and consolidated at a feverish pace. When all of that is done and a state of equilibrium is achieved, these governmental units will have to start thinking about reinvention. The government can give them a push in the right direction.

The federal government should draw upon its best resources to create reinvention templates and primers that these governments can employ to implement the reinvention process. This information should be shared with the governments in planning meetings cosponsored with the National Governors Association and the other national groups that support these governments.

The good news is a lot of good data can be drawn from the federal government's reinvention experience and efforts with GPRA and PART. The better news is that there has been work in the field done by state and local government practitioners, academics, and others. For the most part, this will be about assembling best practices as opposed to inventing. In this regard, the Public Strategies Group has put together an excellent white paper, "Game Changing Opportunities to Help States Deal with Fiscal Crisis," that details some opportunities, including performance contracting, the creation of charter agencies that commit to specified results in return for the waiver of certain rules or red tape, and business process improvement.[16]

CHAPTER 11: RENEWING BUSINESS RECOMMENDATIONS

Business Primary Recommendations

1. Establish an independent oversight board to monitor the work of the Federal Reserve Bank.

2. Establish tax and financial incentives for firms to create or bring jobs to the U.S.

3. Create a social entrepreneur venture and tax credits fund.

Business Subsidiary Recommendations

4. Develop an industrial and innovation policy that spurs investment and creativity in targeted sectors.

5. Engage in transformational thinking and planning to create the business of the future.

6. Revamp the curricula of business schools and schools of public policy.

7. Enhance corporate social responsibility (CSR) programs.

8. Create business and industry advisory panels for businesses in which the government has significant ownership positions.

4. Develop an industrial and innovation policy that spurs investment and creativity in targeted sectors.

America's investment in research and development has always kept it ahead of the competitive pack. Industrial spending on R&D has never declined from one year to another (with the exception of a small decline between 2000–2002, after the dot-com bust). However, Jules Duga of the Battelle Memorial Institute projects that spending will decline slightly in 2010.

We are not certain whether this is a retrenchment or an indicator of a new focus on cost control. We do know that America is losing the race to international competitors in a number of strategic areas. America has been ranked sixth (out of 40 countries) for innovation and competitiveness by the Information Technology and Innovation Foundation.

The government should develop an industrial strategy for growth and innovation that directs investments toward targeted areas, which will diversify our economy. It should hit those areas with a big stick and use these investments as seed money to bring in private-sector capital.

In Chapter 1 of this book, we recommended that the government create a National Global Competitiveness Commission to prepare a Competitive Strategic Advantage Plan. The government should use that plan as the basis for making its decisions on policy and innovation. We also addressed the need for an intensified focus on innovation in Chapter 10 on government and recommended that the government "should promote innovation within the economy, its policies, and in the programs it operates."

America already has a strong track record and history of success from pursuing innovation policies in areas such as the space race, medical research, and maintaining a strong defense. We should study those innovations and learn how to build upon them.

The American Recovery and Reinvestment Act was criticized because it contained a number of R&D projects. We criticize it also. However, our criticism is not because of the projects but because of their diverse scope, nature, and insufficient funding. The projects in the stimulus bill were essentially one-offs or funding for a potpourri of proposals not funded in the past. There was no concentrated focus or leveraging. Therefore, the best that can be hoped for are diffuse results and occasional small victories.

We need an integrated industrial and innovation policy. It is central to restoring America and the American Dream. That is why we have called for an increased emphasis on innovation as a driver in several chapters in this book.

5. Engage in transformational thinking and planning to create the business of the future.

For the vast majority of industries and businesses, 2009 was not a good year. Conventional wisdom is that 2010 will be a relatively flat year with a possible uptick toward the year's end. It is projected that 2011 will see a slow rebound and the establishment of the "new normal" for the economy and businesses. Right now, there is no normal. The only Normal that exists is a city in Illinois.

Businesses should use this transitional period to engage in transformational thinking and planning for their future by asking themselves the following questions:

- What is the "new normal" in terms of factors, such as customer needs and preferences, market size, stability, and profitability?

- What are the basic planning assumptions for the business for the next 3 years?

- What are the most significant trends in the firm's operating environment that the business should be prepared to respond to?

- What is the business's long-term vision?

- If the business could implement only one strategic initiative to realize its vision, what should it be?

- What are alternative scenarios (best case, worst case, another plausible scenario) for the business and industry during this period? What are the key drivers for each scenario?

Businesses should ensure that in asking these questions, they are not just talking to themselves about themselves. They need to reach out to customers and do a rigorous assessment of their competitive landscape. They need to be totally strategic and transformational in considering their future. (We provide a more complete model for transformational thinking and organizational renewal in Chapter 14 of this book.)

6. Revamp the curricula of business schools and schools of public policy.

America's system of higher education is second to none. Our M.B.A. and public policy programs turn out well prepared and highly qualified future leaders for the private and public sectors.

There is one limitation, however. Many of the schools tend to produce students with tunnel vision. They are specialists in the space they have been trained in and in the language that they have learned. Virtually none of these students is bilingual because that is not a success requirement for the career track upon which they are ready to embark. In fact, some see their academic counterparts as enemies—money-grubbers on the one side, tree huggers on the other.

This is a divide that must end. Businesspeople need to understand the way that government works, and government employees need to understand the way that business works. Mutual understanding and respect for the other's field of endeavor is necessary.

To facilitate the establishment of this shared perspective, the M.B.A. school should include a required course in its curriculum on government and vice versa. In addition, business schools should diversify their curricula to be more holistic and reflective of the world of business. Far too much emphasis has been placed in recent years on finance and the teaching of quantitative methods and far too little attention has been paid to the qualitative issues such as organizational dynamics, human resource management, and business ethics.

There are a number of academic institutions that are addressing these more qualitative areas today, and many business schools such as Harvard have begun a complete restructuring of their curriculum. One particularly innovative approach of which we are aware is a business ethics curriculum developed by the Lake Forest Graduate School of Management and the International Business Ethics Institute under the leadership of Bob Kallen, adjunct professor at Lake Forest. The curriculum addresses race and gender in a broader framework of business ethics and covers topics such as:

- Minority and gender composition of board and in the executive suite
- The ethics of Washington focusing on the influence of money and lobbying
- The concentration of wealth in our society and executive compensation
- The ethical issues facing the mutual fund industry
- Comparing explicit values of corporations versus implicit values to see how they differ
- Whistle-blowing and the role of the judicial process
- Effective marketing and ethical constraints

This is just one example of how business schools can make themselves more relevant. The more that our institutions do to educate the future generation of leaders to be bilingual—even multilingual—the better it will be for business and society.

7. Enhance corporate social responsibility (CSR) programs.

When money was cheap and times were fast, businesses could afford to have corporate social responsibility programs that did not necessarily link to their business strategy. Those days are long gone.

Today and in the future, it will be imperative to achieve a perfect alignment between the business agenda and the social agenda. The goal should be to use one to magnify and reinforce the other in order to get the best return on investment.

Michael Porter and Mark Kramer note, "The most important thing a corporation can do for society is to contribute to a prosperous economy."[17] A business makes that contribution by operating both profitably and properly. That enables it to be a good corporate citizen who can be trusted to balance the business and the public interest.

As we noted earlier, well designed and implemented CSR programs produce a double bottom line. Businesses should conduct a rigorous review and evaluation of their current CSR to determine how well they are designed and how well they are performing. They should use that review to restructure their programs as required.

Given the events of 2008, CSR programs are more important than ever. At one time, they may have been nice but not necessary, but that's no longer the case as evidenced by:

- A 2009 IBM Institute for Business Value study which found that 60 percent of the 224 businesspeople surveyed believe that CSR has increased in importance over the past year, with only 6 percent considering it a lower priority

- Hill and Knowlton's 2008 survey which revealed that three-fourths of 530 M.B.A. candidates contacted said that reputation was either "extremely" or "very important" in deciding where to work after graduating

- The Tenth Annual Edelman Trust Barometer which concluded that 77 percent of respondents refused to buy from companies they distrusted

8. Create business and industry advisory panels for those ventures in which the government has significant ownership positions.

In the past, when the renowned criminal Willie Sutton was asked why he robbed banks, he responded, "Because that's where the money is." Willie wouldn't be able to give that answer today because the tables have turned. Now, many of the banks are robbing us because there isn't money in them anymore.

The American taxpayer has been forced to be the investor of last resort and to take majority and minority positions in American businesses. In some instances, the citizens are represented on the board of directors, and in others, it is investment without representation. Frankly, we don't feel that either approach is acceptable.

The government should establish full-time independent business and industry advisory panels for each business in which we have made a major investment (anything over 10 percent). These panels should function in a manner similar to a court-ordered receiver and a turnaround consulting firm.

Each organization's business plan should be reviewed and critiqued. There should be daily oversight and monitoring of an organization's plan. The panel should highlight performance and compliance problems and call for corrective action plans. They should protect the interests of the taxpayer and ensure that progress is made in restoring the organization as a real business instead of languishing as a ward of the state. They should stay involved until that is accomplished.

Even though it's not directly related to the money we put on the stump for them, the first report card on how banks handled the foreclosure workout program provides an excellent example of what happens when institutions are left to their own devices with little or no surveillance. With the notable exception of JP Morgan Chase, the majority of them did next to nothing.

The reason is simple. The banks wanted to continue to carry these mortgages on their books at inflated values, rather than marking them to market, reducing the principal, and renegotiating the loans. By keeping them on their books, they didn't have to deal with the effect these underwater mortgages could have on their balance sheets. So, they have hoarded their money to insulate their capital requirements. That makes sense for them, but not for the rest of us.

The United Kingdom has created an independent UK Financial Investments (UKFI) group as an arm's-length government-owned group to manage the government's financial investments. The UKFI does not intervene in day-to-day management. Simon C. Y. Wong, law professor and independent advisor, advocates creating an equivalent intermediary body in the United States because of the need to integrate voting power (exercised by independent trustees) and strategic influence (which resides in Treasury and regulatory agencies).[18]

The independent body might make some sense. However, we'd like to see more value-added involvement from it than just being an investment advisor. No matter what is done, this is too important an area to just maintain the status quo. We are in perilous times. It's time to get all business hands on board and working in a concerted and concentrated manner to develop successful and sustainable solutions that will help create the new normal—a normal that will protect and advance the American economy, and with it, the American Dream.

CHAPTER 12: RENEWING CIVIC ENGAGEMENT RECOMMENDATIONS

Civic Engagement Primary Recommendations

1. Prepare future generations of citizens by teaching civics and civic engagement in middle school.

2. Permit voting to take place on an extended basis and allow mail-in voting for everyone (with proper safeguards)

3. Implement a national fair districting initiative.

4. Convene town halls and community discussions about issues of concern to citizens and the role of government in America's future.

Civic Engagement Subsidiary Recommendations

5. Develop and enforce a code of conduct for candidates for political office.

6. Demand more transparency and accountability from all groups involved in campaign financing.

7. Involve our higher educational institutions in addressing failures and breakdowns in government and the political process.

5. Develop and enforce a code of conduct for candidates for political office.

There is something that is dehumanizing about too many political campaigns. For some reason, when it comes to political contests, God-fearing, church-, temple-, or mosque-going candidates who normally wouldn't say "horse feathers" if they had a mouthful, turn into fire-breathing, go-for-the-jugular attack dogs and use negative advertising as their preferred mode of communications.

It's not just the candidates; it's the posse around them as well. Name-calling, character assassination, and misrepresentation of facts become not only the norm—they are applauded. If a candidate and his or her team don't engage in this form of negative campaigning, they're accused of being "wusses" or worse.

There is something that is very wrong with this picture. Political candidates should be required to sign a pledge that demands that they comport themselves with dignity, treat their rivals with decency, and not engage in negative political advertising. They should agree to condemn any negative political advertising that is done by groups such as the Swift Boat Veterans. Moreover, the pledge should be enforceable—not with the withdrawal of a candidate from the race—but through a public sanction and rebuke that is promoted prominently to, and through, the media.

The good news is there are some excellent examples of these pledges. In Sarasota, the local Civic League developed the following pledge that was signed by most of the local candidates in the 2008 elections:

Advertisements will be considered negative if they violate the *core values of compassion, honesty, responsibility, fairness, and respect.* Advertisements will be considered:

- *Compassionless* if they foster hatred or rancor
- *Dishonest* if they base their messages on lies or subtle deceptions and half truths
- *Irresponsible* if they degrade the tenor of public discourse and heighten cynicism about the electoral process
- *Unfair* if they use emotive spins to attack an opposing candidate's personal characteristics

- *Disrespectful* if they refuse to treat the opposing candidate as a worthy citizen and individual

In spite of these signed pledges, several of the Sarasota campaigns turned into mud-slinging contests of the worst type. It seemed that for some of the candidates, their pledge wasn't worth the paper that it was written on.

6. Demand more transparency and accountability from all groups involved in campaign financing.

It is difficult to get candidates to agree to campaign finance reform—especially those with significant personal wealth that they are willing to use to get elected or reelected. Even when candidates are in favor of reform, they can change their mind as Barack Obama did in the last presidential contest.

Obama's rationale was that political action committees (PACs) and 527 groups would not be subject to limits and constrained in their spending. Therefore, he wanted to be able to raise as much money as possible to compete against that independent spending.

To get some perspective on the scope and existence of these "independent financing groups," let's look at the state of Florida. In the race for the United States 13th congressional district between Vern Buchanan (Republican) and Christine Jennings (Democrat), Buchanan got $1.3 million from the independent groups and Jennings got $800,000. Buchanan won. In the race for Florida House District 70 between Doug Holder (Republican) and Sam Rosenfeld (Democrat), Holder got $91,000 from independent groups and Rosenfeld received $1,750. Holder won.[19]

These independent groups also spend lots of money on negative advertising and can engage in the most vicious attacks without having to abide by any of the rules or regulations that candidates agree to or at least espouse. An even bigger problem is that it can be extremely difficult to determine who is running these groups. They operate in the campaign financing netherworld and do very bad things.

These independent groups should not be regulated—and it appears they will not—based upon the nature of the Supreme Court's ruling in January 2010. However, they should be required to report as part of their quarterly filings, a listing of officers, directors, and contributors, as well as details of their activities including ads and candidates they have supported. They should also be subject to legal action if their attacks are determined to be defamatory.

In our opinion, the reporting requirements for the individual candidates and the parties are adequate and do not need to be addressed. That does not mean we condone the amount of money that is raised and spent in the political process in the United States—in fact, we believe it is obscene. If we could devote just one-tenth of that amount to supporting civic and charitable activities, America would be a far better place. In fact, there's an idea to try on for size—what about making tithing a requirement for all political candidates and parties?

7. Involve our higher educational institutions in addressing failures and breakdowns in government and the political process.

As we noted earlier, Americans have never been especially fond of government. That fondness has not increased over the past few years. In fact, there has been a further alienation of affections in this time period. In a meeting that Ed Crego facilitated for a brainstorming group of public policy experts convened by the University of Illinois at Springfield, the group concluded that there is "plummeting public confidence in all forms of government—most especially state government."[20]

This trust-busting must be addressed and corrected. Institutions of higher education need to become more proactive in studying and developing recommendations for the improvement of government and restoration of public confidence. Some of the actions that might be taken in this regard include:

- A study on the role of state government in the twenty-first century.

- A continuing education program for legislators and agency heads. The program could address areas such as policy skills, process analysis, and ethics.

- A summit to look at the state of the state in public affairs.

Higher education institutions and their public affairs departments are in the unique position to undertake activities of this type because of their mandates and missions. As honest brokers rather than representatives of special interest groups, they can advocate for changes to enhance the performance of government and public perceptions of government.

CHAPTER 13: RENEWING SOCIAL CAPITAL RECOMMENDATIONS

Social Capital Primary Recommendations

1. Articulate a social compact for the twenty-first century.
2. Establish "Interdependence Day" as a national holiday for celebrating our connectedness as citizens.
3. Require mandatory national service for all youth 18–21.

Social Capital Subsidiary Recommendations

4. Invest in activities that blend community economic development and community building.
5. Increase support for those organizations that are focused on community service and volunteerism.
6. Exploit the power and potential of the Internet for development of social capital and community building.
7. Stimulate the private sector's participation in community-building activities.
8. Encourage interdenominational faith-based initiatives directed at enhanced communications and community problem solving.

4. Invest in activities that blend community economic development and community building.

Over the years, there have been substantial governmental and philanthropic investments in projects directed at social safety net and community-building activities related to poverty. On the national level, the most significant governmental initiative is the work of Community

Action Agencies (CAAs). CAAs were established under the Economic Opportunity Act of 1964 to fight America's War on Poverty. Authorized by the Community Services Block Grant, there are more than 1,000 CAAs covering 96 percent of the nation's counties.

At first, CAAs were primarily focused on social service delivery and support activities. In the more than 40 years since they were created, many innovative CAAs have transformed themselves. They have become the front lines for reducing poverty and its effects throughout the United States and are dedicated to revitalizing low-income communities and empowering the working poor and their families to become fully self-sufficient. They provide a hand up instead of a handout. There are also numerous innovative community-based organizations (CBOs) across the country that are also engaged in community economic development (CED) and asset building.

A new Community Investment Fund should be created to support the activities of CAAs and CBOs who are doing economic development and asset building. This fund is important because it builds the necessary bridges between community, social, and financial capital. It can be a blend of private and public monies similar to the New Markets Tax Credits.

The success of CAAs and CBOs is inextricably linked and interwoven with the success of their participants. Unlike private sector developers and other national groups focused primarily on episodic "bricks-and-mortar" projects, CAAs and CBOs realize the importance of the on-going connection between community and human capital development.

They understand that the fabric of a community is not physical but spiritual and emotional. As a result, they build communities in order to grow more opportunities. They take the returns that they generate and the assets they create and reinvest them in their own communities. They are there for the long haul.

5. Increase support for those organizations that are focused on community service and volunteerism.

On April 21, 2009, President Obama signed the Edward M. Kennedy Serve America Act, a sweeping piece of legislation that will significantly increase the number of Americans volunteering to address local community needs. The act reauthorized and expanded the national service programs administered by the Corporation for National and Community Service, a federal agency created in 1993. The corporation currently engages four million Americans each year in results-driven service including AmeriCorps, Senior Corps, Learn and Serve America, and other community volunteers.

The new act is estimated to cost about $6 billion over 5 years, and by 2017, will expand the number of AmeriCorps members from 75,000 to 250,000. Ten percent of the money for AmeriCorps will be reserved for organizations enrolling adults over 55.

The legislation creates four new service corps specializing in healthcare, clean energy, fighting poverty, and support for veterans. New features include: scholarships of $1,000 for adults over 55 who serve 350 or more hours with a qualified organization; volunteers over 55 who serve full-time for a year can transfer their education award, and Encore fellowships that match those volunteers 55 and older with modestly paid positions in public or private nonprofits. It is envisioned that the fellowships will provide a bridge to second careers in the non-profit world. At the start, up to 10 fellows per state will be financed by a public–private partnership that pairs an $11,000 federal grant for each participant with matching funds from a host organization.

The Serve America Act is an exemplary piece of legislation in what it is trying to achieve. The problem is that the dimensions of the need in terms of those 55 and older are much clearer than they were when the Act was being drafted, as is the state of joblessness and under- and unemployment which, combined, have been estimated to be as high as 20 percent nationally. In other words, there are a large number of people in the 55-plus age cohort who had planned on retiring but because of the collapse in value of their 401(k)s and homes, are, instead, looking to reenter the labor pool. The societal safety net is being stretched as the full effect of the capital collapse of 2008 and the failure to staunch unemployment in 2009 wrecks havoc across generational lines.

Given this, serious consideration should be given to accelerating the AmeriCorps employment target to 250,000 in 3 years instead of 8, as well as increasing the number of fellowships and doubling or tripling the stipends for the scholarships.

6. Exploit the power and potential of the Internet for development of social capital and community building.

We commented earlier that we think the Internet has the potential to be used as a positive force for developing social capital and community building. If there is any doubt about that, look at what the Obama campaign did in the 2008 election and what the administration is doing now with Organizing for America. Obama and his staff rewrote the playbook on how to run a political campaign. That is because they saw the endeavor as being as much about organizing communities and motivating and mobilizing citizens as it was about political organizing. In essence, they built a citizen- and community-centered campaign for the president.

Their use of the Internet as a tool for doing this was unrivalled. Whether it was e-mailing, blogging, getting volunteers, soliciting funds, asking for personal stories, no one had come close to mastering the use of the electronic age in the way the Obama campaign did. What Howard Dean and Joe Trippi did with the Internet for fundraising purposes was the tip of the iceberg. This was the iceberg full blown, and it helped to sink Hillary Clinton's ship in the Democratic primary and John McCain's in the general election.

Now, Obama is president and Organizing for America (the legacy organization from the campaign) is using the Internet in much the same manner that it did during the campaign—seeking funds, asking for stories, and soliciting volunteers to canvass on issues such as healthcare. Time will tell whether they will be effective. We have serious doubts and believe that they will not be as effective as they were when there was a cause and a crusade around a charismatic leader. But, they still provide a model that can be used to build social capital and civic engagement in a manner that hadn't been done before.

Nonprofit and philanthropic groups should be trained in the methods of Internet mobilization so that they can employ them to increase their solicitation of funds and volunteers. They should also develop shared space that can be used for social capital networking purposes.

Tweeting has become the rage. Twitter began as a geeky-, celebrity-based phenomenon used for postings, musings, and meanderings, rather than for meaningful exchanges and advancing society. However, now we are poised on the twitter-totter. Iran showed that tweeting can serve another purpose. The Internet went from academic and business use to being a communications tool for the masses. Tweeting needs to go in the other direction. Twitter should be used to develop communities of interest around important social issues and problems. New apps should be created to allow the use of twitter to explore alternatives, options, and solutions. The same continuing migration should be made for Facebook, MySpace, and other social media.

7. Stimulate the private sector's participation in community-building activities.

In the past, the private sector was a leader in sponsoring activities that built community and created social capital at the local level. That's still true today, but to a lesser extent as organizations are merged, operations are closed or consolidated, corporate giving is nationalized, and local budgets are reduced.

Small local businesses bear more and more of the burden for sponsoring civic and community events and initiatives. But in these tough times, these businesses are being forced to diminish contributions or disappear altogether. As an example, hundreds of Chrysler dealerships were targeted for elimination as part of its restructuring, and GM disposed of more than 2,000 of its dealers as part of its plan to emerge from bankruptcy. Many of these dealers were in small- to mid-sized towns. Many of them were also major employers and charitable contributors in those locations.

There was talk early on in the Obama administration of taxing part of an individual or corporation's charitable contributions. Just the opposite should be the practice. In order to stimulate private sector giving, there should be a gradated incentive in terms of tax credits. In addition, in much the same way that the United Way runs its campaigns, if a high percent of the companies in a community give, they should get some type of group incentive or a matching grant.

Many foundations use a challenge grant approach. This should also be explored as a means for bringing private sector collaboration and cooperation to bear on restoring social capital at the community—most especially in smaller and more impoverished communities where they do not have the resource base to draw upon for campaign purposes.

8. Encourage interdenominational faith-based initiatives directed at enhanced communications and community problem solving.

President George W. Bush placed an early emphasis on implementing faith-based initiatives as a means to deal with social and community problems. President Obama is an advocate of these initiatives. We are also firm believers that they are important.

However, one of our concerns is that these initiatives have the potential to be secular and promote segregation, rather than integration. One of the problems for some of the faith-based organizations is that they tend to elevate hot-button issues such as stem cell research and abortion above those of social justice.

Mike Huckabee, former governor from Arkansas and Republican candidate for president, does not fall into this camp. He espoused a solid social justice agenda as part of his candidacy. Nor, we should add, does Rick Warren, author of *The Purpose Driven Life*, who gave the invocation at President Obama's inauguration.

Through the Depression era and into the early1960s, the Catholic Church had social justice issues at the center of their agenda. That has changed in much of the United States today. It is interesting that when Pope Benedict met with Barack and Michele Obama, a discussion of social justice was high on his priority list. How this admonition will be translated to the orientation and activities of the Catholic Church in America remains to be seen.

The real issue is that people of all faiths—Christian, Muslim, Jewish—be brought together to do ecumenical problem solving around issues that matter. As part of its support of faith-based initiatives, the federal government should give special support to those that transcend a single church or congregation. The government should set aside selected competitive grants that are awarded based upon demonstrated collaboration in cooperative planning and implementation. There is a National Day of Prayer that can, and should, also be used to promote multireligious celebrations by people of faith across the country.

Acknowledgments

We dedicate this book to our wives: Debbie Driesman Islam, Kathy Muñoz, and Sheila Smith (Crego). They have been our partners in pursuing and achieving the American Dream.

We thank everyone who took considerable time from busy schedules to provide input and feedback on the drafts of the book. First, special recognition to Sheila Smith, researcher extraordinaire, who identified numerous resources and provided several of the ideas presented in the book. Second, thanks to our colleagues who had the tenacity and dedication to read and comment on the entire manuscript: Lisa Crego, John Crego, Rita Ferrandino, Ron Gunn, Ed Kazemek, Ted Reed, Rick Roth, and Jim Scott. Third, thanks to those who read and reacted to sections: Dick Anderson, Ron Armagast, Allan Boscacci, Jim Dauner, Tom DeBoor, Kitty Higgins, Art Leyland, Ed McManus, Don Mizaur, Kristi Peterson, and Dan Speers. Fourth, sincere appreciation to development editor Cynthia Zygmund, who helped trim and tighten the book to make it more reader friendly.

We read and consulted a wide variety of diverse sources in preparing to write this book. We were impressed by the quality of thinking and the ideas put forward. They helped shape our analysis, conclusions, and recommendations. We, of course, hold the final responsibility for the book's content.

We take our hats off to American citizens from all walks of life. They make this country what it is—one of a kind. They were the inspiration for this book. We put our faith and hope in them.

Finally, we recognize that our book is not an end but a beginning. The real work starts when the words stop. We commit ourselves to communicating and collaborating constructively with other citizens on our joint enterprise—Enterprise USA—in order to create a twenty-first-century competitive advantage for the country and people we love.

ENDNOTES/BIBLIOGRAPHY

Endnotes

Chapter 1: Competitive Advantage for the Twenty-First Century

1. Two tables constructed from data in Encyclopedia Wikipedia. http://en.wikepedia.org/wiki/List_of_countries_by_GDP_ Growth; and http://en.wikepedia.org/wiki/List_of countries_by_future_GDP_estimates_ (PPP).

2. The healthcare data cited come from a wide variety of sources. The primary ones were: the Centers for Disease Control; U.S. Census Bureau; National Center for Healthcare Statistics; Institute of Medicine, *To Err Is Human: Building a Safer Health System* (Washington: National Academy Press, 2000); and http://health.newamerica.net/blogposts/2010/cost_us_ health_care_spending_growth_at _a_low_but-25962.

3. Katharine Q. Seelye, "Administration Rejects Health Insurer's Defense of Huge Rate Increases," *The New York Times* (February 12, 2010): A17.

4. Reed Abelson, "In Health Care Reform, Boons for Hospitals and Drug Makers, *The New York Times* (March 22, 2010), B1.

5. "Spotlight on Fixing Health Care from the inside out," *Harvard Business Review* (April 2010), 50–73.

6. Executive Office of the President, Council of Economic Advisors, *The Economic Impact of the American Recovery and Reinvestment Act of 2009*, Second Quarterly Report (January 13, 2010), Executive Summary.

7. Robert Farley and Louis Jacobson in a posting for Politifact.com on Wednesday, February 17, at 8:58 P.M., note the following estimates of jobs saved or created by the stimulus in 2009: IHS/Global Insight–1.25 million; Macroeconomic Advisors–1.06 million; and Moody's economy.com–1.59 million.

8. Patricia Murphy, "What Every American Should Know About the National Debt." Interview with David Walker. http://www.politicsdaily.com/2010/02/01/what-every-american-should-know about-the-national-debt/.

9. Committee for a Responsible Federal Budget, *Deficit Reduction: Lessons from Around the World* (September 2009).

10. The Peterson–Pew Commission on Budget Reform, *Red Ink Rising: A Call to Action to Stem the Mounting Federal Debt* (Washington, D.C.: The Peterson–Pew Commission on Budget Reform (December 14, 2009)). www.budgetreform.org.

11. Paul Ryan, Roadmap for America's Future, released on January 27, 2010. http://www.roadmap.republicans.budget.house.gov/plan.

12. David M. Walker, *Comeback America: Turning the Country Around and Restoring Fiscal Responsibility* (New York: Random House, 2009).

13. The New Economics Foundation (NEF) cites these as limitations of GDP. Other limitations that the NEF cites include: GDP as a standard of living measure assumes that general well-being will increase as the economy grows. GDP fails to distinguish expenditures that are incurred in correcting or compensating for undesirable events.

14. Joseph E. Stiglitz, *Freefall* (New York: W. W. Norton & Company, 2010), 284–85.

15. Economists have begun to develop measures similar to the proposed IEW. These include: the Human Development Index, Genuine Progress Indicator or Index of Sustainable Economic Welfare, the Gini coefficient, the Happy Planet Index, and wealth estimates produced by The World Bank.

16. Michael Porter, *The Competitive Advantage of Nations, States, and Regions*, Harvard Business School Advanced Management Program (April 15, 2009 (2009-AMP-final ppt)), slide 27.

17. Council on Global Competitiveness, *Compete* (November 2008): 4–5.

18. The Peterson-Pew Commission issued a report calling for stabilizing the debt-to-GDP ratio at 60 percent by 2018. The Center on Budget and

Policy Priorities felt this was "overly ambitious and unnecessary" and would "actually impede progress" on getting important deficit reduction legislation passed. In its report, *The Right Target: Stabilize the Federal Debt,* January 12, 2010, the Center called for cutting the projected deficits by more than half by 2019.

19. James K. Galbraith, *The Predator State* (New York: Free Press, 2008), xiii.

20. This quote comes from the State of the Union: President Obama's Speech—prepared remarks as posted by ABC news. http://abcnews.go.com/print?id+9678572.

Chapter 2: Reflections on the Dream

1. David Kamp, "Rethinking the American Dream," *Vanity Fair* (April, 2009).

2. Robert J. Burgess, *America in Focus: The Stunning View Through a Two-Way Mirror* (Littleton, CO: MA Arts Publishing LLC, 2008), 16–29.

3. George Akerlof, *Irrational Exuberance* (Princeton, NJ: Princeton University Press, 2005).

4. As quoted in Library of Congress American Memory Fellows Program, *What Is the American Dream? Lesson Overview.* Quote cited on pp. 214 -15 in James Truslow Adams' book, *The Epic of America.* http://online.sfsu.edu/-kferenz/syllabus/dreams/the dream.html.

Chapter 3: The Renewal Framework

1. For another article that addresses this topic further, read Ian Urbina, "Beyond Beltway, Health Debate Turns Hostile," *The New York Times* (August 8, 2009).

2. There have been numerous studies documenting American citizens' lack of knowledge on facts related to American history, government, and the manner in which democracy works. Rick Shenkman, associate professor of history at George Mason University, devotes a whole book to this topic. Rick Shenkman, *Just How Stupid Are We?* (Philadelphia: Basic Books, 2008).

3. Stephanie Coontz, *The Way We Never Were: American Families and the Nostalgia Trap* (Philadelphia: Basic Books, 1992).

4. Christopher Howard, *The Welfare State Nobody Knows: Debunking Myths About U.S. Social Policy* (Princeton, NJ: Princeton University Press, 2007).

5. Howard, ibid., p. 209.

6. Thomas H. Kean and John Farmer Jr., "How 12/25 Was Like 9/11," *The New York Times* (January 6, 2010): A19.

7. Senator Bob Graham with Chris Hand, *America, The Owner's Manual: Making Government Work for You* (Washington, D.C.: CQ Press, 2010).

8. For example read, *Public Engagement: A Primer from Public Agenda* (Washington, D.C.: Public Agenda, 2006).

Chapter 4: Jobs Matter

1. "Jobs and Politics," *The New York Times* (January 9, 2010) p. A16.

2. Charles Hulin, "Centrality of Work in Lives in Modern Society," eds. Jeanne Brett and Fritz Dasgrow, *The Psychology of Work* (Mahwah, N.J.: Lawrence Erlbaum Associates, 2002).

3. New America Foundation e-mail, *New American Contract Jobless Recovery Update* (July 6, 2009).

4. Steve Clemons, *Hindery Report on Effective Unemployment* (November 6, 2009).

5. "When, Oh, When Will Help Be Wanted?" *The New York Times* (July 19, 2009), Weekly Review Section, 4.

6. Peter Coy, Michelle Conlin, and Moira Herbst, "The Disposable Worker," *BusinessWeek* (January 18, 2010): 33–39.

7. In his book Crunch, Jared Bernstein explained the economic plight of average Americans. Jared Bernstein, *Crunch, Why Do I Feel So Squeezed? (And Other Unsolved Economic Mysteries)* (San Francisco: Berrett-Koehler Publishers, Inc., 2008).

8. "When, Oh, When Will Help be Wanted?" op. cit., 4.

9. Roger Lowenstein, "The New Joblessness," *New York Times Sunday Magazine* (July 26, 2009): 11–12.

10. Data drawn from New America Foundation, *Not Out of the Woods: A Report on the Jobless Recovery Underway* (June 2009): 1–14.

11. The Council on Economic Advisors claimed the stimulus bill created or saved 1.5 to 2 million jobs. The Congressional Budget Office estimated anywhere from 800,000 at the low end to 2.4 million at the high end. Neutral economic organizations such as IHS Global Insights and Moodys

put the numbers between 1 to 1.5 million. No matter how many jobs were created or saved, the economy lost 3.5 million in 2009. That means if the stimulus had not been in place, the job loss conservatively would have been 4.3 million to 4.5 million instead of the lower number.

12. *The New York Times* editorial, "How Not to Write a Jobs Bill," *The New York Times* (February 12, 2010): A26.

13. In December 2009, the New America Foundation put forward a New Growth Agenda resembling the one we recommend here. The agenda had three major elements: infrastructure investment, public service investment, and pro-growth tax reform. The foundation also called for investing in jobs that had high multiplier effects and an investment of sufficient scale to make a difference in the economy. Read Michael Lind, *Jobs and the New Growth Agenda*, New America Foundation (December 2, 2009).

Chapter 5: The Middle Class Matters

1. Stephen Koepp, Gisela Bolte, and Jon D. Hull, "Is the Middle Class Shrinking," *Time* (November 3, 1986). http://www.time.com/time/printout/0,8816,962753,00.html.

2. Andrew Chamberlain, "What Does America Think About Taxes? The 2007 Annual Survey of U.S. Attitudes on Taxes and Wealth," *Tax Foundation Special Report*, No. 154 (April 2007).

3. Pew Research Center, *Inside the Middle Class: Bad Times Hit the Good Life* (April 9, 2008): 3.

4. David Leonhardt, "A Decade with No Income Gains," *The New York Times* (September 10, 2009). http://economix.blogs.nytimes.com/2009/09/10a-decade-with-no-income-gains/.

5. Elizabeth Warren, "The New Economics of the Middle Class: Why Making Ends Meet Has Gotten Harder," Testimony Before the Senate Finance Committee (May 10, 2007): 2–3.

6. Pew Research Center, op. cit., 110–39.

7. Isabel V. Sawhill and Ron Haskins, "Five Myths About Our Land of Opportunity," *The Washington Post* (November 1, 2009).

8. Thomas F. Cooley, "Has Rising Inequality Destroyed the Middle Class?" Forbes.com (June 3, 2009). http://www.forbes.com/2009/06/02/middle-class-income -inequality-technology-opinions.

9. Paul Rosenberg, "The One Percent Economy," blog posting (September 26, 2009).

10. Elizabeth Warren, "America Without a Middle Class," *Huffington Post* (December 3, 2009).

11. Jared Bernstein, *Crunch: Why Do I Feel So Squeezed?* (San Francisco: Berrett-Koehler Publishers, Inc.), 9.

12. Jennifer Wheary, Thomas M. Shapiro, and Tamara Draut, *By A Thread: The New Experience of America's Middle Class* (Demos: A Network for Ideas and Actions/The Institute on Assets and Social Policy at Brandeis University, 2007).

13. Pew Research Center, op. cit., 36–47.

14. Pew Research Center, *Current Decade Rates as Worst in 50 Years* (December 21, 2009). http: people.press.org/report 573.

15. These recommendations are consolidated from recommendations provided by Bernstein in his book *Crunch*, Warren in her 2007 testimony before the Senate Finance Committee, and D-IASP in its paper, *By a Thread*. Bernstein, op. cit., 169–89. Warren, op. cit., 11–15. D-IASP, op. cit., 11–13.

16. James W. Hughes and Joseph J. Seneca, "America's New Post-Recession Employment Arithmetic," *Advance & Rutgers Report*, Issue Paper Number 1 (September 2009).

17. Paul Krugman, "Mission Not Accomplished," *The New York Times* (October 2, 2009): A27.

18. Middle Class Task Force, The vice president of the United States, "Why Middle Class Americans Need Health Reform" (July 10, 2009).

Chapter 6: Manufacturing Matters

1. Office of the President of the United States, *2009 Economic Report of the President*. These data are available in table B-51 of report.

2. U.S. Department of Commerce, *Manufacturing in America: A Comprehensive Strategy to Address the Challenges to U.S. Manufacturers* (January 2004). See pp. 59–80 for recommendations.

3. Leo Hindery, Leo W. Gerard, and Donald W. Riegle, Jr., New America Foundation Blog Posting, (August 6, 2009).

4. Senator Byron L. Dorgan, *Take This Job and Ship It: How Corporate Greed and Brain-Dead Politics Are Selling Out America* (New York: Thomas Dunne Books, 2006), 241.

5. National Association of Manufacturers (NAM), "The Turning Tide: Prospects for a Manufacturing Recovery," Labor Day 2009: The Manufacturing Report, 6.

6. Eric Janszen, "Reindustrialize," *Harper's Magazine* (November 2008): 44.

7. As quoted in article by Michelle Singletary, "'Enough.' May be the one word that would serve all of us well," *Sarasota Herald Tribune* (September 9, 2009): 3D.

8. Data under this heading are drawn from Josh Bivens, "Squandering the Blue-Collar Advantage: Why Almost Everything Except Unions and the Blue-Collar Workforce Are Hurting U.S. Manufacturing," *Economic Policy Institute Briefing Paper #229* (February 13, 2009).

9. Gary Pisano and Willy Shih, "Restoring American Competitiveness," *Harvard Business Review* (July/August 2009): 114–22.

10. David Blanchard, "The Face of American Manufacturing," *IndustryWeek* (June 1, 2007). http://www.indusryweek.com/Print Article.aspx?Article ID=14159.

11. Jeri Gillespie and Heath Weems, "Manufacturing a High-Performance Workforce," *National Association of Manufacturers Solutions: A White Paper Series* (2004).

12. James Jacobs, "The Diminished Role of Training and Education in American Manufacturing and the Imperative for Change," *Manufacturing a Better Future for America* (Washington, D.C.: Alliance for American Manufacturing, July 2009): 217–45.

13. NAM, op. cit., cover letter.

14. NAM, ibid, 6–7; 11–12.

15. Steven Greenhouse, "G.E. to Add Two New U.S. Plants as Unions Agree on Cost Controls," *The New York Times* (August 7, 2009): B.3. This article also includes a quote on Immelt's call for the U.S. economy to have 20 percent of its GDP from manufacturing.

16. Alan Tonelson, "Up From Globalism," *Harper's Magazine* (January 2010): 7–9.

17. Tonelson and his colleagues at the United States Business and Industry Council (USBIC) put forward a comprehensive set of "emergency" and "long-term" measures for saving manufacturing in a paper released in December 2009. Kevin L. Kearns, Alan Tonelson, and William Hawkins, *To Save American Manufacturing: USBIC'S Plan for American Industrial Renewal,* USBIC (December 2009).

18. Eric Janszen, op. cit., 44.

20. Adrian Slywotsky, "How Science Can Create Millions of New Jobs," *BusinessWeek* (September 7, 2009): 37–39.

21. Peter Engardio, "Can the Future Be Built in America?" *BusinessWeek* (September 21, 2009): 46–51.

22. Jeffrey J. Kuenzi, "Science, Technology, Engineering, and Mathematics (STEM) Education: Background, Federal Policy, and Legislative Action," *Congressional Research Service Report for Congress* (Updated March 21, 2008): 5–9, summary.

23. Kuenzi, ibid, Summary.

24. Office of the Press Secretary, White House, "President Obama Expands 'Educate to Innovate' Campaign for Excellence in Science, Technology, Engineering, and Mathematics (STEM) Education," press release (January 6, 2010).

Chapter 7: Small Business and Entrepreneurs Matter

1. "Is the U.S. Really A Hotbed Of Small Business?" *BusinessWeek* (September 7, 2009). To access the report by John Schmitt and Nathan Lane of the Center for Economic & Policy Research, go to http://www.cepr.net/documents/publications/small-business-2009-08.pdf.

2. U.S. Small Business Administration (SBA) Office of Advocacy. *The Small Business Economy: A Report to the President.* 2009 Edition (July 2009), 6–13.

3. U.S. SBA, ibid, 13–31.

4. William C. Dunkelberg and Holly Wade, "NFIB Small Business Economic Trends," National Foundation of Independent Businesses (September 2009).

5. Dane Stangler, "The Economic Future Just Happened," *Ewing Marion Kauffman Foundation Report* (June 9, 2009): 1.

6. Vivek Wadhwa et al., "The Anatomy of an Entrepreneur: Family Background and Motivation," *Ewing Marion Kauffman Foundation Report* (July, 2009).

7. Ewing Marion Kauffman Foundation, "The 'Build a Stronger America' Campaign to Give a Unified Voice to Entrepreneurs and Business Owners," press release (September 23, 2009).

8. U.S. Small Business Administration, Office of Inspector General, "Review of Selected Small Business Procurements," Advisory Report Number 5–16 (March 8, 2005). See also, "New Management Challenge—Large Businesses Receive Small Business Awards," Report Number 5–15 (February 24, 2005).

9. Robb Mandelbaum, "The S.B.A. Puts the Best Face on Small-Business Contracting," *The New York Times* (August 24, 2009). http://boss.blogs.nytimes.com/2009/08/24/the-sba-puts-the-best-face-on-small-business-contracting.

10. Office of Public Affairs, U.S. Department of Commerce, "Commerce Secretary Locke Announces New Commerce Initiatives to Foster Innovation and Entrepreneurship," press release (September 24, 2009).

11. Robert W. Fairlie, "Kaufmann Index of Entrepreneurial Activity: 1996–2008," *Ewing Marion Kauffman Foundation Report* (April 2009).

12. James O'Shea, "A Small Business Finds a Catch in Federal Aid," *The New York Times* (February 14, 2010): 27A.

13. Ylan Q. Mui and David Cho, "Small Businesses Leery of Obama's Jobs Plan," *The Washington Post* (Friday, January 29, 2010). http://www.washingtonpost.com/wp-dyn/content/article/2010/01/28/AR2010012803818.

14. Data used in this analysis extracted from the official Web sites for the SBA and the Department of Commerce. http://www.sba.gov and http://www.commerce.gov.

Chapter 8: The Media Matters

1. Robert Burgess, *America in Focus* (Littleton, CO: MA Arts Publishing, LLC, 2008), 96–97.

2. MSNBC, *Morning Joe* (June 30, 2009).

3. Gene Policinski, "Role of Newspapers in U.S. Society: A Nation Talking to Itself," First Amendment Center Paper. http://www.firstamendmentcenter.org/analysis.aspx?id=12047&printer-friendly=y.

4. John Nerone, "The Media and American Society," *OAH Magazine of History* (Spring 1992).

5. Gene Policinski, op. cit.

6. Doris A. Graber, *Mass Media and American Politics*, Eighth Edition (Washington, D.C.: CQ Press, 2010): 49–50.

7. Michael Schudson, *Why Democracies Need an Unlovable Press* (Malden, MA: Polity Press, 2008).

8. Schudson, ibid., 11–26.

9. Pew Research Center, "Press Accuracy Rating Hits Two Decade Low: Public Evaluations of the News Media: 1985–2009" (September 13, 2009).

10. Richard Pérez-Peña, "Newspapers Have Not Hit Bottom Yet, Analysts Say," *The New York Times* (September 21, 2009): B3.

11. Leonard Downie and Michael Schudson, *The Reconstruction of American Journalism*, Columbia University (October 20, 2009).

12. Arianna Huffington, "Citizen Journalists: Online Paul Reveres," *What Matters* (February 26, 2009). http://whatmatters.mckinseydigital.com/internet-citizen-journalists-online-paul-reveres.

13. The data in the analysis of this subsection come from multiple sources. However, the primary source was Downie and Schudson, ibid. For ProPublica, see also, Paul Steiger, "Investigative Reporting in the Web Era," *What Matters* (October 14, 2009). http://whatmatters.mckinseydigital.com/internet/investigative-reporting-in-the-web-era.

14. David Carr, "Newsweek's Journalism of Fourth and Long," *The New York Times* (May 24, 2009): wk 1-4.

15. The Knight Commission on the Information Needs of Communities in a Democracy, *Informing Communities: Sustaining Democracy in the Digital Age* (Washington, D.C.: The Aspen Institute, 2009).

16. Downie and Schudson, op. cit., 77–96.

17. Knight Commission, op. cit., xvi–xvii.

Chapter 9: The World Matters

1. Pew Research Center Global Attitudes Project, "Confidence in Obama Lifts U.S. Image Around the World: Most Muslim Publics Not So Easily Moved" (July 23, 2009).

2. Ron Haskins, *Immigration: Wages, Education and Mobility* (Economic Mobility Project, an initiative of The Pew Charitable Trusts, 2007).

3. Jeffrey Thomas, "American Dream Still Alive and Well for Immigrants, Report Says," *The Washington Post* (July 26, 2007).

4. Waldo Proffitt, "A Nobel Cause for Rejoicing," *Sarasota Herald Tribune* (October 10, 2009): 19A.

5. Office of the Press Secretary, The White House, "Remarks by the President on Winning the Nobel Peace Prize," press release (October 9, 2009).

6. Ross Douthat, "Heckuva Job, Barack," *The New York Times* (October 12, 2009): A21.

7. Thomas Friedman, "The Peace (Keepers) Prize," *Sarasota Herald Tribune* (October 13, 2009): 9A.

8. Pew Research Center, op. cit. See favorability ratings discussion.

9. Thomas R. Pickering, Chester A. Crocker, and Casimir A. Yost, *America's Role in the World: Foreign Policy Choices for the Next President* (Washington, D.C.: Institute for the Study of Diplomacy, Walsh School of Foreign Service, Georgetown University, 2008).

10. Robert M. Gates, "A Balanced Strategy: Reprogramming the Pentagon for a New Age," *Foreign Affairs* (January/February 2009).

11. Dr. Andrew Krepinevich, "Rethinking the Foundations of the National Security Strategy," notes taken by JHU/APL staff member at a seminar presented on July 7, 2009.

12. Bono, "Rebranding America," *The New York Times* (October 18, 2009). http://www.nytimes.com/2009/10/18/opinion/18bono.html.

13. The 13 choices are described in detail on pp. 55-74 of the *Institute for Study of Diplomacy Report*, Crocker et al., op. cit.

14. David Oshinsky, "Ted Widmer's 'Ark of Liberties,'" *The New York Times*. http://www.nytimes.com/2008/07/12/arts/12iht-idbriefs12A.14423846. html.

15. Robin Niblett, *Ready to Lead? Rethinking America's Role in the World* (London: Chatham House, Royal Institute of International Affairs, 2009). See Executive Summary for key points.

16. Barry C. Lynn, *End of the Line* (New York: Doubleday, 2005), 256.

17. Fareed Zakaria, *The Post-American World* (New York: W. W. Norton & Company, 2008), 231–50.

18. Craig Ferguson, *American On Purpose: The Improbable Adventures of an Unlikely Patriot* (New York: Harper Collins, 2009), 265.

Chapter 10: Government Is Not the Problem

1. Felix Rohatyn, *Bold Endeavors: How Our Government Built America and Why It Must Rebuild It Now* (New York: Simon & Shuster, 2009).

2. Steven Kelman, "The Transformation of Government in the Decade Ahead," *Reflections on 21st Century Government Management* (Washington, D.C.: IBM Center for the Business of Government, 2008), 34. www.businessofgovernment.org.

3. See two sources: Partnership for Public Service, *State of the Public Service Conference, Report of Proceedings* (June 3, 2007). Grant Thornton, *Federal Human Capital: The Perfect Storm—A Survey of Chief Human Capital Officers* (July 2007): 8–10.

4. Two excellent resources are: Shelley H. Metzenbaum, *Performance Management Recommendations for the New Administration* (Washington, D.C.: IBM Center for the Business of Government, 2009). www.businessofgovernment.org. Accenture Institute for Public Service Value (Accenture), Georgetown Public Policy Institute (GPPI), OMB Watch, *Building a Better Government Performance System: Recommendations to the Obama Administration* (Washington, D.C.: Accenture, GPPI, and OMB Watch, 2009. Commissioned Background Memos on pp. 27–50 are especially useful. Another helpful resource is: GA0-08-1026T, *Government Performance: Lessons Learned for the Next Administration on Using Performance Information to Improve Results* (Washington, D.C.: GAO, July 24, 2008).

5. Al Morales and Jonathan Breul, *Ten Challenges Facing Public Managers* (Washington, D.C.: IBM Center for the Business of Government, 2008).

6. Dan Balz and Jon Cohen, "In Poll, Republicans Gaining Political Ground on Obama," *The Washington Post* (February 10, 2010). http://www.washingtonpost.com/wp-dyn/content/article/2010/02/10/AR2010021000010.html?wprss=rss_polititcs/congresss. Adam Nagourney and Megan Thee-Brenan, "Poll Finds Edge for Obama Over G.O.P. Among the Public," *The New York Times*, February 12, 2010. http://www.nytimes.com/2010/02/12/us/politics/12poll.html.

7. David Brooks, "What's Next, Mr. President?" *The New York Times* (February 12, 2010). http://query.nytimes.com/gst/fullpage.html?res+9807EFDF10311F931A25751COA9669D8.

8. James Fallows, "How America Can Rise Again," *The Atlantic* (January/ February, 2010): 55.

9. The final NPR Annual Report was titled, *Businesslike Government*. All of the NPR reports are accessible online. http://govinfo.library.unt.edu/npr/library/review.html.

10. Peter Orszag, Memo titled "Planning for the President's Fiscal Year 2011 Budget and Performance Plans," M-09-20 (June 11, 2009): 1–2.

11. Donald F. Kettl, "Has Government Been 'Reinvented'?" Testimony to Congress (May 4, 2000). http://www.brookings.edu/testimony/2000/0504 governance_kettle.aspx?p=1.

12. Partnership for Public Service, *Roadmap to Reform* (Washington, D.C.: Partnership for Public Service, October 1, 2008).

13. For additional thoughts from Professor Kettl on improving government performance, read Donald F. Kettl, "The Next Government of the United States: Challenges for Performance in the 21st Century," *Reflections on 21st Century Government Management* (Washington, D.C.: IBM Center for the Business of Government, 2008). Another excellent resource is provided by Chris Wye, *Performance Management for Political Executives: A "Start Where You Are, Use What You Have Guide"* (Washington, D.C.: IBM Center for the Business of Government, October 2004).

14. James Fallows, op. cit., 49–50.

15. David M. Walker, *Comeback America: Turning the Country Around and Restoring Fiscal Responsibility* (New York: Random House, 2009). See Chapter 11, "Fixing Our Dysfunctional Democracy," 181–97.

16. Joe Scarborough, *Morning Joe Show*, MSNBC TV (February 18, 2010).

Chapter 11: Business Is Not the Answer

1. Stephen Labaton, "Ailing, Banks Still Field Strong Lobby at Capitol," *The New York Times* (June 5, 2009). http://www.nytimes.com/2009/06/05/business/economy/05bankrupt.html.

2. New America Foundation e-mail, "Subject: Banks Use TARP Funds to Boost Lending—NOT!" (July 20, 2009).

3. Gillian Tett, *Fool's Gold: How the Bold Dream of a Small Tribe at J. P. Morgan Was Corrupted by Wall Street Greed and Unleashed a Catastrophe* (New York: Free Press, 2009).

4. Dennis Overbye, "Looking for Science on Wall Street," *The Sarasota Herald Tribune* (March 10, 2009): 2A.

5. Kevin Phillips, *Bad Money: Reckless Finance, Failed Politics and the Global Crisis of American Capitalism* (New York: The Penguin Group, 2008).

6. Frank Rich, "The Other Plot to Wreck America," *The New York Times* (January 10, 2010). http://www.nytimes.com/2010/01/10rich.html.

7. Professor Ferguson makes this case very well in his new book. Read Niall Ferguson, *The Ascent of Money: A Financial History of the World* (New York: The Penguin Group, 2009).

8. Jim Collins, *How the Mighty Fall: And Why Some Companies Never Give In* (New York: HarperCollins, 2009).

9. As quoted in column by Ernest Werlin, "Warren Buffett's Annual Letter Offers Insight into a Great Mind," *Sarasota Herald Tribune* (March 10, 2009): 3D.

10. Starbucks Newsroom, "Starbucks Posts Strong Third Quarter Fiscal 2009 Results" (July 21, 2009). http://starbucks.tekgroup.com/article_display.cfm?article_id=249.

11. Starbucks Newsroom, "Fact Sheet: 15th Ave. Coffee & Tea" (July 23, 2009). http://starbucks.tekgroup.com/article_display.cfm?article_id =250.

12. Michael E. Porter and Mark R. Kramer, "The Link Between Competitive Advantage and Corporate Social Responsibility," *Harvard Business Review* (December 2006).

13. Sheila Bonini, Timothy M. Koller, and Philip H. Mirvis, "Valuing Social Responsibility Programs," *McKinsey on Finance*, Number 32 (Summer 2009): 11–18.

14. For the full report from the 2009 social markets conference, visit the Web site for the Social Enterprise Reporter. http://www.sereporter.com/?q=blog/%5D/reports_from_the 2009_social_capital_markets_conference. For more information on Kevin Jones and Good Capital visit http:www.goodcap.net.

15. "Surviving the Slump: Red Tape and Scissors," *The Economist Special Report on Business in America* (May 30, 2009) 10–11.

16. In May 2009, *BusinessWeek* also announced the first group of 15 winners for its "most promising social entrepreneurs" awards. *Fast Company* has been making these awards for some time.

Chapter 12: Citizens All

1. George Lakoff, *Don't Think of An Elephant: Know Your Values and Frame the Debate* (White River Junction, VT: Chelsea Green Publishing company, 2004).

2. Robert J. Burgess, *America in Focus* (Littleton, CO: MA Arts Publishing, 2008).

3. Milton Rokeach was a very influential social psychologist. His best-known works were the *Open and Closed Mind* (1960), *Beliefs, Attitudes and Values: A Theory of Organizational Change* (1968) and *The Nature of Human Values* (1973). He developed the Rokeach Values Survey, a tool used to measure people's relative ranking of values and then to predict a wide variety of factors, including party affiliation and religious belief.

4. Howard Fineman, *The Thirteen American Arguments: Enduring Debates that Define and Inspire Our Country* (New York: Random House, 2008), 14–16.

5. E. J. Dionne, Jr., *Why Americans Hate Politics* (New York: Simon & Schuster, 1992).

6. Robert D. Putnam, *Bowling Alone: The Collapse and Revival of American Community* (New York: Simon & Schuster, 2000), 31–47.

7. Professor Alan Gittelson has lectured extensively on this topic. He draws upon a variety of sources for the data used in his lectures, including Gallup, Pew, the University of Michigan Survey Center, and the National Opinion Research Center at the University of Chicago. His favorite print resources include: Garry Wills, *A Necessary Evil: A History of Distrust of Government* (New York: Simon & Schuster, 1999); Joseph S. Nye et al., eds., *Why People Don't Trust Government* (Boston: Harvard University Press, 1997); E. J. Dionne, Jr., *Why Americans Hate Politics.*

8. Barat Education Foundation, *Our American Voice Facilitator's Guide* (Lake Forest: Barat Education Foundation, 2009): 2.

9. Winnie Hu, *The New York Times*, "Middle Schools Teaching Empathy," *Sarasota Herald Tribune* (April 5, 2009): 8.

10. Seth Schiesel, "Former Justice Promotes Web-Based Civics Lessons," *The New York Times* (June 9, 2008). http://www.nytimes.com/2008/06/09/arts/09sand.html?

11. "Voter Turnout Study Ranks U.S. Lowest Among 28 Nations," *The New York Times* (December 8, 1987). http://www.nytimes.com/1987/12/08/

us/voter_turnout_study_ranks_us_lowest_among_28_nations. Also see "Voter Turnout" in *Wikepedia*, the free encyclopedia.http://en.wikipedia. org/wiki/Voter_turnout.

12. Jeffrey Toobin, "The Great Election Grab," *The New Yorker* (December 8, 2003). http://www.newyorker.com/archive/2003/12/08/031208fa_fact?

13. There are a wide variety of postings on the California redistricting reform proposals. For a source on this statistic, see http://www.cgs.org/index. php?option=com_content&view=article&id=52&Itemid=57.

14. John Tanner and Mike Castle, "A Bipartisan Call to Action on Redistricting," *My Two Census* (June 24, 2009). http://www.mytwocensus.com/tag/ fairness-and-independence-in-redistricting-act/.

Chapter 13: Bowling Together

1. Robert D. Putnam, *Bowling Alone: The Collapse and Revival of American Community* (New York: Simon & Schuster, 2000).

2. Robert D. Putnam, "Bowling Alone: America's Declining Social Capital," *Journal of Democracy* 6:1 (Jan 1995): 65–78. http://xroads.virginia.edu/_ HYPER/DETOC/assoc/bowling.html.

3. Marshall McLuhan's most famous book was *The Medium Is The Massage,* published in 1967. He was the leader in identifying and predicting the impact of the media on human behavior. He coined the phrase "the medium is the message" to describe the overarching effect of the media in all facets of our lives.

4. Jim Lehrer, "Harvard University Commencement Speech of Jim Lehrer," Cambridge Massachusetts (June 8, 2006). http://www.news.harvard.edu/ gazette/daily/2006/06/08-lehrerspeech.html.

Chapter 14: The Renewal Model

1. John Kotter, *Leading Change* (Cambridge, MA: Harvard Business School Press, 1996).

2. Andrew Clark, "Car Wars: How Alan Mulally Kept Ford Ahead of Its Rivals," *Guardian.Co.UK* (May 11, 2009). http://www.guardian.co.uk/ business/2009/may/11/ford-allan-mulally-interview-car-industry.

3. When George Muñoz took over OPIC, it was under significant scrutiny from both Democrats and Republicans. Serious consideration was given to closing it down.

4. The *Harvard Business Review* published a special centennial issue titled, "The Drucker Centennial: What Would Peter Do?" in November 2009. The articles in this issue include: "What Would Peter Say?" by Rosabeth Moss Kanter and "Why Read Peter Drucker?" by Alan Kantrow.

5. For a complete explication of the model, read Edwin T. Crego, Jr., and Peter D. Schiffrin, *Customer-Centered Reengineering: Remapping for Total Customer Value* (New York: Irwin Professional Publishing, 1995).

6. Charles McGrath, "David's Reappearance Was Years in the Making," *The New York Times* (June 23, 2009). http:www.nytimes.com/2009/06/23/sports/golf/23duval.html?

7. Dan P. McAdams, *The Redemptive Self: Stories Americans Live By* (New York: Oxford University Press, 2006).

8. For an excellent article on Senator Kennedy's "redemption," read, Courtney E. Martin, "The Imperfection and Redemption of Ted Kennedy," *Prospect* (August 31, 2009). http://www.prospect.org/cs/articles?article=the_imperfection_and_redemption_of_ted_kennedy.

9. William Hart and Dolores Albarracin, et. al., "Feeling Validated Versus Being Correct: A Meta-Analysis of Selective Exposure to Information," *Psychological Bulletin*, Vol. 135, No. 4 (2009): 555–88.

10. Philip E. Tetlock, *Expert Political Judgment: How Good Is It? How Can We Know?* (Princeton, N.J.: Princeton University Press, 2005).

11. There have been many quality articles and books on decision making. Two of the most recent are: Tom Davenport, "On Making Better Decisions," *Harvard Business Review* (November 2009): 117–23. Zachary Shore, *Blunder: Why Smart People Make Bad Decisions* (New York: Bloomsbury USA, 2008).

12. George A. Akerlof and Robert J. Shiller, *Animal Spirits: How Human Psychology Drives the Economy, and Why It Matters for Global Capitalism* (Princeton, N.J.: Princeton University Press, 2009). Sunstein and Thaler were not specifically focused on 2008 and the market meltdown. However, they do an exceptional job in their book *Nudge* of providing examples of flawed decision making of humans and providing recommendations to move our decision making in the right direction on issues that matter to us as individuals. See Richard H. Thaler and Cass R. Sunstein, *Nudge: Improving Decisions About Health, Wealth, and Happiness* (New York: The Penguin Group, 2009).

13. Gerd Gigerenzer, *Gut Feelings: The Intelligence of the Unconscious* (New York: The Penguin Group, 2007).

14. For a straightforward explanation of why this works, read David Pogue, "To Sleep, Perchance to Analyze," *The New York Times* (July 16, 2009): B1.

15. For guidelines on how to simplify, read, Michelle Passoff, *Lighten Up! Free Yourself from Clutter*. (New York: HarperCollins, 1998).

16. Ruth Pennebaker, "The Mediocre Multitasker," *The New York Times* (August 30, 2009): 5.

17. University of Oxford, "Rats Show Effects of High-Fat Diet After Nine Days" (August 12, 2009). http://www.ox.ac.uk/media/news_stories/2009/12089.html.

Chapter 15: Implementing the Renewal Process

1. Mark R. Warner, "Floor Speech: Greater Accountability, Transparency in the Budget Process," press release (March 24, 2009). http://warner.senate.gov/public/?=PressReleases&ContentRecord_id=8b482737-689d-46.

2. Mark R. Warner, "Warner Launches Government Performance Task Force, Issues & Legislation" (October 30, 2009). http://warner.senate.gov/public/index.cfmp=IssuesLegislation&ContentRecord _id=019a4.

3. Robert Rubin, *In an Uncertain World: Tough Choices from Wall Street to Washington* (New York: Random House, 2003).

4. Henry Mintzberg, "Crafting Strategy," *Harvard Business Review* (August 1987).

5. Michael C. Mankins and Richard Steele, "Stop Making Plans; Start Making Decisions," *Harvard Business Review* (January 2006). Reprint R0601F.

6. Jennifer Medina, "Teacher Training Termed Mediocre," *The New York Times* (October 22, 2009). http:www.nytimes.com/2009/10/23/education/23 teachers.html. For the complete text of the speech, go to http://www.tc.columbia.edu/news/article.html?id=7192.

7. See NIMS Web site www.nims-skills.org for information on both the competency-based apprenticeship program and the structured O-J-T system.

8. Jon R. Katzenbach and Douglas K. Smith, "The Discipline of Teams," *Harvard Business Review*, Best of HBR 1993 (July–August 2005). Reprint R0507P.

9. Ron Gunn has written an excellent and practical book on how to implement matrix management successfully. Ronald A. Gunn, *Matrix*

Management Success: Method Not Magic (West Conshohocken, PA: Infinity Publishing.com, 2007).

10. There were several sources for the Marriott discussion. The two relied on the most were: Robert J. Thomas and Walter E. Shill, "Why Marriott Shareholders Sleep Well at Night," *Outlook Journal* (May 2006). http://www.accenture.com/Global/Research_and_Insights/Outlook/By_Issue/Y2006/Marriott.html. Marriott News, "Marriott International Named Most Admired Hotel Company by FORTUNE for the Ninth Consecutive Year," March 11, 2008. http://www.marriott.com/news/detail.mi?marrArticle=309272.

11. Read Samantha Bomkamp, "Buffett's Railroad," *Sarasota Herald Tribune* (November 4, 2009): Marc Gunther, "Warren Buffett Takes Charge," CNNMoney.com (April 13, 2009). http://cnnmoney.printthis.clickability.com/pt/cpt?acton=cprt&title=Why+Warren+Buffett.

12. Larry Bossidy and Ram Charan, *Execution: The Discipline of Getting Things Done* (New York: Crown Business, 2002).

13. Ken Blanchard, "Seven Dynamics of Change," *Executive Excellence* (June 1992): 5.

14. Thomas Friedman, "The Fat Lady Has Sung," *The New York Times* (February 21, 2010): wk 8.

Appendix: Renewal Recommendations

1. Richard C. Longworth, *Caught In the Middle* (New York: Bloomsbury, USA, 2008).

2. For an excellent review of the current state of the art and capacity of America's training system and community college capabilities, read James Jacobs, "The Diminished Role of Training and Education for American Manufacturing and the Imperative for Change," *Manufacturing a Better Future for America* (Washington, D.C.: Alliance for American Manufacturing, 2009): 217–44.

3. Manufacturing Extension Partnership, National Institute of Standards and Technology, "The Future of the Hollings Manufacturing Extension Partnership" (December 2008).

4. Peter Navarro provides a comprehensive analysis of the substantial edge that other countries provide their manufacturers in the trade arena in his chapter in the book, *Manufacturing a Better Future for America*. Peter Navarro, "Benchmarking the Advantages Foreign Nations Provide

Their Manufacturers," *Manufacturing a Better Future for America,* op. cit., 105–48.

5. Alan Tonelson, "Obama: Looking for Jobs in All the Wrong Places," *U.S. Employment Trends* (Thursday, November 26, 2009). Also see Tonelson's article, "Up From Globalism," *Harper's Magazine* (January 2010): 7–9.

6. Robert W. Fairlie, *Kauffman Index of Entrepreneurial Activity: 1996–2008* (Ewing Marion Kauffman Foundation, April 2009).

7. William C. Dunkelberg and Holly Wade, *NFIB Small Business Economic Trends*, National Foundation of Independent Businesses (September 2009).

8. *Kaufman Foundation Survey of Entrepreneurs* (September 2009). Poll conducted by pollster Doug Schoen with more than 250 entrepreneurs and 150 "would-be" entrepreneurs.

9. Peter Orszag, Memo titled, "Planning for the President's Fiscal Year 2011 Budget and Performance Plans," M-09-20 (June 11, 2009).

10. "The Memo That Roared: OMB Dictates Much-Needed Changes for the Federal Hiring Process," *The Washington Post* (June 19, 2009). http://www.washingtonpost.com/wp-dyn/content/article20096/06/18/AR2009061803617.html.

11. Partnership for Public Service, *A Golden Opportunity: Recruiting Baby Boomers into Government* (January 2008).

12. Steve Lohr, "Can Governments Till the Fields of Innovation?" *The New York Times* (June 20, 2009): BU 3.

13. Accenture Institute for Public Service Value (Accenture), Georgetown Public Policy Institute (GPPI), OMB Watch, *Building a Better Government Performance System: Recommendations to the Obama Administration* (Washington, D.C.: Accenture, GPPI, and OMB Watch, 2009).

14. Office of Economic Adjustment, Department of Defense, "A Model for Responding to Trade Adjustment and Other Industry Dislocations" (September 2008). Visit www.OEA.gov to get more information on the services provided and material available from OEA.

15. We should note that over 2,000 house staffers make six figures. As reported by Politico, however, "Starting salaries on the Hill are still low—many entry level congressional jobs pay less than $30,000 a year. And many of the most highly paid staff could make several times the maximum by jumping

to lobbying and consulting jobs in the private sector." "2,000 House Staffers Make Six Figures," *Politico* (March 26, 2010).

16. Public Strategies Group, *Game Changing Opportunities to Help States Deal with Fiscal Crisis* (St. Paul, MN: Public Strategies Group, 2009). For more information, contact the Group via e-mail, www.psg.us.

17. Michael E. Porter and Mark R. Kramer, "Strategy and Society: The Link Between Competitive Advantage and Corporate Social Responsibility," *Harvard Business Review* (December 2006).

18. Simon C. Y. Wong, "Government Ownership: Why This Time It Should Work," *The McKinsey Quarterly*—Online Journal of McKinsey & Co. (June 2009).

19. Nigel Mould, "Campaign Finance Analysis, Nov. '08 Elections, Power-Point Presentation" (May 5, 2009).

20. Ed Crego, "UIS Future Directions in Public Affairs Brainstorming Meeting Report" (May 2009).

Bibliography

In addition to the source material cited in the endnotes, we consulted a wide variety of other materials that helped to shape and inform our thinking and opinions in the areas of importance to renewing the American Dream addressed in this book. A select bibliography of those sources follows.

Albrecht, Karl. *Practical Intelligence: The Art and Science of Common Sense.* San Francisco: Jossey Bass, 2007.

Anderson, Terry L., and Richard Sousa, eds. *Reacting to the Spending Spree: Policy Changes We Can Afford.* Stanford: Hoover Institution Press, 2009.

Beattie, Alan. *False Economy: A Surprising Economic History of the World.* New York: Penguin Group, 2009.

Bilmes, Linda, and W. Scott Gould. *The People Factor: Strengthening America by Investing in the Public Sector.* Washington, D.C.: The Brookings Institution, 2009.

Brabandere, Luc de. *The Forgotten Half of Change: Achieving Greater Creativity Through Changes in Perception.* Chicago: Dearborn Trade Publishing, 2005.

Brackley, Dean. *The Call to Discernment in Troubled Times: New Perspectives on the Transformative Wisdom of Ignatius of Loyola.* New York: The Crossroad Publishing Company, 2004.

Charan, Ram. *Leadership in the Era of Economic Uncertainty.* New York: McGraw Hill, 2009.

Choate, Pat. *Saving Capitalism: Keeping America Strong.* New York: Vintage Books, 2009.

Choate, Pat. *Dangerous Business: The Risks of Globalization for America.* New York: Alfred A. Knopf, 2008.

Crawford, Matthew. *Shop Class as Soul Craft: An Inquiry into the Value of Work.* New York: Penguin Press, 2009.

Eggers, William D., and John O'Leary. *If We Can Put a Man on the Moon . . . Getting Big Things Done in Government.* Boston: HBS Press, 2009.

Elliott, Larry, and Dan Atkinson. *The Gods that Failed: How Blind Faith in Markets Has Cost Us Our Future.* New York: Nation Books, 2009.

Fallows, James. *Breaking the News: How the Media Undermine American Democracy.* New York: Vintage Books, 1997.

Faux, Jeff. *The Global Class War: How America's Bipartisan Elite Lost Our Future—and What It Will Take to Win It Back.* Hoboken, NJ: John Wiley & Sons, 2006.

Foley, Duncan K. *Adams Fallacy.* Cambridge, MA: The Belknap Press of Harvard University Press, 2006.

Forbes, Steve, and Elizabeth Ames. *How Capitalism Will Save Us: Why Free People and Free Markets Are the Best Answer to Today's Economy.* New York: Crown Publishing Group, 2009.

Frank, Robert H. *The Economic Naturalist's Field Guide: Common Sense Principles for Troubled Times.* New York: Basic Books, 2009.

Gilbert, Daniel. *Stumbling on Happiness.* New York: Alfred A. Knopf, 2006.

Greenberg, Stanley B. *The Two Americas: Our Current Political Deadlock and How to Break It.* New York: Thomas Dunne Books, 2005.

Greider, William. *Come Home, America: The Rise and Fall (and Redeeming Promise) of Our Country.* New York: Rodale, 2009.

Harari, Oren. *Break from the Pack: How to Compete in a Copycat Economy.* Upper Saddle River, NJ: FT Press, 2007.

Harvard Business Review. *Harvard Business Review on Strategic Renewal.* Boston: Harvard Business School Publishing Press, 2008.

Kettl, Donald. *The Next Government of the United States: Why Our Institutions Fail Us and How to Fix Them.* New York: W. W. Norton, 2009.

Krugman, Paul. *The Conscience of a Liberal.* New York: W. W. Norton & Company, 2007.

Lakoff, George. *Moral Politics: How Liberals and Conservatives Think.* Chicago: The University of Chicago Press, 2002.

Levitt, Stephen D., and Stephen J. Dubner. *Freakonomics: A Rogue Economist Explores the Hidden Side of Everything*. New York: William Morrow, 2005.

Light, Paul. *A Government Ill-Executed*. Boston: Harvard University Press, 2008.

Lowenstein, Roger. *While America Aged: How Pension Debts Ruined General Motors, Stopped the NYC Subways, Bankrupted San Diego, and Loom as the Next Financial Crisis*. New York: The Penguin Press, 2008.

Luntz, Frank I. *What Americans Really Want . . . Really: The Truth About Our Hopes, Dreams, And Fears*. New York: Hyperion Books, 2009.

Maxwell, John C. *Put Your Dream to the Test: 10 Questions to Help You See It and Seize It*. Nashville: Thomas Nelson, 2009.

Moyers, Bill. *Moyers on Democracy*. New York: Doubleday, 2008.

Podesta, John. *The Power of Progress: How America's Progressives Can (Once Again) Save Our Economy, Our Climate, and Our Country*. New York: Crown Publishers, 2008.

Posner, Richard A. *A Failure of Capitalism: The Crisis of '08 and the Descent into Depression*. Cambridge, MA: Harvard University Press, 2009.

Reich, Robert B. *Reason: Why Liberals Will Win the Battle for America*. New York: Alfred A. Knopf, 2004.

Sabato, Larry J. *A More Perfect Constitution: 23 Proposals to Revitalize Our Constitution and Make America a Fairer Country*. New York: Walker & Company, 2007.

Scarborough, Joe. *The Last Best Hope: Restoring Conservatism and America's Promise*. New York: Crown Publishing Group, 2009.

Shipler, David. *The Working Poor: Invisible in America*. New York: Alfred A. Knopf, 2004.

Shultz, George P., and John B. Shoven. *Putting Our House in Order: A Guide to Social Security and Health Care Reform*. New York: W. W. Norton & Company, 2008.

Smick, David. M., *The World Is Curved: Hidden Dangers to the Global Economy*. New York: The Penguin Group, 2009.

Stiglitz, Joseph E. *Globalization and Its Discontents*. W. W. Norton & Company, 2003.

Whybrow, Peter C. *American Mania: When More Is Not Enough*. New York: W. W. Norton & Company, 2005.

Index